Location Location Location

How to Select the Best Site for Your Business

Second Edition

LUIGI SALVANESCHI

Oasis Press®/PSI Research
Central Point, Oregon

Published by The Oasis Press®
© 1996, 2002 by Luigi Salvaneschi

This publication is designed to provide accurate and authoritative information
in regard to the subject matter covered. It is sold with the understanding that
the publisher is not engaged in rendering legal, accounting, or other professional service. If legal advice or other expert assistance is required, the services of a competent professional person should be sought.

> *— from a declaration of principles jointly adopted by a committee of*
> *the American Bar Association and a committee of publishers.*

Second Edition Editor: Constance C. Dickinson
First Edition Editors: Camille Akin, Linda Pinkham, and Vickie Reierson
Book Designer: Constance C. Dickinson
Compositor: Jan Olsson
Illustrations: Margo DePaulis
Cover Designers: Margo DePaulis and Tim Hannah

Please direct any comments, questions, or suggestions regarding this book to
The Oasis Press®/PSI Research:

Editorial Department
P.O. Box 3727
Central Point, OR 97502
(541) 245-6502
info@psi-research.com *e-mail*

The Oasis Press® is a Registered Trademark of Publishing Services, Inc.,
an Oregon corporation doing business as PSI Research.

Library of Congress Cataloging-in-Publication Data

Salvaneschi, Luigi, 1929–
    Location, location, location : how to select the best site for your business / Luigi
Salvaneschi.—2nd ed.
        p. cm. — (PSI successful business library)
    ISBN 1-55571-611-3 (pbk.)
    1. Store location—United States—Handbooks, manuals, etc. 2. Retail trade—United
States. I. Title. II. Series.
HF5429.28.U6 S25 2002
658.1'1—dc21   2002022098

Printed in the United States of America
Second edition 10 9 8 7 6 5 4 3 2 1

♻ Printed on recycled paper when available.

To my wife, Lenore, and my daughter, Margherita.

Table of Contents

Foreword

In the new millennium, new trends in retailing, commercial real estate development, and competitive forces require a new level of sophistication concerning where to best market a product or service. In the pages that follow, one of the deans of the retail real estate industry, Luigi Salvaneschi, insightfully articulates what it takes to successfully locate small and medium-sized retail businesses. This unique how-to book is designed to help those in the franchise and corporate real estate industry as well as those who are independent retailers. In fact, anyone involved in retail store development should have a copy of this helpful guide on his or her desk for reference. This book provides a wealth of information not found in any of the real estate or business books that presently exist.

Salvaneschi explains the process of finding the right type of location based upon customers' wants and needs. He shows how to determine customer profiles. He spells out the who, what, when, where, and how in the definition of the right location for a specific industry. He explains the importance of understanding your industry from the operations and marketing standpoint, and how to get the right piece of land or right building. He gives the pros and cons of all types of locations, including suburban areas, downtowns, malls, small towns, and along interstate highways.

In addition, this book explains how to research and use demographic and psychographic data to obtain a successful location. Of particular interest is the concept of interest gravitation, which will help any burgeoning or existing retailer determine the dynamics among the various areas of activities in any given market. Salvaneschi explains the retail trading zone and its importance as it relates to potential customers. The reader will learn how to judge traffic patterns of customers in an area, learn about the movement of people and how it can affect sales, learn about the time-convenience line produced by the time factor, and learn how to evaluate various kinds of barriers that keep customers away from a retail business. To accomplish this, Salvaneschi details the importance of walking a property, driving a property, and flying a property and the importance of seeing and understanding road patterns, population clusters, and physical barriers to movement.

Location, Location, Location gives its readers a deeper understanding of the critical importance of a total decision based on all factors, some of which, at times, are overlooked or underestimated by retail management. The book teaches professionals involved in site selection how to work best with operation, marketing, construction, engineering, and other disciplines in a unified team effort.

Location, Location, Location combines practical experience with a theoretical approach. The reader will learn ways to estimate future sales and a method to evaluate hourly and weekly sales. The book not only deals with a whole array of challenges faced every day by those who are in the retail industry, but delivers solutions as well.

I first had the opportunity to meet Luigi Salvaneschi when we served on the board of directors of the International Association of Corporate Real Estate Executives (NACORE). This was a group of corporate real estate executives that met to build a new organization. We became friends because we both had a sincere interest in marketing, long-term strategic planning, and increasing the professionalism of real estate members. The great success of the corporate real estate industry can be credited, to a large extent, to the dedication and contributions of people like Luigi Salvaneschi. He has taken his long-term strategic knowledge and applied it to achieve success in some of America's top corporations. He did so first at McDonald's and later at KFC and Blockbuster Video. As one of the international gurus of retail real estate, he offers valuable information to everyone involved in retail management and development. Readers will come away more knowledgeable, more experienced, and ready to make better contributions to their companies or businesses.

JOSEPH R. BAGBY
Founder, International Association of
Corporate Real Estate Executives
(NACORE)

Preface

In the bookstores I noticed an abundance of literature for private entrepreneurs. These books cover organization, finances, accounting, personnel matters, and entrepreneurial attitudes for men and women who intend to start their own businesses. Surprisingly, not many books are available concerning the foundation of a retail business — that is, location. If your proposed or existing retail business is smaller than a typical grocery store, then this book will give you the tools you need to build the foundation of your operation. As a retailer in today's multi-faceted market, you will face the choice of locating your business in a shopping center or strip center, in a mall or storefront, in a downtown area of a big city or a small town. Whether you are an independent retailer or a franchise operator with a single store or multiple stores, the information in this book will give you the secrets to site selection.

So many retailers select poor locations. Too often entrepreneurs, who are masters of their own art or trade, expect to be successful in any location of their choice; they think they can make their businesses successful despite their locations. It does not work this way — experienced entrepreneurs can fail if their locations are not good for their industry. Although there is no substantial difference between the locations of retailers of goods versus retailers of services, both new and existing business owners must consider the role their types of business play in the site selection process. A shoe store needs certain location requirements that are unique to the shoe industry; a travel agency has different requirements; so do medical clinics, restaurants, and tire shops. For instance, a regular, nonspecialty shoe store needs to be located in an area where the demographic makeup consists of blue-collar workers and lower to middle income families of four. A person wanting to start a travel agency, on the other hand, needs to consider a location in an area of white-collar workers, upper income individuals, or near large corporations that need to book business travel on a daily basis. If you don't grasp the essential elements of each of their differences, you won't be able to identify the essential elements of a location for your industry.

To help you grasp these essential elements of a location, I advocate the study of competitor stores that are similar to your operation — also known as existing analogue stores. Retailers who already have stores can compare their existing stores to existing analogue stores. First-time retailers can focus their attention on the best competitors in the market, especially in their selected areas. In fact, the analysis of the competition is the main task to develop criteria for a new retail store. New entrepreneurs need to understand the concepts and the process of using their competitors' information and diligently research less obvious factors. When it comes to location, a decision cannot be made hastily. The selection of a site is a lengthy, painstaking exercise in research, comparisons, analyses, interviews, and investigations. The biggest mistake you can make in site selection is to start a retail business relying on the word of somebody else, say a co-owner, partner, broker, or family member. The analysis of a location is a personal matter. You cannot delegate anyone to learn for you. You need to do the research and to learn from it. Besides, you may have several thousands of dollars on the table.

I kept my reasoning as practical as possible. Almost every site selection factor I have researched shows no direct relationships among the various factors, such as sales versus traffic counts, versus age groups, versus income. If they do, they are more coincidental than anything else. Yet the facts show that there are locations better than others; this book will help you unlock the secret.

The selection of a retail location is a complex task; but keep two things in mind. First, you want to improve your ability to predict your store's sales. After all is said and done, your main concern still is the bottom line. Second, you need some assurance that you will not commit a blunder from which you will never be able to extricate yourself. The site selection steps outlined in this book will help you achieve this assurance.

I will show you proven methods and critical information based on many years of experience. I will not give you complicated mathematical formulas or research methods. Nobody can give you hard numbers, even though the academic world has tried. The world of retail is the world of marketing; you deal with people — who by essence are a nonmeasurable entity. Looking for a location for your retail business is doing marketing and marketing is nothing more than having the customers in mind all the time. You must look for what your customers want and like. You must make their visits to your store as pleasant and comfortable as possible. Your location will advertise your goods or services. Your store will become part of a neighborhood's life.

When a retail business is poorly located, you can't do much with its operations, facilities, nor marketing to make it flourish. The business will consistently underperform. On the contrary, a poorly managed or operated business in a good location can be turned around with smart management and creative marketing.

Acknowledgments

During my professional years, I have had the opportunity to work and deal with outstanding people. Many of these have been generous by offering me advice in writing this book.

I owe a debt of gratitude to Dave Cattel, Phillip deMena, Robert Frey, Esq., Bruce Pasternack, Dave Segal, Tom Colaw, Ron Simon, Gena Kay Sedlack, and all the others I called on the phone to discuss facts and ideas concerning the selection of retail sites.

A special thank you to Delphine Johnson who labored in the typing of the original manuscript, coping with all the corrections and changes.

Thanks also to my daughter, Margo DePaulis, a talented graphic artist, who provided the illustrations as well as the cover idea for this book.

I want to thank the book design team at PSI Research — Constance C. Dickinson, J. C. Young, Steven Burns, and Jan Olsson — for the creative talent, hard work, and dedication they gave to this project. Finally, a very special thank you to Camille Akin, the very able editor of the first edition who diligently, competently, and patiently reviewed and reorganized this book and to C.C. Dickinson for coordinating the second edition.

LUIGI SALVANESCHI

About the Author

Luigi Salvaneschi was born and raised in Italy. He earned a B.A. in humanities from Valsalice College, located in northern Italy and a Ph.D. in law from Lateran University in Rome. While at Lateran he was employed by the Vatican as administrator of the *Official Catholic Bulletin*. He then became a teacher in the Italian schools in Alexandria, Egypt, and Beirut, Lebanon.

Mr. Salvaneschi came to the United States in 1959 with the goal of teaching at a university. In the meantime, he worked in a McDonald's store where he met Ray Kroc, the founder of McDonald's. Soon thereafter he became a major player in the successful retail site selection of thousands of McDonald's stores worldwide. As vice-president in charge of real estate administration at the McDonald's headquarters in Chicago, Illinois, Mr. Salvaneschi was instrumental in setting up standards and policies for all McDonald's store locations. In 1971, he was made an advisory member to the McDonald's board of directors.

In 1983, he joined Kentucky Fried Chicken (KFC) in Louisville, Kentucky, as a senior vice-president. Under his leadership, KFC's growth rate and standards were dramatically raised and each store's sales reflected the change, both nationally and internationally. In 1987, H. Wayne Huizenga invited Mr. Salvaneschi to visit some of the new Blockbuster Video stores. Eventually he joined the young company as a consultant, then as executive vice-president, and was promoted to president and director. In a period of three years, he helped Blockbuster open almost 1,800 stores throughout the nation and become one of America's top home video rental stores.

Retired since 1991, currently he devotes his time to consulting, writing, and teaching at Barry University in Miami Shores, Florida.

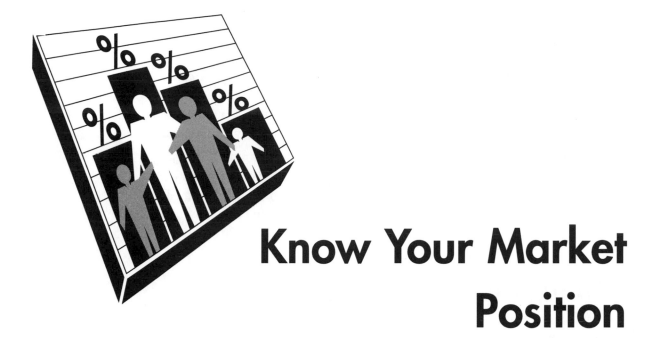

Chapter 1

Know Your Market Position

Selecting the location for your store is the most important decision you will make in your efforts to achieve success in retailing. In addition to location, you must choose the right product, identify your market, and assess your competition. To begin your search for the right location, you will need to thoroughly analyze your market. A market analysis will include a careful evaluation of your:

- Industry and product
- Customers
- Competitors

In the 1960s, Ray Kroc, founder of McDonald's, decided to hire a high-class chef from France and start a chain of pie shops — called Jane Dobbin's Pie Shop. The pies were delicious. The first pie shop opened in Pasadena, California. The business went nowhere because the product was too expensive for that particular market. Although the product was superior, the business was located in the wrong market. You may have many years of experience in your field, but being an expert in your field may not necessarily translate into sales of your service or product. Consider the examples of a hardware person who has spent several years in the business and dreams of opening a hardware store, or a chef who longs to open a French restaurant. While the hardware and recipes may be outstanding, these entrepreneurs need to know who will buy their products and services, at what price, and in what city. A market analysis will help you gain a better sense of market positioning — knowing who the right customers are and where to find them.

To understand your market position, you can use existing demographic and lifestyle information. Much of this demographic information is industry specific and will give you insight into running your type of business. In addition, you can glean important information about your market by analyzing your competition. There is no better way to learn about your potential customers than to carefully study existing competitors. Find out who their customers are, when they buy, what they buy, how much they spend, and the frequency of their visits.

If you are thinking about opening your first store, relocating your existing store, or opening an additional store, imagine your future location and business in relation to the best existing competitor. Don't strive to be merely equal to your competition; rather, strive to be much better than anyone currently in the marketplace.

Understand Your Industry

In a market analysis, your first priority is to understand your industry and your product. The industry aspect of your market analysis will show you:

- Your specific type of business;
- The number of existing similar businesses;
- How long your type of business has been around; and
- Whether your business type is a variation of an old concept or a niche in a general concept.

If you have a thorough knowledge of your industry and your product, you will be in a better position to make your business succeed.

Your market research must tell you whether there is a demand for your product. Demand can be characterized into two types — obvious and latent. Obvious demand is revealed by the presence of strong competition. Latent demand is revealed by a call for related products. For instance, a pharmacy may call for medical equipment sales-rental; a hardware computer store may call for a software computer store; the special environment (beach-recreation) may call for more of the same products: more swimwear, more sunlotions, and more beach umbrellas. The products must be different, diverse, and innovative, and vary by kind, size, look, price, and by the way they are offered: a better location is a better way of offering them. The products can be specialty (better, more expensive) or commodity (easier to produce and widely affordable). Specialty products do not go well in areas of poor economic performance.

Many successful entrepreneurs base their businesses on old concepts. You need a clear picture of what others are doing in your industry before you simply repeat an existing idea. To gain a clearer picture of your industry, look around and find out what already exists in the marketplace. Find out who are your industry's key leaders and how they achieved top quality. Further, examine the overall quality of what your industry offers, noting its areas of weakness.

When analyzing your industry, you need to evaluate its leaders because it will be much harder for you to succeed when you are covered by the shadow of a leader. You will simply play second fiddle, and your customers will sense it.

If your retail business will be based on an existing concept, work on developing that concept. For example, Ray Kroc saw a very successful McDonald's drive-thru restaurant in San Bernardino, California. He moved the concept to Chicago, Illinois, and worked on perfecting it. He did not invent McDonald's; he developed it by improving its quality, equipment, operations standards, service, and marketing.

Look at your industry's progress. An industry rarely will make a drastic change. Progress takes place incrementally over a long period of time. For instance, automobiles have been around for almost a century, and engineers are still trying to improve them. So when you look at your industry, determine its progress by noting its vitality, future, and growth.

- Make sure your industry is alive, widely recognized, and profitable for those who operate within it.
- Never hook up with an industry that is visibly declining — meaning you rarely see customers in the store, or the facility is run down, or the suppliers are on a C.O.D. delivery basis. Make sure you understand the long-term trends, not just the short-term trends. Don't presume that you will be able to turn around and revitalize that industry.
- Aim at an industry growth rate higher than the projected cost of living index. You know that your business' operating costs will increase due to the cost of living.
- Look at your industry's potential for growth in the international arena. As you know, today all businesses have international potential and international competition.

Be Aware of Your Industry's Strategic Evolution

Be constantly aware of the evolution in consumers' demands. Although your competitors may be currently profitable, they may not look at their customers' future needs. The future may require a modified and improved approach. Be ready to offer that new approach.

Analyze the strategic evolution of your industry and chart its life cycle — that is, where, when, and how it began; its sales peaks and valleys; its current performance; and its latest trends. For instance, consider the future of the home video rental industry.

- How will tapes continue to be rented?
- Will they be delivered to homes?
- Will games become more relevant?
- Will DVDs become a sizable part of the rental business?
- What is the implication of cable systems with 500 channels?

If you open a home video rental store, you will need to consider these factors to project its future sales curve.

This type of situation happened to the fast-food industry during the recent decade. Because of Americans' shift in eating habits, the fast-food trend is toward leaner and healthier foods. Restaurants that primarily offered hamburgers tried to switch to roast beef. Now consumers perceive beef as unhealthy and they want chicken. But chicken is being offered fried or roasted, still full of fat and cholesterol. Base your products or services on what will last and satisfy people in the long run, knowing that trends will eventually change. Consider the evolution of product offerings at McDonald's restaurants. McDonald's original identity was as a fast-food business specializing in hamburgers. After several years of study, debate, and development, McDonald's came out with the Egg McMuffin and other breakfast items in which hamburger meat plays no part.

Orient your retail store's activity to your customers' needs — which are immediate and long range. You must be able to endure all sorts of competition. You will have to tailor your products and your services to the market changes. Yes, it is still possible for McDonald's to sell hamburgers and french fries after 45 years! In fact, your goal might be to become a leader in your industry.

If your industry is trying to meet consumers' demands, but is fragmented, confused, and run haphazardly by mom-and-pop operations with short-term goals, look for ways to improve industry operations. In their beginnings, the founders of McDonald's and Blockbuster Video faced some problems with their industries. To succeed, they knew they would need to incorporate three essential elements of success, including:

- Good management
- Sufficient capital
- Consistent marketing

Both companies helped clean up the industry by including professional management in all facets of the business, including operations, human resources, marketing, procurement, and accounting.

Consider Your Industry's Markets

When evaluating your industry, keep in mind the variety of markets it serves. Any industry has markets that can be measured according to geographic areas, demographic groups, cultural groups, and behavioral groups.

- Geographic areas may be designated as northern climate; urban, suburban, or rural; big cities; small towns; and interior or coastal zones.
- Demographic groups include various age groups, men and women, income levels, household size, and education.
- Cultural groups may be identified by country of origin, religion, ethnic groupings, social or family status, and lifestyle.
- Behavioral groups may be classified as conservative, aggressive, seeking convenience or prestige, and showing brand loyalty.

To serve your market, you must fine tune your store. This means you will have to customize your retail store to accommodate your particular product, to portray an image that attracts your target customer, and to create an atmosphere and look that suits your marketing needs. By evaluating all these industry market factors first, you will have a better idea of where to locate your business and possibly even an idea on space and layout.

In the process of customizing your store, consider whether you will stock a small, but expensive inventory for the more affluent and discriminating clients, offer a wide assortment of goods in a narrow range, or present a vast display that covers an entire field. Once you have considered your product offering, inventory, and clientele, you can choose to become one of these store types.

- Specialty store. Specialty stores handle only a part of a single product line, such as women's shoes or children's clothing. Selected items, usually at a higher price, are offered in specialty stores such as Brooks Brothers, Bonwit Teller, Ann Taylor, and Garfinkel's.
- Store with a limited line. Stores with a limited line offer a large assortment within a single product line or a few related product lines. Limited line stores range from the Gap and Contemporary Casuals to Barnes & Noble Bookstores.
- Category superstore. Category superstores offer a huge selection of goods and lower prices within a similar product line. Home Depot, Pet's Mart, and Toys "R" Us are good examples.

Whichever store type you choose, make sure you stay on top of your industry's current trends.

You need to evaluate and analyze the latest retail concepts and methods by which goods and services are offered in your industry's marketplace. For example, if you intend to open your business as a mom-and-pop store, you might find that you will have to compete with a new kind of superstore that offers broader inventory and lower pricing. Hence, you must pick the right industry market and then detail your store accordingly. In short, once you evaluate your industry market and determine which store type you will need, you will be able to better evaluate your site options.

Different store types require different types of locations. Your choice of store type must be right the first time; there probably will not be a second chance. When it comes to the placement of a retail location in a market, some people call it a science; others call it an art. You should really call it hard work.

Your Customers

When you look for the proper location, you must be aware of who is going to spend money for your goods and services and why. Some will spend money for goods or services they feel are a necessity for everyday living. Some will spend money for recreational activities and fun. Some will spend money for personal satisfaction. The mere physical location of your business will not be sufficient to generate sales. You need to know what motivates your customers to buy. A major reason an individual becomes a spending consumer is to fulfill a need. Thus, your products and services must satisfy one or more of your customers' needs. Their needs are satisfied according to a purchasing cycle — a cycle that indicates how needs change over time, based upon different circumstances.

To get an idea of your customers' needs in relation to a purchasing cycle, take a look at your own needs.

- You may go to a pizza restaurant every three weeks to bring home a pizza.
- You need a new pair of shoes three times a year.
- You need groceries every week.
- You might need to refill prescriptions once per month.

To help you identify the people who need your products and services, divide them into three main groups:

- Heavy users
- Light users
- Nonusers

Heavy users consume your products and services often. The frequency of use will depend upon the nature of your business. Heavy users may represent 20 percent of your customers, but they produce the majority of your sales. If a heavy user is disappointed, don't count on a repeat sale. If you fail to cater to your heavy users, it will be a big loss for your business. Light users represent about 40 to 50 percent of all your customers. They generate the minority of your sales, yet they represent your immediate opportunity for marketing initiatives. With the proper marketing efforts, light users can more easily become heavy users. Nonusers represent the last opportunity. Your best hope is to bring them inside your store and treat them with special care. They are the most difficult to reach with local marketing and major media. These three types of customers also can be divided into nationally recognized demographic groups.

Use Demographics

The 2000 census provides an accurate look at population swings, demographic groups, changing family structures, and regional migrations. It provides a measurement of various ethnic groups. The census information is invaluable for targeting your market at specific groups with an affinity for a special industry and product — also called *capillary* or *viral* (from virus) marketing.

- Age groups are classified as children, birth–12; young teenagers, ages 13–15; older teenagers, ages 16–19; new adults, ages 20–24; young adults, ages 25–34; mature adults, ages 35–44; middle age adults, ages 45–54; older adults, ages 55–65; and senior citizens, age 65 plus.

- When classifying by gender, sometimes you will cater more to either the male population or the female population. Targeting either gender is an important factor in the delivery and the merchandising of your goods and services.
- Ethnic backgrounds vary according to cities, sections of cities, and country. Due to the diversity of people and cultural trends, you need to customize your products and services to the demographic profile of the consumers in your business' area.
- Marital status is important for knowing buying preferences. Single consumers will buy differently than their married counterparts.
- Household types are identified as consisting of one, two, three, four, or more family members, nonfamily members, or work associates.
- Income level is obviously a critical demographic factor. When looking at income levels, know that families and individuals are classified by their annual earnings, such as up to $10,000; $20,000 to $25,000; and more than $100,000.

Getting to know your customers and potential customers can also mean classifying them by the hours and days they shop. Consider every type of consumer — the weekend drivers, evening strollers, Saturday shoppers, and 11:00 A.M. browsers. If your business is a restaurant, you can identify your inside diners, carryout customers, or drive-thru diners. Some people will first select a location and then try to justify it with demographics. You know better: Proceed to secure your location only after you have studied the demographics of the areas you are interested in.

Learning how to recognize demographic factors and research demographic information is relatively easy. To start, familiarize yourself with federal census data. The federal census is one of the most important tools you must learn to read and interpret. Census data is compiled into categories such as total population, age group, income, and population density. For instance, you can identify your customers by studying how populations are grouped.

The major population areas of the United States are divided by the U.S. Census Bureau into metropolitan statistical areas. A *metropolitan statistical area* (MSA) is the largest census category. An MSA is a designated area consisting of a large population nucleus that includes its adjacent communities with a high degree of social integration. An MSA includes a city of at least 50,000 people with a total metropolitan population of at least 100,000. In turn, MSAs are divided into census tracts that generally contain 2,500 to 8,000 residents. In general, smaller tracts are more densely populated. However, the size of a tract is not necessarily an indication of its population density. Further, adjacent tracts do not necessarily indicate populations with similar characteristics. Tracts include heavily populated and sparsely populated areas. Take the state of Nevada, for instance. In many areas of this state, you will find stretches of highway but no towns of significant size or population.

Census tracts will always remain the same geographically; consequently, you will be able to compare them from census to census. In a metropolitan area, information is available on a block-to-block basis. Each census tract carries a four-digit basic code number, such as 6631, 6525, and 6632 to help identify it. Keep in mind that the population is never evenly distributed across a tract area. It may congregate on one side. Two-thirds of the tract may actually be desert, forest, or water. When studying census tracts, your goal is to capture the greatest number of potential customers. To illustrate this point, look at

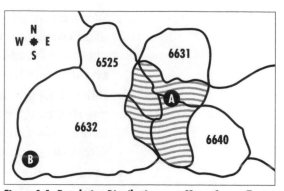

Figure 1.1 Population Distribution over Many Census Tracts

Figure 1.1. If you are considering Location A, you will find that only the population east of Tract 6632 falls into the trading area — that is, the buying area — of a potential retail business. The southwest population, Section B of Tract 6632, is 20 miles away from your business. Because of proximity, you cannot take into account all the census tract population as being the generator of your sales. You will need to combine other key demographic data to get an overall sense of your customers and their buying habits.

You can obtain census data from the *Statistical Abstract of the United States*. This helpful volume is printed every ten years — each time a census is taken — and will provide you with timely and accurate information on your potential customers. Also, you can get maps that show the various MSAs throughout the United States. To learn how you can get these maps and other MSA data, check out the listing of demographic information sources located in Appendix B. Most of these companies can be accessed via the Internet. Another invaluable tool is *Editor & Publisher Market Guide*. See Appendix B for the address and phone number.

Be cautious when using federal census data. First, the data's accuracy can be off by more than ten percent because of the sporadic sampling system used and the interpretation of the data. Second, the data will become obsolete in three or four years. To get the timeliest and most accurate data, you may wish to deal with a professional demographic services company that updates the data yearly. In addition, you should verify the facts by personally familiarizing yourself with the area. As you will learn in Chapter 3, you walk it, you drive it, you fly it — in person. A catastrophic event can affect the demographics of an area. For instance, in Florida, Hurricane Andrew wiped out 180,000 homes overnight. On the other hand, areas can change fast due to new industries, manufacturing plants, and residential or commercial developments.

Use Psychographics

The 2000 census provides the latest information on our population, including vital statistics like age, race, income, density, distribution, and residential types. Several marketing companies compare or add these statistics to marketing surveys to produce a new classification of the population based on preferences, attitudes, tendencies, perceptions, motivational forces, and special traits. The results are psychographic data that reflects the axiom, "Birds of a feather flock together." When choosing a place to live, people look for areas where other people have compatible life styles and similar consumer behavioral patterns. For more information about these companies, see Appendix B – Demographic Resources.

In the development of new retail stores, there are two approaches: one aims at bringing products and services to areas that are new and different attempting to penetrate a market still forcign to the brand, the other focuses on markets that precisely fit the demographic and psychographic profile of the consumer. The risk is less, of course, using the second approach. Aiming at markets that best suit your industry definitely improves your chances of success. Some companies develop their own psychographic parameters, using customer surveys. For instance, at KFC, the marketing department developed an attitudinal criterium called "chicken propensity" which helped identify areas where people just prefer chicken products.

Look at Cars

You can learn valuable demographic information about your customers by looking at their car license plates. A license plate tells you where your customers live; the type of car tells you the socioeconomic status of the people in the area. For instance, in a retail location in Walterboro, South Carolina, a survey of car registrations revealed that:

- 26 percent of the cars traveled long distances from cities like New York and Philadelphia, Pennsylvania, along the corridor of I-95;
- 12 percent traveled from cities like Cleveland and Columbus, Ohio, and Knoxville, Tennessee, from corridors along I-71, I-75, I-77; and
- 72 percent (the balance) were South Carolina residents.

This type of research is useful in locations oriented toward travel and tourism. In Florida, the number of out-of-state cars changes during the winter months. The increase of out-of-state vehicles is considerable — typically a 10 to 30 percent increase. Tourist traffic is extremely important to Florida retailers. On the same token, the types of cars you find in an area will indicate the income levels of your potential customers.

On the north side of Chicago, a research project involving a high-priced jewelry store revealed some interesting demographic data. Researchers literally counted the number of Mercedes, Lexus, Cadillac, and Lincoln cars. Although the car registration was local, the types of cars clearly confirmed the income of the area. This concept also applies when you see older, poorly maintained cars on the road, parked along curbs, or in local shopping centers. These run-down vehicles indicate an area of lower income. In addition to looking at the area's cars to get an idea of income level and type of traffic, you can get to know your customers more by understanding the concept of market share.

Know Your Market Share

Knowing your market share will help you find the best location for your business. A *market share* is the proportion of total potential sales that a store generates from a given area. For example, if you are in the pizza business and want to locate in Peoria, Illinois, you should know that the people who live in Peoria eat 20 pizzas per capita and spend $200 to purchase these pizzas each year. If you intend to open a pizza restaurant in Peoria, your goal of selling might be to sell at least 2 of the 20 pizzas sold there. Keep in mind, per capita sales normally will vary with the median family income. If you want your retail business to succeed above and beyond any of your competitors, then you want your customers to buy 22 pizzas or more — thus, causing the market to grow.

To more fully understand this concept, consider your needed sales figures in relation to a market penetration index. If you succeed in selling two pizzas per capita, your market share would obviously be ten percent of the pizza dollar in Peoria. If your restaurant becomes an option for pizza buyers, people might buy more pizzas — maybe 25 to 27 pizzas per capita. The result: you will sell 5 or 6 pizzas per capita, which will cause an increase of your percentage of market share. You can use a formula to arrive at your store's market share.

$$\text{Market share} = \frac{\text{Store's sales per capita}}{\text{Sales potential per capita}}$$

In addition to using this formula to calculate your market share, you can glean important information from statistics offered by various governmental agencies and industry research companies. This detailed research data will reflect the sales potential of a particular product line in a defined area. If the area is around your potential store, then you will have a better idea of the customers of that trading area — which is also referred to as the "retail trading zone" of your store. To learn more about the importance of your trading area, refer to Chapter 4. For a sample listing of typical market research companies, refer to Appendix B – Demographic Resources. To learn more about doing your own market research, get a copy of *Know Your Market: How to Do Low-Cost Market Research* by David Frigstad. For more information, contact:

The Oasis Press
(800) 228-2275 or *www.oasispress.com*

To understand the market share information, you must understand key market designations, including:

- Standard metropolitan area
- Area of dominant influence
- Radio metro market

A *standard metropolitan area* (SMA) is a city within its greater limits, which normally increases in size due to the natural increase in population and the expansion of suburban areas. In other words, an SMA ends where the buildings end and the cornfields, deserts, forests, and lakes begin — even though these types of land are technically within the city limits. An SMA is where people live, work, and circulate. An *area of dominant influence* (ADI) is the area covered by the television signals in your city and is based on measured viewing patterns. An ADI goes beyond the limits of the city and its city zone and includes surrounding towns — even those that are far away. For instance, Elgin, Illinois, is in the ADI of Chicago; San Bernardino, California, is in the ADI of of Los Angeles; St. George, Utah, is in the ADI of Salt Lake City. If you open your retail store in Salt Lake City, don't expect to get much business from St. George 150 miles away, even though it is part of the same ADI.

On the other hand, a *radio metro market* includes people reached by the majority of the local area stations. It is important that you know these terms because your market share information will only be meaningful to you if it is based on the SMA. Don't be confused by the other terms. If you use a market research company, you will come across as an informed entrepreneur.

You can obtain information on market share by simply asking questions. If you are part of a franchise system, you can get market share data from your franchisor or your fellow franchisees. If you are a private entrepreneur, try to answer questions that will help you decide if you are looking at the right marketing area. Ask yourself:

- How many same-industry stores are there in the SMA?
- What types of stores, such as mom-and-pop stores, small stores, superstores, national chains, are there?
- How many people per store? (You get this figure by dividing the population of the SMA by the number of existing competitor stores.)
- How many dollars per capita are spent yearly for your type of product or service?
- What percentage of the SMA's industry sales goes to your best competitors?
- What is the trend of the SMA's industry sales?

As you gather this type of critical data, you will begin to formulate a profile of your potential customers.

Create Customer Profiles

A customer profile can be developed for any industry. A sample profile of customers in the bakery goods industry might look like this:

- Age: young adults, ages 25–34;
- Residence: single dwelling or apartment;
- Marital status: married;
- Gender: 55 percent female;
- Ethnicity: 50 percent White, 30 percent Latin-Hispanic, and 20 percent African-American;

- Household: more than three people;
- Employment: blue-collar and full-time;
- Median income: $15,000–$35,000 per year;
- Shopping habits: visits the store with family members 20 percent of the time; and
- Education: high school diploma.

The profile of the customers in the area in which you are interested must meet the profile of your industry. A lifestyle profile of your customers is of great importance because their lifestyles vary greatly and will affect the customer portion of your market analysis. Census data must be interpreted according to various lifestyles. Lifestyle differences mean people of the same age and income do not necessarily opt for the same goods or services.

Even people in the same ethnic area, suburb, block, and row house may have different needs and tastes. For instance, a retired couple may continue to live in the little house in Iowa where they raised their children. They may spend their evenings watching television, visiting with the neighbors, or reminiscing about the past. Yet another couple in the same age group and income level may be sunbathing on the white beaches in Florida, deep-sea fishing by day, and dancing in their social club at night.

Now that you know specifics regarding your industry, product, and customers, focus your attention on your competitors as a way to complete your overall market analysis.

Get to Know Your Competitors

Do not fear competition; rather, seek it and learn from it. Where there is good competition, there will always be opportunity for more good business. Thus, the third aspect of your market analysis will entail a thorough evaluation of your competition. Your first job is to discover the existing sales captured by your competitors to determine if there is an excess demand that is latent and unaccounted for. You can know this by analyzing your theoretical potential sales. To understand this concept, consider this scenario.

Suppose that the demographic mix in your trading area (based on the actual statistics) calls for potential sales of $150,000 a week — or $15 a week multiplied by 10,000 people. Two existing competitors serve the same area; the combined sales of these two competitors is $85,000. This means that you have the potential for additional sales (or excess sales) of $65,000. Thus, when you open your retail business, you need to attract the $65,000 excess, plus a percentage of your competitors' sales. You need to *impact* them — meaning the new store's effect on an existing store, usually expressed in reduced sales. Impact will be discussed in more detail in Chapter 9. Basically, you want to know how big the slice of your business could be in the market. You must figure out how to get people to your store more often, to spend more money, to buy better and less expensive products, and to enjoy better services. The purpose of this is twofold: to satisfy all the potential demand and to make a dent in the sales of your competitors.

Analyzing your competition is essential, particularly when you want to start your new business. Whether you are a single entrepreneur or a franchisee, to establish a new business in a market, it is necessary to analyze similar businesses to help you predict sales. A competition analysis is one of the most instructive exercises you can do. You will see and feel what actually happens in the store. You will notice what works and what doesn't work and what you want to copy, improve, or change in your own future store. As a franchisee, if you are entering a market where there are already similar stores, then it will be easier to make projections with the help of your franchisor and fellow franchisees. If you are a franchisee, you need to analyze your competition if your franchise system does not have a store in the market you want to serve. Three indispensable planning tools for prospective franchisees and franchisors are *Franchise Bible* by Erwin J. Keup and Roger C. Rule's *Franchise Redbook* and *No Money Down Financing for Franchising*. To learn how you can get copies of these helpful, up-to-date resources, contact:

The Oasis Press
(800) 228-2275 or *www.oasispress.com*

By analyzing your competition, you can select a site that will be a step beyond what your best competitor currently offers. Two kinds of analyses are common when sizing up your competition in an area you have tentatively selected for your own store. First, complete the Competitor's Location Analysis. Once you have tackled this task, complete the Competitor's Strategy Analysis. Both of these analyses are located at the end of this chapter. Keep in mind, understanding your competitors' locations will provide valuable insight into your site selection process.

Survey Your Competitors' Locations

Start your survey by driving throughout the area of town served by your competitors. Rate the location according to five fundamental characteristics of a successful location, including:

- Regional exposure
- Excellent visibility
- Superior accessibility
- High density
- Growth

These and other essential location factors are discussed in-depth in Chapter 6. When you have identified your competitors, look at the demographic makeup of the areas in which they are located. Remember to keep your industry and customer requirements in mind as you analyze each location. Your study of your competitors' stores will include an:

- Appraisal from the outside;
- Observation from the inside; and
- Interviews of other people, including nearby merchants, shoppers, and each store's manager.

From the outside, evaluate whether the facility is properly located and attractive. While judging the external appearance of a competitor's store, bear in mind that it is supposed to attract the passing traffic. From the inside, judge the layout of the store and its merchandising, pricing, personnel training and attitudes, inventory level, cleanliness, lighting, and the number of people walking out of the store without any purchased merchandise. Your observations are likely to turn up some astonishing information. For instance, you may find the store has only one cash register open most of the time, which causes long lines of people. When you have listed your likes and dislikes about each store, discuss your findings with somebody else in the industry, like a franchisee, supplier, former manager, or consultant.

Make photocopies of the blank Competitor's Location Analysis. Complete an analysis for each competitor in the area(s) in which you want to locate. Your analysis includes intangible elements that cannot be quantified, yet are important to evaluate. For example, you will want to know the degree of goodwill and market acceptance of each of your competitors. You need to have an idea of the depth of loyalty of their customers to understand the image-reputation that they enjoy. If you learn that the reputation of one of your competitors is shallow, then your opportunity for snatching its customers is greater.

Your Competitor's Location Analysis also includes general observations. For example, you can gain key insights by studying the sales curve of a competitor's business throughout the business hours by counting the number of customers and estimating the dollars spent per hour. Remember that on weekends the sales curve will always be different. You need to know the peak hourly sales for each day the store is open and how many customers are producing those peaks. This sales curve information will help you know which location may or may not be the best for your store based on the fluctuations in sales curves. You can be certain that when you operate your store in the area, you will have the sales peaks and valleys at the same time as your competitor's store. Refer to Chapter 5 for a more in-depth look at hourly and weekly sales curves.

As you examine your competitors' locations, make notes on the items you will sell versus what your competitors are selling. Seek ways to make your merchandise distinct and different from your competitors. Strive to offer:

- Improved items;
- Better quality;
- Better prices;
- Better interior decor
- Additional amenities, and
- Newer items that your competitors don't offer.

The more informed you are about your competitors, the better your market position and location selection will be. After you have completed an analysis of each of your competitors, you must determine which one is your toughest competition and then analyze that store's strategies.

Analyze Your Top Competitor's Strategies

Now that you have narrowed down your study to your top competitor, you must delve further into the reasons for the competitor's success. You can do this by using the Competitor's Strategy Analysis located at the end of this chapter. To help you complete the analysis, you must do more research.

One way you can learn your top competitor's strategy is via a straight interview with the manager or owner and with some of the employees. Introduce yourself and indicate your interest in the business. You may be given a tour of the entire facility. You may be shown the accounting records, financial charts, sales records, and inventory turnover. Just ask — you will be amazed at what you will learn. You can also interview the adjacent merchants. They can tell you what they like and don't like about their neighbors and what they think is right or wrong about their neighbors' stores. It is natural for them to pay attention to businesses nearby.

Some nearby merchants' businesses probably depend upon the business cycles of others. For instance, a shoe store may be heavily dependent upon a nearby clothing store. Further, analyze the advertising of your top competitor. Advertising tells you about the image your competitor wants to project and the pricing level it chooses. You can use the annual reports of the company, analyses of investment firms, market share reports, Dun & Bradstreet reports, newspapers, industry publications, and other sources.

Completing a Competitor's Strategy Analysis will require time, effort, and ingenuity. Investing the effort now will give you a better idea of how to design your business' strategies — and that means a solid future payoff. If you come across a lack of competition in your prospective trading area, carefully look at why there is a lack.

Beware of a Lack of Competition

Suppose you have tentatively selected a location that doesn't have any significant direct competitors. You may think that you will have the market all to yourself. Before you make a location decision you might regret, consider the reasons for the lack of competition. Either the market is excellent and so far nobody discovered it, or the market does not show a propensity toward your type of business. You must look beyond what is obvious. Be sensitive to indications of other underlying realities that may affect your business.

Some of the problems waiting for you at certain locations are specific to the people who live in the area. These factors are real and important, even though they are not obvious.

Thus, you need to double your efforts in your search for factors that are not obvious and visible. You must weigh intangible factors like:

- Ethnic backgrounds, habits, and traditions;
- Tastes;
- Health and social concerns; and
- Religious or cultural beliefs.

Consider what McDonald's encountered when trying to set up operations in some overseas locations. Sales at a new McDonald's located in St. Etienne, France, were low even though the location was on the main commercial street in front of a major tramway exchange. A problem existed: the population was blue-collar, unionized, politically red, and anti-American. And in Rotterdam, Netherlands, McDonald's planners looked at an area with high-rise residential buildings that housed a population of 80,000 people. There was no restaurant in that area — for a good reason. The religious convictions of the residents encouraged the tradition of family meals at home. In short, these people would not patronize a fast-food restaurant. Once you have a good idea of who is your customer, you will be better prepared to make your decision.

Here in the United States there are markets with ingrained traditional tastes. McDonald's had a problem in New York City, where people did not like catchup on their hamburgers, and in Dallas, Texas, where people wanted fresh lettuce and tomatoes on their sandwiches. These items are not part of McDonald's standard hamburger recipe.

Some markets are the capital of a product or service. For instance, Louisville, Kentucky, is the cradle of Kentucky Fried Chicken (KFC). If a competitor tries to enter this market, it might be subdued by the intense customer loyalty to the Colonel and by the devastating market campaign by KFC against the newcomer. The same situation happened to Blockbuster in Tifton, Georgia, where a franchisee opened a store near the headquarters of a local video chain. Blockbuster was forced to close the store.

Other not-so-obvious factors to consider when selecting your location include a wide range of customers' perceptions. These perceptions, whether true or not will impact your location choice.

- The size of the sidewalk in front of your store is narrower than the one across the street.
- You are located on the shady side of the road.
- Your location is at the margin of social ethnic groups instead of in the midst of the group themselves.
- You are defying the political or environmental trends by locating on a certain parcel and that sparks a negative reaction in the community.
- Your employees do not fit the profile of your customers.
- Your image does not fit the profile of your customers.

- People are seeking commodity goods and you are selling specialties.
- Your pricing policy does not fit the income of the area.
- People fear crime in the area.
- Your location itself is related to past criminal events.

Remember, a lack of competition in an area should raise a red flag for you. Before you proceed in your site selection efforts, make sure you have researched the reasons for the lack of competition — both the obvious and not-so-obvious factors.

Chapter Wrap-Up

To recap, make sure your market analysis includes a thorough knowledge of:

- How your type of business fits into your industry;
- How to strategically stay on top of your industry's evolution;
- The various markets your industry serves;
- Who will buy your products and how to learn about these customers via demographic research;
- Your potential share of the market you want to serve; and
- Your competitors' locations, strategies, failures, and successes.

Your combined knowledge of your industry, product, customers, and competitors will equip you to take your next step. You are now ready to look at some critical site issues, including a study of the characteristics of the city in which you want to locate your business and a look at the specific aspects of the most desirable pieces of property.

Competitor's Location and Strategy Analyses Instructions

These worksheets will help you analyze and understand your competitors. Use them especially to analyze your best competitor. As you evaluate the critical factors of your best competitor's location — such as a look at its exterior and interior layouts, its history, long-range plans for development, and its percentage of market share — you will be forced to notice essential elements that you will want to incorporate into your store. It is a good, disciplined way to find out how others run their businesses so you can make yours one step beyond the very best currently in the market.

Competitor's Location Analysis

General Observations

Name and address of competitor:

_____

_____

_____

Weekday operating hours: _____ to _____   Days of the week: _____ through _____

Weekend operating hours: _____ to _____

Total weekly operating hours: _____

Number of customers entering throughout an entire week: _____

Weekday low: _____   Weekday high: _____   Weekend low: _____   Weekend high: _____

Your analysis of the service: _____

_____

What you like about the store: _____

_____

What you don't like about the store: _____

_____

Exterior Appraisal

Type of physical facility [check one]:

☐ In-line in a mall, shopping center, or downtown commercial street

☐ Free standing structure

☐ End cap (at the end of a row of stores)

☐ Other [specify]: _____

Your impressions of the external design, parking arrangement, and signage: _____

_____

_____

The elements of the store's exterior that make it attractive: _____

_____

The elements of the store's exterior that make it unattractive: _____

_____

Competitor's Location Analysis (continued)

Interior Appraisal

The adequacy and condition of the store's fixtures and equipment: _____

_____

The estimated square footage of the selling area: _____

The estimated square footage of the storage area: _____

Number of cash register stations: _____

The store's best feature: _____

The store's worst feature: _____

The core groups of merchandise are classified as: _____

_____

The complementary or peripheral groups of merchandise are classified as: _____

_____

The best-selling items: _____

The items that are not selling: _____

The pricing policy is [check one]:

☐ Above market   ☐ Middle-range   ☐ Other [specify]: _____

☐ Below market   ☐ Heavy discount   _____

The creativity in selling and merchandising: _____

_____

Interviews

Comments about the store from nearby merchants: _____

_____

Comments about the store from shoppers: _____

_____

Comments about the store from the store's managers: _____

_____

Your impression of this competitor's goodwill and how well it has been accepted in the marketplace [check one]:

☐ High   ☐ Below average   ☐ Comments: _____

☐ Average   ☐ Poor   _____

Competitor's Strategy Analysis

Business Owner or Top Manager

Name: _____

Leadership qualities: _____

Management style: _____

Competence: _____

Personality traits: _____

Company History

How it came into existence: _____

_____

_____

Market conditions at the time of its origin: _____

_____

_____

How the original idea was applied: _____

_____

_____

Store's Labor

Number of full-time employees: _____

Number of part-time employees: _____

Percentage of full-time employees: _____

Union situation: _____

Labor relations: _____

Long-Range Plans for Development

Availability of capital for growth and development of the existing facility for:

New products: _____

New markets: _____

New locations: _____

New format for facility: _____

New acquisitions: _____

Competitor's Strategy Analysis (continued)

Immediate (Short-Term) Strategic Plans

Merchandising: _____

_____

_____

Transportation: _____

_____

_____

Manufacturing: _____

_____

_____

Expansion: _____

_____

_____

Delivery systems: _____

_____

_____

Business' Image

Advertising: _____

_____

_____

Merchandising: _____

_____

_____

Promotion: _____

_____

_____

Pricing: _____

_____

_____

Chapter 2

Understand the City

The location you ultimately choose for your store is part of a bigger context that most people don't realize. For instance, you may observe it to be part of a shopping center and business district that has some sort of relationship to a neighborhood. What is not so easy to see is that it has an important relationship to the entire metropolitan area in which the site is located.

This chapter will teach you how to understand the dynamics of a city and how certain key factors will directly impact your future business location. Your study of the city in which you wish to locate will involve several areas of examination, including a look at:

- The city's relationship to surrounding cities;
- The road system and road configurations within the city;
- The traffic patterns of the people who live, work, play, and travel in the city; and
- What causes people to move in certain directions.

Your study of the bigger picture will start with a survey of the arterial roads that both feed the city and compose its historic framework. Your study also involves knowing the dynamics of the city's subdivisions so you can make quick, accurate assessments of neighborhoods in your quest for a customer base that you can profitably serve. You will also need to know what the flow of traffic between cities, between cities and suburban areas, between the city's subdivisions, and within microareas means to your business and choosing a location that will bring you retail success.

Study the City's Layout

Your study should begin with a look at the macromarket — also called the standard metropolitan area (SMA). Your analysis will help you discover the hubs of activity within the city and their importance in respect to each other. The important hubs, or *nodes*, are defined as specific and well-recognized areas, often referred to with a name. Some examples of existing city nodes include the Oxmoor Center in Louisville, Kentucky, the Oak Brook Center in Chicago, Illinois, and the Del Amo Shopping Center in Torrance, California. The *nodules* — or smaller activity hubs — tend to serve the nodes, which in turn serve the bigger hubs.

The study of a city's layout involves breaking down its subareas with the goal of discovering the smallest market area that contributes to your business. The distance between the hubs is strictly dependent upon the demographics and the physical-psychological characteristics of the area. Dividing areas within a city into smaller areas will make it easier for you to understand each of them. To illustrate this process, look at Figure 2.1. The inverted pyramid shows you how to properly approach a study of your prospective site. To recap, you will:

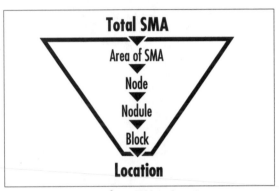

Figure 2.1 Narrowing from SMA to Location

- First, select one of the nodes (big activity hubs) in the area according to the market it represents.
- Second, narrow your focus to the nodules (smaller activity hubs) and pick the most important nodule.
- Third, analyze the appropriate block, or cluster of blocks, where you hope to find the right location for your business.

Your next step is to study the layout of the city. Each part of the city is characterized by a specific type, such as single residential, multiple residential, professional, industrial, commercial, agricultural, governmental, educational, military, and recreational. All these parts are linked to each other by a network of roads, highways, freeways, tollways, railroads, rivers, and canals. You need to understand the various parts of the city to understand the whole city — just like a physician needs to understand the inner workings of a human body to understand the overall body functions. Although big cities like New York and Los Angeles are more complex in layout due to the sheer magnitude of their size, you will be able to study some obvious links. Los Angeles, for instance, has specific links with Santa Ana and San Diego to the south, with San Bernardino to the east, and with Santa Barbara and Bakersfield to the north. These types of links are referred to as arteries of an urban market.

For a visual display of the complex relationships of cities, look at the illustration in Figure 2.2. Chicago is linked to Milwaukee to the north with the corridor

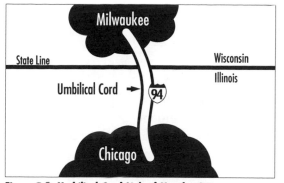

Figure 2.2 Umbilical Cord Link of Nearby Cities

of I-94 as the main road that links the two cities — also called the *umbilical cord*. The umbilical cord is a lifeline without which secondary (smaller, fewer populated) communities cannot survive. Along that route innumerable developments have occurred and will continue to take place. Yet another example is found in Louisville, Kentucky. Louisville is connected to the south with the city of Bardstown, a vital link connecting the two cities that clearly determines the developments in the area. Knowing a city's layout will give you an idea of the potential for future city development.

So, when looking at your prospective site, find out whether:

- An agricultural area might suddenly cut off potential future developments;
- Another city is connected to yours;
- Your city is located in a valley or on top of several hills and has winding roads at the bottom;
- The degree of fragmentation — or spaced and disjointed areas of activity; and
- The locations of the largest homogenous areas.

Detroit, Michigan, Los Angeles, California, and Phoenix, Arizona, are flat cities. There are no physical barriers like mountains or rivers that cut the development of areas and limit the length of the roads, which are usually wide and straight. Other cities have all kinds of separations, such as rivers, ravines, woods, hills, rocky areas, commercial-industrial-military developments, and airports. You need to evaluate the effects that these types of separations will have on your business. For instance, to pick a spot in the city of Cincinnati, Ohio, you need to know that it is divided by the Ohio River. One very effective way to learn about the layout of a city is to study the different types of roads. A typical city will have a road system that includes:

- Arterial roads
- Radial roads
- Quadrant roads
- Regional-local roads

Your first task will be to learn your city's arterial roads.

Arterial Roads

You have to approach a city area map like a doctor. You need to understand all the parts of the body, separating the important parts from the limbs; figuring out how the parts are connected to each other; and how they function jointly or independently. *Arterial roads* make it possible for a city or area to exist, to breathe, to function. If you eliminate the arterial roads, a city or area will figuratively collapse. Examples of arterial roads include:

- Ventura Boulevard in San Fernando, California;
- Rockville Turnpike in Fairfax County, Maryland; and
- Roosevelt Road in Chicago, Illinois.

When the Los Angeles market for McDonald's was being developed, much time was spent scanning a huge wall map of the city. The map clearly showed each individual arterial road with distinct colors identifying parks, rivers, mountains, plains, and political jurisdictions. Arterial roads can be both radial and quadrant.

Radial Roads

Radial roads are the main links from a city's core to the outer parts of a city. Radial roads form the web around which the city was built over the years. In addition, radial roads form radiuses from a city's core that, in turn, form a starlike configuration. Radial roads expand into all parts of a city, in all directions, and all parts of a city are directly connected to a center. In fact, history will show you that cities were formed at critical junctions where various paths would meet and focus. For example, Rome has a remarkable system of radial roads, including the Appian Way, Cassian Way, and Flaminian Way. These important roads expand in all directions, and as of today, are true connectors to both Italy and Europe.

To understand the importance of radial roads, look at an atlas, such as the *Rand McNally Atlas of the United States*. Examine the road structure of major and minor cities in several different states. For instance, look at Lexington, Kentucky. The city has a true center, just like a circle, from which radiuses expand all around. Atlanta, Georgia, also has its main arteries fanning out in all directions. Boston, Massachusetts, with the Massachusetts Bay to the east, shows its radial roads expanding to the west, north, and south.

For your retail business you need to attract not only your neighbors, but as many potential customers as possible, coming from other parts of a city — or a city's central business district (CBD) — countryside, and other towns. Radial roads are, by their own nature, more important than the local roads used primarily by residents. Because radial roads radiate outward from major human centers, as illustrated in Figure 2.3, they are the true connectors to the countryside and other towns — whether adjacent or distant. These roads carry a variety of traffic for short and long distances. This traffic is formed by:

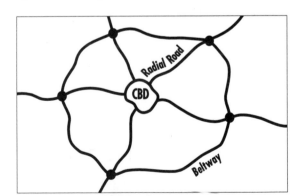

Figure 2.3 How Radial Roads Connect

- Residents and nonresidents
- Workers and vacationers
- Merchants and shoppers
- Tourists and other visitors
- Commercial and industrial carriers

These travelers use a variety of transportation means. You can expect people to travel radial roads via automobiles, pickups, vans, trucks, motorcycles, semi-trailers, and buses. Radial roads often run parallel to railroad tracks, which are themselves radial roads. In some cases you will find radial roads that have evolved from quadrant roads.

Quadrant Roads

Quadrant roads are nothing more than straight arterial roads. Quadrant roads are not the product of nature; they were designed by humans. Quadrant roads are at 90-degree angles and the cardinal orientation for them is almost always north–south and east–west. You will find a few cities in the United States that don't have quadrant roads, like downtown Minneapolis, Minnesota; downtown Philadelphia, Pennsylvania; and downtown St. Louis, Missouri. These are exceptions due to the presence of winding rivers. Quadrant roads can be found in the cores of cities, which at their inception, were carefully planned by city founders. A quick look at history will show you that the military camps of the Romans were laid out in geometric grids. Today, the city of Turin, Italy — built over the grid of a Roman camp — has quadrant roads throughout the entire city. Many modern cities are based on a quadrant road system, such as:

- Manhattan, New York
- Oklahoma City, Oklahoma
- Phoenix, Arizona

Sometimes quadrant roads form a complex set of quadrangles as illustrated in Figure 2.4. The darker lines represent the major roads that carry the greatest amount of traffic. The medium thick lines indicate roads that are somewhat important and the thinnest lines indicate the smallest, least important, neighborhood-type roads. A city's topography has much to do with the quadrant road layout. For instance, look at the stretch between Covina and San Bernardino in Southern California. This space is flat and buildable — perfect for long, straight, and parallel roads.

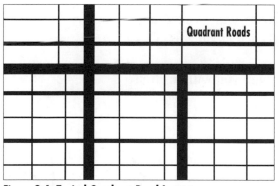

Quadrant Roads

Figure 2.4 Typical Quadrant Road Layout

To select the most important road in your quest for the right location for your business, first identify the prevalent type of zoning along the roads, such as commercial, residential, industrial, or agricultural. Second, look for the quadrant road that becomes a radial road extending well beyond the city limits into the countryside and leading to other towns. Third, study the traffic dynamics of each road. Some carry more residential traffic; some carry more of a variety of traffic.

In some cities the road dynamics are more obvious on the east–west arteries; in other cities the road dynamics are on the north–south arteries. In Miami, Florida, the east–west arteries, which are connected to I-95 and the Turnpike, show more retail action. The north–south arteries instead function as connectors that substitute for a freeway system. Consequently, the main intersections are very desirable for retailers, as long as they gravitate toward the east–west roads.

Regional-Local Roads

Regional roads are major arteries that crisscross a city and connect long-distance points. Often, regional roads continue into the countryside and eventually connect with other cities and towns. Examples include Ventura Boulevard in Los Angeles, California; Telegraph Road in Detroit, Michigan; and North Avenue in Chicago, Illinois. Regional roads are wider, carry more long-distance and local traffic, and serve major sections of a city. Traffic can cover a longer distance in a shorter time. *Local roads* carry traffic within a small area.

Other Road Configurations

Other types of road configurations are described below and illustrated in figures 2.5 and 2.6 below.

- Fishbone. The main road has various tributary roads on both sides. This type of configuration is good for retailing.
- Loop. This configuration is made up of a curved road that carries limited and local traffic. This does not include long-distance traffic. This is not good for retailing.
- Tree branch. If you locate at the base — that is, the first "y" — you will be in an excellent position for running a retail operation.
- Parallel. Each road is independent in this configuration. None of these roads serves the store's trading area properly; thus, this configuration is not an ideal location.
- Serpentine. This configuration includes winding roads with limited and slow traffic. This is often found on the slopes of hills and mountains. This setup is not good for retailing.
- Stellar. If you locate in the center of this configuration, you will position yourself for retail success.

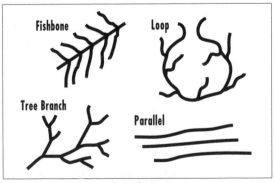

Figure 2.5 Varying Road Configurations

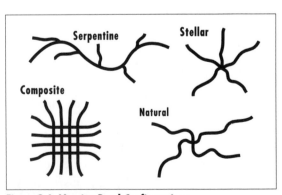

Figure 2.6 Varying Road Configurations

- Composite. You will normally find this configuration in areas of high density, like in a downtown. Your challenge is to find the most important intersection within this configuration.
- Natural. This road configuration follows the contours of topography. You will find that good locations will cross over the points of each road's intersections.

Most of these configurations offer limited opportunities for good retail locations, especially when compared to the straight and parallel features of more typical quadrant roads.

You need to pay special attention to the roads that follow natural contours. Forests, rivers, and terrain allow for natural paths. The roads constructed over these paths form the skeleton of a city. Subsequently, other roads may have been developed to connect existing developments and long-distance points that cut across the original road configurations. Study the parts in the context of the whole.

Importance of Signage

Make no mistake, a sign must be considered an essential quality of a location because it can improve the location a great deal. Begin with the intent of obtaining the biggest, tallest, most visible sign allowed in the area. Aim at the most and proceed with that in mind.

There are ways of interpreting without violating the ordinances that combine the goals of the community's aesthetic and environmental concerns. The sign must be both attractive and functional to catch the eye of potential customers; and it must reveal a reasonable attempt at adapting to ordinances. Stay involved in its creation with the architect and sign designer, to be sure all concerns are adequately addressed.

The great sculptors of in Florence, Italy, before sculpting a statue from stone or in bronze, would place a clay model of it on the exact spot where the completed masterpiece would be placed in the square. The intent was to experience the impact that the monument would create *in situ*.

You must bring this sense of reality, of size, and of proportion to the designer. The lettering of too many signs is muddled or convoluted, making them illegible, even close up. Fancy letters selected by draftsmen or architects could be inadequately legible and recognizable from a distance. Spacing between the letters is best decided on site. Your sign on the front of the shopping center must be legible from the street while driving. To maximize visibility, it is necessary that the sign be different from the others around it, in size, height, geometrical shapes, and contrasting colors. For instance, Blockbuster Video had a free standing rectangular sign. To increase visibility, management decided to tilt it so it would stand out from all other horizontal signs.

Your sign must be located where it is maximally visible and noticeable — at times when you know you will miss the long distance visibility, it could be placed so it is more visible at eye-level while driving. Signs can be everywhere: at the entrance, at the exit, on the roof, on the front, inside glass windows (permitted by ordinance), on the side, on the rear, freestanding, or on the wall. At times there are creative ways of improving your sign. In one German town, McDonald's erected a sign on a telescopic pole with holes in it. From time to time, they would lift the sign to a more desirable height.

To conclude, your sign should have these three characteristics:

- Pleasant and creative design
- Absolute simplicity of form (e.g. the McDonald's arches)
- Legibility and recognizability from a distance

Most important is the latter, recognizability, particularly in foreign countries.

Look at the City's Economy

Determine whether the downtown is alive and well. In short, find out if there is a healthy activity of business, commerce, social life, and entertainment late into the night. Find out if the downtown still exercises its pulling power from all areas around the city. If so, the roads coming to and going from downtown are true arteries of the city. These arterial roads make the city live and breathe.

You may find some sections of the city that lack an economic base. Look for tell-tale indicators of a poor economic base, including:

- Topographical problems;
- Poor roadway systems;
- New interest gravitation centers appearing in adjacent areas;
- Downward demographic trends;
- Lack of adequate city planning; and
- Lack of new investment.

To learn more about the city's economy, look at the historical pattern of vacancies of all types — residential, industrial, professional, and commercial. Ask questions like:

- Where were the vacancies ten years ago?
- How many blocks were affected by these vacancies?
- What areas are currently affected by vacancies?
- Where did the tenants move?
- Did vacancies increase?

Vacancies, or the lack of them, in a commercial area are a clear indication of the prosperity level of the retail businesses. You do not want to locate in an area with a history of vacancies.

Retail vacancies occur for various reasons. A rotation of merchants in some strip centers is normal. In other strips or centers, vacancies can indicate a repositioning of tenants with merchandise pricing that better fits the demographics of the area. Further, vacancies may indicate a moving away of business to new centers because of rerouting of traffic or because of a healthier environment somewhere else, due to a disappearance of the demand as a result of changes in demographics and density. These types of vacancies reveal a deep-seated problem that rarely can be reversed.

Know the Balance of a City

Excluding a city's center or downtown, the balance of a city can be divided into three parts. The first part is formed by buildings built close together during the 1800s through the 1940s. The second part includes the suburban areas of single and multiple dwellings with neighborhood shopping centers, community centers, and malls that are generally old, but have been remodeled. The third part is made up of new suburban areas built during the last 30 years. This newer part consists of single dwelling developments, bigger malls, fancy office parks, and a new highway network. Knowing the city's balance will help you understand where your potential customers live, work, and play. For example, in the communities that are farther away from the center of the city, the pulling power of the downtown will become weaker. Some communities will cluster among themselves, forming a separate core downtown. Oak Brook, Illinois, on the west side of Chicago or Schaumburg on the northwest side are communities that belong to the SMA of Chicago, but they stand distinct and independent. A far away city like Naperville is actually linked to a separate city, Aurora, which both form a new cluster of vitality and interest.

Examine the parts of the whole to see how they relate or do not relate to each other with this thought in mind — which area of the city will help your business prosper. This type of thorough study will help you better understand how and where to advertise and promote your business, literally, block by block. Your goal as a retailer is maximum market penetration — that means you reach every potential customer in the area.

Target an Area of Functional Completeness

Also study the area in the context of functional completeness — meaning an area that offers its residents everything they need, including places of work, shopping, social, cultural, recreational, and professional activities. In short, look at a self-sufficient area. For instance, when you look at an area that consists only of factories, you will know that no people will be around that area at night or on weekends, unless they operate two or three shifts. Similarly, when you look at a residential area, you know that people — and, commonly, both spouses — work Monday through Friday. Carefully examine the presence of all the factors that indicate functional completeness and are necessary for a solid customer base, including:

- Both single and multiple dwellings;
- Shopping centers of all sizes;
- Industrial and manufacturing areas;
- Office-professional buildings;
- Recreational attractions;
- Academic institutions;
- Health care providers;
- A good system of roads; and
- Public transportation.

If you will live in the community you have selected for your retail business, you must consider these factors in meeting both your needs and your family's needs. Besides the city's economic balance and functional completeness, you will also need to consider other key factors that pull people from their homes, workplaces, and long-distance travels.

Know What Moves People – The Wind

Imagine looking at one area (one-fourth of a square mile) from above, in a helicopter, during the hours of the day when most people move from one point to another — morning and late afternoon hours. You will be able to clearly distinguish heavy flows of cars heading in one or more directions. The flow eventually will fan out into smaller channels, just like the blood flowing from the arteries into the capillary streams. Some will make sharp turns, meandering into smaller sections of the area. When it comes to site selection, the study of the movement of people is produced and determined by interest gravitation.

Interest gravitation or the *wind* is a force or attraction that orients and moves people toward places of interest in a determinate direction. These places can be places of employment, shopping, and various recreational, social, professional, and cultural activities. More specifically, these are places where people go to get their basic necessities for living. These places, or objects of interest, are assembled in an area that form a gravitational mass that generates a strong magnetic pulling power. This magnetic pulling power is directly proportional to the quantity, diversity, and attributes of these places, like attractiveness, newness, and convenience. You must examine the movement of people caused by interest gravitation because in the selection of your location, you need to identify the main movement stream. Your location should be along that stream. If the stream goes in another direction, people will ignore your place of business. To help you understand people movement, plot the movement with vectors. A *vector* itself can be represented by an arrow with three characteristics:

- Direction, relative to a cardinal point;
- Magnitude, or the thickness of the arrow, which represents the amount of flow (a small stream carries less water than a big river); and

- Length, which is the distance between the point of origin and the point of arrival. Think of a short river and a long river.

Picture in your mind the movement of people according to the described characteristics of vectors. To more fully comprehend the concept of interest gravitation and what it means to retail businesses, consider your own daily routine.

In planning the activities of your day, your mind is naturally directed toward the directions in which your activities will take place. For instance, if you live in Winnetka, Illinois, and work in downtown Chicago, your mind will turn in the southern direction. Downtown Chicago is a vibrant center of interest. Consequently, you will find a heavy stream of movement from Winnetka toward downtown Chicago — also known as the Loop. In fact, all metropolitan areas have gravitational centers spread through them — within an area, outside an area, and between small towns. Interest gravitation affects the relationship between small towns and large, metropolitan areas, too. For instance, if you live in:

- Indio, California, your interest gravitation will be toward Palm Springs;
- Grants Pass, Oregon, your interest gravitation is toward Medford;
- Pompano Beach, Florida, most likely your interest gravitation will be Fort Lauderdale to the south;
- Quincy, Massachusetts, your interest gravitation will be Boston to the north; and
- Waipahu, Hawaii, your interest gravitation will be Honolulu to the east.

The relationship between centers of interests is not only a city-to-city relationship, but also an urban-suburban relationship. Each city has various parts serving others that offer a stronger degree of interest. By knowing this interest gravitation in the part of the city in which you want to locate, you will begin to understand the movement of people that will generate your customers. You need to locate where the wind flows.

Three Types of Traffic

You can subdivide interest gravitation into types of movement or traffic, including:

- Living traffic
- Work traffic
- Long-distance traffic

Living traffic is generated by the basic needs people fulfill to live. People fulfill these needs when they:

- Buy groceries, medicines, and clothing;
- Join recreational or social activities;
- Go to the doctor or dentist;
- Get an ice cream or a taco; or
- Go to the movies.

In most communities the radius in which these activities occur is relatively small — usually within one or two miles.

When you look at the map of the area where you live, you will be able to identify the centers of living traffic of which you are a part. A city is nothing but a grid that includes various interest gravitational centers. Adjacent interest gravitational centers serve each other. In the selection of your location, you need to identify the living traffic that happens most of the day and night. Living traffic forms the primary network of people movement and usually consists of heavy users. You will want to know about the consumers who comprise the living traffic in your prospective site. People who pass your store often will have a high top-of-mind awareness. In other words, your store will come to mind first for a majority of your customers. When they think of your product, they think of your store. More information about top-of-mind awareness is in Chapter 6.

Work traffic is produced by jobs. Superimposed on living traffic, work traffic involves commuting from home to job site. However, the movement of work traffic normally is longer than living traffic movements. If you have excellent living traffic plus excellent work traffic, the center of interest gravitation is more desirable. However, be careful because this traffic movement is not constant. Work traffic will vary by time of day and day of week — with peak and valley time periods. Also, work traffic passes in front of your store at least twice a day, but probably not weekends.

Long-distance traffic is varied and includes:

- Trips to vacation spots;
- The salesperson passing through;
- Commercial transporters in vans or semitrailers;
- People seeking specialty goods and services; and
- Individuals attending occasional events like concerts, industrial shows, and conventions.

Long-distance traffic can be found on interstate highways, freeways, and toll roads. If the long-distance traffic passes through the center of living traffic, the interest gravitation will intensify — meaning that a particular location will be even more desirable. Long-distance traffic is a very important bonus for your location, because it adds to the potential business that already exists in that particular trading area. The combination of the three types of traffic is called a *traffic aggregate*. Figure 2.7 illustrates how the three types of traffic can converge. A traffic aggregate is more intense when you have a wide, straight road that connects distant parts of the city or countryside. The kind of road that carries aggregate traffic is a regional road. Obviously, neighborhood and local roads do not carry all three types of traffic — living, work, and long-distance traffic —

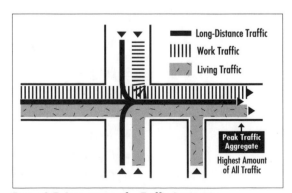

Figure 2.7 Importance of a Traffic Aggregate

they carry only one or two types of traffic. Once you have identified them, imagine a triangle with the sides representing the three traffic movements just described. Ideally, your location should be in the center of the triangle.

Since one of the essential elements of a good retail location is the traffic flow on the road, you want to choose a location with a high level of visibility and exposure along a regional road, so you can have the highest possible number of daily impressions.

Now that you know the different types of traffic possible on a roadway, proceed to identify the center of interest gravitation most relevant to your business. Make a list of these centers and rank them in terms of their relevance. Understand how the movements from all directions complement or exclude each other. However, keep in mind that the limits of a trading area are dictated by hills and mountains. For instance, in cities with hills and valleys like Pittsburgh, Pennsylvania, the traffic gravitates toward the bottom of the valleys and follows their contours. One valley opens into another, and the traffic acts like a river with several tributaries. You can identify the centers of living and work traffic along that river. These centers, or nodules, will provide a traffic aggregate — the sum of living traffic plus work traffic plus long-distance traffic.

Observe Daily Traffic Patterns

To better understand the city that you want to serve, take an in-depth look at not only what moves people, but also the daily traffic patterns of its people. Traffic can be classified as single-head traffic and multiple-head traffic. For instance, if you are in the banking business, you will be interested in single-head traffic. If you are in the motel or restaurant business, you will be interested in multiple-head traffic. The theory is the more people, the greater the sales potential. Multiple-head traffic is often long distance and recreational, which means more people in a spending mood. Work traffic can also be single- and multiple-head traffic.

You can gain a good sense of the number of your potential customers by analyzing the *traffic count* — the number of vehicles passing in front of a location in a 24-hour period. Many cities and counties take periodic traffic counts for purposes of road improvements and construction. Usually, a traffic count is taken by hour; however, for the needs of your business, you may want to take a count for shorter periods. Take a look at the traffic count example on the next page. This traffic count analysis gives you an idea of the peak traffic periods that may make up a great portion of customers.

A daily traffic curve will coincide with the business hours of a particular location. You need to know the peak and low hours of traffic in front of your prospective store. Managing your retail business during peak traffic hours is essential because this is where you will earn your profit.

Your prospective location may have great traffic flows on a Saturday, but may seem disastrous at 3:00 P.M. on a Thursday. When you are looking at a new site, you must visit the site during the various parts of the day and night to fully understand:

- Traffic patterns;
- Type of traffic;
- Traffic vectors; and
- Traffic related to specific business generators, such as regional shopping centers and office industrial parks.

Also, you need to understand the relevance of the traffic peaks in relation to the top sales hours of your specific business. Use the figures you obtain from your Hourly Sales Analysis located in Appendix C – Analogue Data Development and described in Chapter 5. The peak traffic count may be found at another point, perhaps even with only one or two types of traffic — like mostly work traffic or mostly living traffic. Depending upon the nature of your retail business, you need to choose the traffic type and count that fits the best. As a general rule, the peak aggregate traffic count — work, living, and long-distance traffic combined — is more desirable than the mere peak traffic count. Of course, the number of cars on the road is more important in big cities where there are many competitive places. In small towns, your customers will know where you are; thus, fewer cars will pass by your store more often.

Feel the Wind

Interest gravitation is sometimes referred to as the *wind*. The wind can flow within an entire city, part of a city, or between cities and towns. When considering your location, it is essential that you feel the wind — where it comes from, where it goes to, where it passes through. You must locate where the best flow, or sum of the flows, happens. You must feel a strong wind.

For instance, consider the case of a small town linked with a big city. Think of Ann Arbor, Michigan, about 25 miles west of Detroit. The wind flows between Ann Arbor and Detroit, but the stronger wind flows toward Detroit. In Figure 2.8 the arrows between the cities indicate a strong level in interest (the wind). People travel between these cities frequently. The type of traffic is mostly living and work traffic. The areas through which the wind blows are the desirable areas of activity. Be cautious, however, when considering a location in the middle of a city. Oftentimes, the very centers of the towns have become stale, due to the aging of buildings, lack of parking, and lack of space, preventing the possibility of expansion. A suburban location may be your choice. Suburban areas have developed, particularly when the wind connects to other centers of interest, like other suburban nodes, towns, or freeway and highway intersections.

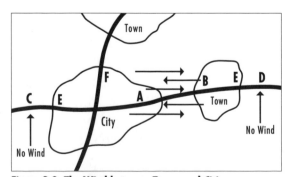

Figure 2.8 The Wind between Towns and Cities

In Figure 2.8 the wind is strongest between points A and B. If you locate at points C, D, or E, you will

Traffic Count Example

Location: 142 Main Street

Hour Ending	Volume	One Dot Equals 20 Cars
1:00 A.M.	92	••••
2:00 A.M.	44	••
3:00 A.M.	37	••
4:00 A.M.	27	••
5:00 A.M.	49	•••
6:00 A.M.	208	•••••••••••
7:00 A.M.	734	••••••••••••••••••••••••••••••••••••
8:00 A.M.	1,180	•••
9:00 A.M.	817	••
10:00 A.M.	637	•••••••••••••••••••••••••••••••••
11:00 A.M.	608	••••••••••••••••••••••••••••••••
12:00 P.M.	645	•••••••••••••••••••••••••••••••••
1:00 P.M.	806	••
2:00 P.M.	733	••••••••••••••••••••••••••••••••••••
3:00 P.M.	753	•••••••••••••••••••••••••••••••••••••
4:00 P.M.	818	••
5:00 P.M.	1,155	•••
6:00 P.M.	1,452	••
7:00 P.M.	1,114	•••
8:00 P.M.	941	••
9:00 P.M.	763	•••••••••••••••••••••••••••••••••••••••
10:00 P.M.	639	•••••••••••••••••••••••••••••••••
11:00 P.M.	401	••••••••••••••••••••
12:00 A.M.	228	••••••••••••
24-Hour Total	14,881	

be away from the action because the east–west roads lead to nowhere. However, the location marked F is possibly a good location depending upon the size and distance of another town to the north. Don't make the same mistake as this franchisee. In Philadelphia, Pennsylvania, a retail franchisee insisted on opening her store near a mall, but not between the mall and the city. She chose, instead, the far side (the area marked C in Figure 2.8). People drove from the town to the mall and vice versa, but almost nobody drove beyond the mall. The location was deceiving. The mall was more than one million square feet in size, but her store was not within the wind. The franchisee lost business at the misplaced store.

Making a map of the city in which you wish to locate and finding where the wind exists will help you know where your greatest number of potential customers exists. Figure 2.9 is a good example of how to map the wind in a city.

Figure 2.9 shows the downtown area of Louisville, Kentucky — a dynamic and vibrant location. Notice the system of radial roads leading to the downtown — also called the central business district (CBD) — from all directions. The northeast area shows rapid development, and its gravitation toward the downtown is shown here with directional arrows that indicate percentages. The square indicates the area of interest where the winds merge. The interest gravitation in the northeast, within the freeway loop, is strong. But the wind outside the loop is much weaker, as the percentages show. Other centers of interest can be found at several intersections between some of the radial roads and the freeway.

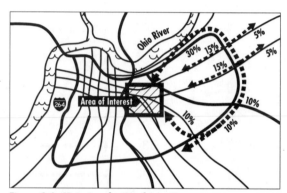

Figure 2.9 Mapping the Wind in a City

Figure 2.10 gives you another example of how to map the wind to and from a city. In this illustration, the CBD is the main hub of activity. More about CBDs as retail site options is in Chapter 7. The concept of the wind clearly illustrates the need to locate on or near important roads flowing both into and from other important roads with easy intersections.

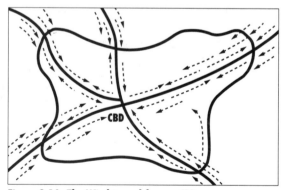

Figure 2.10 The Wind to and from a CBD

Be cautious of choosing locations on a road that:

- Goes nowhere;
- Ends against a mountain or at the shore of a lake;
- Is against a freeway slope; or
- Abuts another road at a 90-degree angle at a T-intersection.

You will also need to consider the dynamics of traveling patterns based on the different types of retail purchases.

Understand Trip Patterns for Various Retail Purchases

When looking at the way people move to make retail purchases, always consider the distance your customers will travel. People move differently depending upon the object of the desired purchase. The number of trips and the amount of travel time will vary based on whether the purchase is for a specialty or commodity product.

When it comes to specialties — normally expensive, special, and long-lasting goods — the distance traveled is much longer. For example, cars and appliances are purchases that are infrequent, expensive, and definitely special. They are handled by dealers who specialize in these items. Compared to trips to grocery stores, trips to car dealers and appliance dealers are rare. People go out of their way to seek the desired model of car or the preferred brand of appliance. These factors influence the trading area of your retail store.

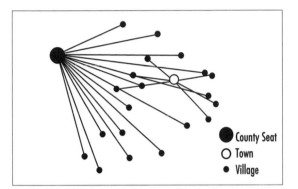

Figure 2.11 Trip Patterns for Specialty Products

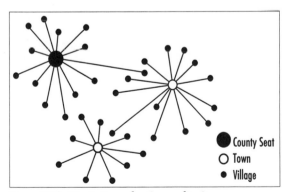

Figure 2.12 Trip Patterns for Commodity Items

As Figure 2.11 illustrates, specialty trips are less frequent and longer in distance and time. People will travel out of their towns to bigger towns or to a larger city. You will find that the wind will flow from smaller centers toward bigger centers. On the other hand, trips to purchase everyday supplies are made by the living traffic. The element of convenience is basic to this kind of traffic. These purchases are for common items — always in great demand, offered at affordable prices, and on sale at many locations. Trips for commodity items are frequent, the distances are rather short, and the driving time is brief. For instance, people typically will not drive to another center of town for groceries, unless they need special items that are infrequently sold.

As Figure 2.12 indicates, trips for commodity items tend to remain within the town itself. Local grocery retailers enjoy the business of the residents within the city in which they are located. People coming from the countryside may make fewer trips per month for groceries, but they still patronize the town stores.

Chapter Wrap-Up

Your search for the best spot to open your own store will always start with an analysis of the bigger picture — in this case, the overall city. As you analyze an entire metropolitan area you will begin to see the relationships between the city and the outlying areas in terms of interest gravitation. Your knowledge of the radial, quadrant, regional, and local roads to, from, and within the city is critical to helping you determine the various types of traffic. As you discover the important nodes and nodules within a city, you can choose one of them as the most promising for your retail purposes and narrow your search to the specific site. Now it is time to focus your attention on finding the right piece of property.

Chapter 3

Research the Specific Site

Now that you have found a section of the city that is situated to serve your target customers, you can narrow your search from an area of perhaps two or three blocks down to the best possible location. You may have noticed two, three, or possibly four sites that look promising. But now you must decide which one best suits your retail store.

In this chapter, you will learn the secrets of gathering the necessary facts about a prospective business site. You will learn to:

- Walk, drive, and fly the location.
- Use aerial photos.
- Map the site.
- Research the location's history.
- Deal with land use control issues.
- Determine potential environmental liability.

By using the essential information in this chapter, you will know whether to go ahead with location planning or to walk away and find somewhere else to build or rent your store. To begin your research of a specific site, it is essential that you see the property from several different vantage points. A sure-fire way to get a well-rounded look at a site is to walk, drive, and fly the location.

Walk It, Drive It, Fly It

Walking a site is essential, whether it is a vacant parcel or improved and occupied, because you will be able to form an idea of the possibilities of its usage and the costs involved. As you walk a site you want to critically analyze every detail. For example, find out how the site relates to the front sidewalks, street, and front and side of the adjacent parcel. Also, check for any encroachments of buildings, fences, or vegetation and if anybody is using the property as a right-of-way or for any other purpose. Look for things like:

- Type of soil, sand, or sod;
- Whether the site is level and drainage is possible;
- If dirt needs removal or the land needs additional soil;
- Whether it requires retaining walls; and
- If water from adjacent parcels is flooding the property.

You need to know these types of details to know the amount of time and money you may have to invest to make the site workable for your retail business. In addition, you will want to know how your future improvements fit into the context of other improvements.

If building improvements are on the property, you may wish to visit the site with a structural engineer to see whether you can use it by remodeling it. If so, carefully examine every brick, crack, and beam on the roof and ceiling, and take exact measurements.

You can also drive the property to gain other key insights. The parcel with or without an improvement on it must be judged from a driver's standpoint. Your customers driving by will see what you see. You need to visualize the raw parcel properly developed with your store on it. In fact, you may want to use computer software that graphically shows a completed development. From the physical standpoint, evaluate the site's visibility. Pay close attention to barriers, raised and landscaped dividers, trees, bushes, buildings, land elevations, or depressions that may decrease a store's visibility and accessibility. Rate the importance of the property in relation to:

- Its adjacent businesses;
- The entire block of which it is a part;
- The traffic generators seen from the property itself; and
- Other traffic generators within half a mile.

Make sure the parcel has presence and is not lost within the landscape. Further, check to see how the site compares to your competitors' sites. Your site should look equal to or more important than your competitors' locations. After you have walked and driven the location, you will be ready to get a view from the sky.

Nothing speaks more clearly than a view from above. From the sky you can see your site in the context of the whole city. The benefits of flying a site are the same in all types of markets — rural, suburban, urban, or downtown, such as

Manhattan or the Loop. You will always discover something you haven't considered during your view from below. For example, flying a site reveals the movement of people — which you can break down to number of cars, lines at the stoplights, swing traffic (the heavier traffic), cars turning left or right, speed of traffic, and mix of traffic, such as buses, trucks, and cars. Further, you will have the opportunity to count the number of cars parked in the lots of office complexes, industrial buildings, shopping centers, and residential areas. Take note of the height of buildings, main crosswalks, overpasses, sidewalks, and number of pedestrians on the sidewalks. It is important to note the exact time of your aerial survey, because you want to know, for instance, if it was peak hour traffic or not.

The secret to a successful aerial survey is preparation, preparation, preparation. You have two options for air travel — rent a plane or a helicopter. Of course, you will need a pilot unless you are licensed to fly. If you rent a plane and pilot, be sure to rent a high-wing plane, such as a Cessna A 172 Skyhawk or 184 Skylane. The high wing will allow you an unobstructed view of the ground. However, it is best to use a helicopter. Renting a plane or copter may not be part of your budget, but the knowledge you gain from flying a site will pay off in the long run. After you have arranged for a means of transportation for your aerial survey, you will want to prepare a map of the site to use during your flight.

You can use the map of the site you created to identify the roads and interest gravitation, as you learned in Chapter 2. As you fly the area, you can use your map to better understand traffic patterns, including:

- The movement of traffic at the major intersections;
- The number of cars that travel from beyond a river or over a hill; and
- The location of the most congested bottleneck.

Discuss the map with your pilot and prepare a route for him or her that identifies the successive points to examine. Study the relationship of the area with adjacent areas. Identify competitive stores and similar chain stores to understand how they relate to each other. Your main goal is to understand the overall trading area of your future store by discovering its physical boundaries in relation to the city or a great portion of it.

During your flight, take lots of photographs. Take some of them from an altitude low enough to show details on and around the location, like markings on the street, width of the sidewalks, and placement of stop signs; and take a vertical shot over the identified location from about 1,500 feet. Be sure to include four shots, taken at an angle of the four cardinal points (one-, two-, three-, and five-mile distant). If you cannot afford the price of an aerial survey, use existing aerial photos from city records or real estate companies.

Use Aerial Photos

Your local city hall may have aerial photos. Ask if you can buy, rent, or photocopy them. If the city hall you contact doesn't have aerial photos, you can contact the

Federal Clearing House in the Earth Resources Observation Systems (EROS) Data Center in Sioux Falls, South Dakota. When you order the photos, you will need an exact address of the property you are considering or the address of adjacent properties. You can also get the map coordinates of the site from your pilot, who normally uses a sectional chart for flying. See Appendix A for more information. In addition, you may wish to contact the local county office of the National Resources Conservation Service. Through the National Cooperative Soil Survey, this agency regularly publishes soil survey reports that become public. These reports contain aerial photos that may help you. Once you have photos of your prospective site, you will be in a better position to tackle the next facet of site research — accurately mapping the site. If possible, locate old aerial photographs of the area, so you can compare them with newer ones to see the area's growth pattern and identify trends.

Plan Ahead

Planning ahead is a must in areas that are in a development phase. You can discover at city hall the development plans that have been approved and those under consideration and review: new subdivisions, roads, utilities. Also, you can see the rate of construction actually taking place. You need to visualize the location of your future retail business in the context of the completed development. You want to be part of the activity core with a location that will have the best attributes, including visibility and accessibility. Even though you may be looking at a forest, it could soon become a community shopping center. It is important for you to contact the developers and familiarize yourself with their plans.

Map the Site

The risk of making a mistake in site selection is always high. At times, the presence of a few traffic generators in adjacent blocks may lead you to accept a site even when it may be clear that to support your store, you will need more and bigger traffic generators. To avoid making an unwise decision, prepare maps with several visual indicators, such as dots, arrows, colors, and lines. These indicators will signify major relevant business generators, like shopping centers, office buildings, apartment complexes, supermarkets, schools, and the strongest competitors. If you are locating a franchise, plot stores of the same company as well.

Hang your maps on a wall in a well-lit area. Spend considerable time looking at them to:

- Evaluate the various marks.
- Study the relationships of the roads.
- Calculate distances and driving times between points, stores, and traffic generators.
- Know the position of the location in respect to the competition.

If you have properly mapped the site, you will be able to see the location in its entire context, not only in the context of a block or two. If you have plans for further developments, mapping is essential because you now need to see entire areas of the city and understand how they relate to each other. For a complete discussion of expanding by opening more stores, see Chapter 9.

Physical-geographic characteristics of a location are visible, measurable, and easy to evaluate. Mapping your site will help you know your site's physical-geographic attributes.

As you learned from Chapter 1, you can identify your market by studying the profile of the user of your goods and services and by the nature and size of the trading area produced by your type of industry — check your demographics and psychographics. The right location in the wrong market will contribute more to the failure of a business than if you plan the wrong location in the right market. To continue your site research, you will now have to devote some time talking to people that have knowledge of and influence in the specific area you are interested in.

Get Facts from City and Community Resources

Another essential element of researching a site involves getting facts from city government and community resources. You may prefer to have an outside firm do the research for you. However, such surveys are very expensive, and the firm you hire will learn a lot, but you will learn very little.

A compilation of data that is neatly bound in a colorful folder may seem impressive. But the knowledge, sense, and understanding you develop in doing the research yourself is essential before you invest everything you have into a retail business. To start your fact-finding mission, learn what the city government offers for entrepreneurs.

The Official Route

Start your fact-finding by going the official route. You can question city government officials. You will have access to five key city contacts, including:

- City hall
- Engineering department
- Building and planning department
- Utilities company
- Police department

When you approach city hall, find out whether there are plans for property condemnations that will affect your site — either directly or indirectly. You need to know accurate facts about accesses, interchanges, and overpasses in front of your prospective business site. For a more detailed discussion on property condemnations, refer to the section later in this chapter.

Further, you need to get information from your city's engineering department regarding crucial city developments. You will learn about plans for new and improved roads, median strips, new regulations involving turns — anything that will create a physical and psychological barrier to the traffic. Find out which projects are totally funded — you would be surprised at how many plans fall through due to a lack of funds. The engineering department can also provide you with traffic count maps.

The building and planning department can tell you the number and types of building permits granted over the last three or four years — particularly during the previous year. You can learn about permits for:

- Multiple dwellings;
- Single residences;
- Industrial complexes;
- Commercial buildings;
- Roadway systems; and
- Governmental buildings, hospitals, and schools.

In addition, the building and planning department will have maps showing the present and future layout of the city in conformity to the master zoning plan and the projected timetable for development. Any information regarding city development will help you make your location decision. For example, scheduled roadwork in front of your prospective site may seriously impact your location.

The local utilities company works hand in hand with the building and planning department. To be ahead of development, a local utilities company will continuously project the number and types of new sewer, electric, and water services. It is also instrumental in the selection of areas in which, eventually, the population will grow. Its projections might be long-range and well-beyond your immediate need, but they will show where the future growth will be.

Finally, you will want to contact the local police department to find out the history of crime in your prospective business site. You are best served by creating a good relationship — mutually supportive and cooperative — with the law enforcement authorities.

The Community Route

After you have collected important information from city officials, make sure you tap into the wealth of information available to you elsewhere in the community. You will have access to six key community contacts, including:

- The chamber of commerce
- Banks
- Newspapers
- Schools
- Real estate brokers and developers
- Merchants

Start your search at the local chamber of commerce. Your local chamber of commerce is a particularly useful source to find out the big trends in town, such as what industries there are, and the transportation system that serves the area in which goods are produced. You can often get geographic maps, zoning maps, and a selected amount of demographics data. Be careful though — this is good information, except it is general, with a heavy dose of promotional flavor. To learn even more information about the area in which you want to serve, contact the local banks.

Count the banks that serve your trading area. You should know the amount of their deposits in millions. You are most interested in the banks physically near your location. A good chat with a bank manager will tell you how many loans were granted recently and for what purposes. Each bank has a map or an electronic record of its own trading area — where its customers reside — broken down into geographical details. A nearby bank's trading area will usually mirror your own trading area.

Another good source of community information is your local newspaper. One sure-fire way to make a positive contact is to set up a meeting with the advertising director of the local newspaper. An advertising director is always eager to attract new advertising revenue, and this person will know the area intimately — its people, policy, politicians, and customs. You can acquire important information about the community you intend to serve. For instance, your advance knowledge of fairs, recreational activities, and special celebrations can help you plan for increased business.

Further, a school administrator can provide you with helpful information. You can learn the enrollment trends and how many students leave home to go to college. You might also pick up information regarding new schools or school closures. Further, you can find out what school events create interest in the community and whether there are any future opportunities for sales promotions.

You can talk with real estate brokers and developers to find out key market information about the area in which you wish to locate. For example, you might learn what type of retailer is coming to or leaving the area and what are the real estate prices for commercial properties. Often you will see broker signs on a property that indicate a future store. To learn the facts, however, your best bet is to talk with the brokers and developers in charge of these proposed developments.

Another good source of information is the local merchants, especially the ones located adjacent to your site. You want to find out:

- The type of customers they serve;
- The time of the day they experience peak sales hours;
- The sales levels and trends; and
- Special local factors and events.

Basically, you want to find out anything that correlates with your industry and respective product. Additionally, you want to introduce yourself to your neighboring merchants and create a friendly rapport. Now that you have gathered essential information from city government and community sources, make sure you research the history of your prospective location.

Study the History of the Location

Your search for a retail location should include the history of the location itself. You can learn the location's history by checking the records at city hall or by talking to neighbors — both businesspeople and residents. Determine the reasons the previous businesses did not succeed on that specific property. Some common reasons might include:

- Bad management
- Poor products
- Low standards
- Inadequate capital
- Shifts in traffic
- Changing demographics
- Environmental problems
- New shopping centers opening nearby
- Strong competition
- Large employers leaving the area

Your findings regarding the location's history may alter your decision concerning the specific parcel or even the area itself. For example, if you find out that the shopping center across the street just closed, you may change your mind about the particular location in which you are interested.

Your research of the location's history should include a trip to the local title company or county assessor's office. Once you have selected a specific parcel, obtain a preliminary title report. It will show the main restrictions that affect your property and its adjacent properties. This is something very important to know, because some restrictions might prevent you from using the property or from using it for commercial purposes.

Know the Land Use Control Issues

A thorough research of a specific site includes learning the land use control issues that affect the area in which you wish to locate. *Land use control* is a broad term that describes any legal restrictions that control how land may be used. Two types of land use control categories exist — public controls and private controls. When first reviewing a proposed site, determine whether any public controls exist. You can get this type of information from the local planning department by asking for a listing of the zoning ordinances.

Public Controls

Public controls are enforced by governmental agencies and include issues like:

- Zoning laws;
- Building codes;
- Subdivision and plat regulations; and
- Master plans, including planned unit developments (PUDs).

If you don't pay attention to these laws, you may not be able to secure a building permit. Also, a violation of these codes can lead to criminal prosecution.

In your quest to learn about the public controls that may affect your prospective business location, your first concern is learning how the parcel is zoned. Zoning conditions and other public controls can usually be determined from zoning and plat maps; every jurisdiction will be different. Zoning laws divide large governmental units like cities into districts or zones. Within each zone, the law regulates the use of the land — how buildings and improvements may be constructed, the area of the lots the improvements may occupy, setback lines, and land density. Zoning laws protect the public health, safety, morals, and general welfare of the people who live in each zone. For convenience, zones are restricted to either residential, commercial, industrial, or agricultural uses; each zone is further subclassified.

In reading the zoning ordinances, you will find that some are clearer than others. Many zoning ordinances do not distinguish between types of use. For instance, they may merely state "retail sales or service establishment." Under some codes, restaurants and gas stations may come under the description of retail sales and service establishments. The zoning ordinance language is often not as important as its interpretation. You will need to thoroughly understand the zoning restrictions of the area you are interested in.

You may be required to obtain specific permission — such as a variance or conditional use permit — from the local zoning authorities to do business at your prospective site. For instance, you may be interested in an existing business in an area zoned for a different use. The building probably existed when the land was first zoned — also known as a nonconforming use. While you may continue to use the land as nonconforming, you will have restrictions on enlarging or remodeling the structure. If it is your intent to demolish or remodel an existing structure, you may need to secure a variance. A *variance* allows you, as an individual land owner, to use your parcel for a use other than that provided by the current zoning requirements. Usually, variances are granted where strict compliance with the zoning law would cause undue hardship. However, the variance must not change the basic character of the neighborhood or defeat the general objectives of the zoning code applied to that particular neighborhood.

In some areas, you may need a conditional use permit rather than a variance. A *conditional use permit* allows you to use the land in a manner that does not conform with the existing zoning. However, when you are issued a conditional use permit, you are responsible to diligently follow its various conditions, like *setbacks* — rules that indicate how far in feet you can build from the center of the road or from the side or back property lines. These conditions can be restrictive, and if you violate a permit, it may become invalid.

Sometimes, rather than securing a variance or a conditional use permit, an entire area may need to be rezoned if the character of the use of the land has changed. For example, there may have been a need to restrict a certain area for residential purposes, but as the community developed, the need for more business also developed; thus a rezoning may be necessary.

You are less apt to receive objections from local citizens and politicians to such rezoning if the request is reasonable and will benefit the community as a whole. Keep in mind, if you apply for a change in zoning, be aware of local conditions. You are best served by securing the assistance of a local planner and zoning attorney who are active in the community, understand the local codes, and know the psychology of the neighborhood. In researching your specific site, you also need to consider private controls that may affect your business.

Private Controls

Private controls are hidden. Private controls take the form of deed and lease restrictions that have been recorded in the land records. In the United States, ownership of land includes the right to sell or lease it on whatever legally acceptable terms the owner wishes, including the right to restrict the use of that property in the future. If you, as a buyer or tenant, agree to the restrictions, you are bound by them. If you disobey these restrictions, any lot owner in the subdivision in which the restricted parcel exists, can obtain a court order to enforce compliance. These deed restrictions are known as restricted covenants and can be used to control such matters as:

- The use of the future structure;
- Architectural requirements;
- Setbacks, size, and height of the structure; and
- Aesthetics.

If the restrictions are reasonable, they usually will be enforced by the courts. You can learn about private restrictions by conducting a title search. Keep in mind, if you violate a zoning law, you will have to answer to a governmental agency. If you violate a private restriction, any of the lot owners are in a position to enforce the restriction.

Prepare, Prepare, Prepare

If the property is not zoned for your type of business, you will have to follow a process of administrative and public hearings. In this process, you will face an arduous battle with the possibility of many surprises along the way. To eliminate or reduce surprises in the zoning process, prepare yourself by taking these steps.

- Learn the roles of the legislative council, planning department, general public, and special interest groups, such as members of historical associations, homeowners associations, and downtown merchants associations.

- Familiarize yourself with the neighborhood and the manner in which regulations have been applied to the area.

- Talk to residents, local merchants in their places of business, customers in bars, and patrons in restaurants to learn the community's attitudes, concerns, and fears.

- Get support for your project from your broker, lawyer, mayor, and business leaders and understand their ideas, intentions, and concerns.

- Make sure you have enough capital to deal with fees, land engineers, environmental impact reports, architectural designers, lawyers, special witnesses, traffic experts, and landscapers.

In the meantime, your real estate conditional contract options may expire. Political elections may take place, new city officials may be elected, and ordinances may change. You need to keep all the balls in the air. If you will need to take your case to a hearing, your best option is to fully prepare yourself.

Zoning ordinances spell out the details of a hearing format. Make sure you produce the proper notifications and forms before the hearing session and follow all applicable deadlines. You can prepare for your hearing session by following three essential steps. First, communicate with members of the hearing to understand their positions and qualifications. Make sure you explain your position and how you operate your business. A polite and amiable expression of mutual positions will disclose new angles of the strategy to follow. Second, gather expert testimony — from traffic engineers, lawyers, architects, and operations people — and go through a dry-run rehearsal. Go over the questions and answers. Be ready to submit convincing alternatives. Anticipate every question and use convincing logic and facts. Third, set up your timetable for meetings with your attorney(s) and city planners. The zoning procedures will lay out your requirements for land procurement, facilities design, planning, organizing, and operating. Make proper time adjustments to allow for derailments and delays. Always plan for contingencies.

New Land Use Control Trends

In recent years, several U.S. Supreme Court decisions have enabled real estate developers to force local zoning boards to let them do what they want with their property. In return, the zoning boards demanded that the developers do many things for zoning changes and permits. For example, if a developer wants a zoning change, then a zoning board may require that developer to improve a public road adjacent to or near the property. In fact, recent decisions allow developers to collect monetary damages from governmental agencies when the restrictions on the use of the property go too far. In addition, the courts have identified the fine line between a restriction on use of the property under the police powers and such a use that could constitute a taking. The interpretation of these court rulings seems to say that if a governmental zoning regulation deprives land owners of all economically beneficial use of their property, then it is considered a taking for which the land owners can claim compensation. However, if the governmental regulation deprives the land owners of some, but not all, of the use of their property, then it is not clear whether there should be compensation. As an alternative, a zoning law may be changed or struck down if you can prove in court that it is unclear, discriminatory, unreasonable, and not for the protection of the public health, safety, and general welfare.

In addition to land use control issues, your specific site research will include finding out how condemnation ordinances can affect your business' future.

Understand the Concept of Condemnation

Once you settle on your location, you need to gather all the information concerning existing and potential condemnation ordinances. You need to understand the importance of *condemnation* — the process by which private property may be taken for a public purpose under the right of eminent domain. The right of eminent domain is the power of the federal, state, or local government, such as county, city, or district, to appropriate private property for public use or welfare. Once you are in business, even three feet of frontage taken by the right of eminent domain can cut your accessibility or your parking, which can cause drastic losses in sales. Therefore, carefully listen to any discussion or rumor concerning future takings that may affect your property. It is easy to delude yourself into thinking it may never happen. Think of the worst possibility and plan around it, particularly when property frontage and rerouting of roads are involved.

If you know of approved plans or plans in the process of approval, you will be able to design a layout that will allow for such future land taking. If your business site will be affected by the right of eminent domain, you as the owner of the property, must be paid just compensation. If the amount of the just compensation cannot be settled by negotiations, condemnation proceedings are instituted that involve time and expenses.

The rights of eminent domain have increased greatly during the last decade for public forest, public drainage, soil conservation, and other purposes. You may be particularly interested in urban redevelopment and in renewal projects in crowded residential and business areas of the city. To learn more about condemnation ordinances that may affect you, contact the road department in the area in which you wish to locate. Another significant part of your site research will involve an evaluation of potential environmental liability.

Determine Potential Environmental Liability

If you are involved in a real estate transaction involving properties, you must consider potential environmental liability whether you are a seller, buyer, landlord, tenant, or lender. Determining the likelihood of hazardous waste contamination in a parcel in which you may be interested is equally important as determining the appropriate zoning. Usually, hazardous waste contamination is associated with past uses of a site. In addition, a site can be impacted by migration of contaminants from off-site neighboring areas. Be aware that lending institutions do not lend money on properties that have environmental liabilities. With increasing state and federal regulations, your safest bet is to hire a professional to conduct an environmental audit.

The primary goal of an environmental audit is to gather information so that all interested parties can evaluate their liabilities and manage their risks. By doing this, the various parties can realize the value of the real estate asset. The secondary goal of an environmental audit is to identify and remediate problems. The three types of environmental audits are categorized as:

- Phase I
- Phase II
- Phase III

In a *Phase I Audit*, an auditor will visit a site and find out the nature of its historical use. This type of audit primarily involves a record search and a site walk by an individual qualified to assess the specific environmental factors that may be involved in its prior use. Depending on findings of the Phase I Audit, a *Phase II Audit* may be needed to continue the investigative process. This type of audit involves taking soil samples and analyzing samples of the ground water to detect any past leakage into the ground water. In this phase, the total environmental sampling will confirm or deny the existence of suspected contamination. If contamination has been discovered, a *Phase III Audit* will be necessary. This type of audit will also include the actions needed to proceed with the clean-up measures.

A Phase I Audit usually costs $3,000–$5,000 and a Phase II Audit costs $8,000–$10,000 or more depending upon the number of field samples and depth of analysis required. A Phase III Audit will usually involve an in-depth environmental clean-up process after contamination has been discovered. For instance, if you want to build your flower shop on a corner that had been occupied by a gas station for the last 50 years, most likely you will have soil contamination from the oil drainage. To clean the soil will cost you hundreds of thousands of dollars. Keep in mind, a Phase I Audit is required in any commercial lending transaction. Make sure you discuss this with your lender.

To learn more about environmental compliance issues for your business, use *The Business Environmental Handbook* by Martin Westerman. For more information, contact:

The Oasis Press
(800) 228-2275 or *www.oasispress.com*

Chapter Wrap-Up

Your search for the right location for your business has taken you from a thorough market analysis to a look at the city in which you wish to locate your store to a thorough research of the specific site. To recap the essentials of specific site research, you can avoid unpleasant surprises about a location choice if you:

- Travel the site via foot, car, and plane to gain a better overall picture of the site in relation to its surrounding areas.

- Look at existing aerial photographs of the site to glean important information that will help you create a workable map — a map in which you can pinpoint the sources of your main customers.

- Meet with city government and community officials to gain a sense of what makes the people within the city and community tick.

- Approach land use control issues, like proper zoning for your business site, with confidence.

- Plan for the future should an issue like condemnation affect your prospective business area.

- Stay on top of environmental issues to protect you from potential federal, state, and local liability.

These are certain issues with which you will eventually need to deal — certainly before closing any real estate transaction. Your next concern is to examine your trading area in more depth. As you continue to build your knowledge of your prospective location, know that you are paving the way for the success of your retail operation.

Chapter 4

Identify Your Trading Area

To select the right location for your business, you must fully understand the dynamics of where your customers come from and how you can attract more customers. In a nutshell, you must identify your trading area. Understanding the energy, force, and influence of your potential trading area is a time consuming and laborious process. A simple, across-the-board method for identifying your trading area does not exist; nor does a mathematical formula exist that will help you calculate the retail potential of a trading area. The only way you will learn about your trading area is by diligently studying the many factors that bear on potential sales. To begin your study, you will need to understand:

- The various types of trading areas;
- The way towns and sections of towns connect with each other;
- The effects of size, shape, and density of a trading area;
- The importance of the grocery stores in a trading area; and
- The meaning and significance of a trading area's boundaries.

To conclude your study of your potential trading area, you will complete a survey to verify your initial findings. First, however, take a moment to acquaint yourself with the concept of a retail trading area and what it means to the livelihood of your business.

A retail trading area — also called a *retail trading zone* (RTZ) — is the area that surrounds a retail outlet within which 75 to 80 percent of customers move from one point to another. Thus, an RTZ is formed by people who live, work, and move there. In addition, a percentage of customers come from outside an RTZ. Every RTZ has three main sections of customers — a core area, secondary area, and tertiary area — as illustrated in Figure 4.1.

- The core area accounts for about 50 percent or more of your customers.
- The secondary area accounts for up to 25 percent of your customers.
- The tertiary area accounts for 10 to 15 percent or less of your customers, including those customers coming from off-map — or beyond four or five miles.

Another 10 to 15 percent of your customers — sometimes known as the off-map customers — come from beyond the tertiary area. As shown in Figure 4.1, these off-map customers will vary in frequency and percentage according to the novelty of your business — whether your product is a commodity or a specialty,

the character of the road, and the topography of the area in which your store is located.

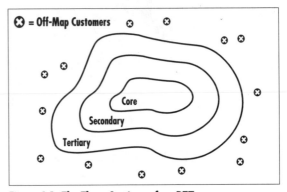

Your RTZ is the lungs of your store — it breathes, is alive, and subject to change. Although you will face a rotation of customers — the natural cycle of gaining new customers and losing old customers — a core of customers in a smaller percentage will continue to generate the majority of your sales. The RTZ will continue to be essentially the same. Your first step in identifying the RTZ of the site in which you wish to locate is to understand what type of zone it is.

Figure 4.1 The Three Sections of an RTZ

Understand Your Type of Zone

A city or town's RTZ can fall into one or a combination of the following four categories:

- Downtown
- Urban
- Suburban
- Rural

In turn, each can be of a different type — for instance, residential, professional, commercial, industrial, or recreational. This is important because the profile of your customers will differ according to the zone in which they are located. For instance, a customer in a suburban zone will have different needs at different times than a customer who lives in a downtown zone.

You will find the analysis of your customers' needs and moods to be an ideal foundation for your store's local marketing efforts. Once you examine the specific characteristics of the four categories, you will better understand their dynamics and how your business can be best situated.

A Downtown Zone

If you are interested in a site that is located in a downtown area of a city, you will see the geometric pattern created by the city's layout. In this case, the boundaries of the RTZ trace the pattern made by the plotting of city blocks, which are themselves geometric. The structure of a downtown forces its residents, employees, and visitors into semigeometric patterns. Figure 4.2 illustrates the geometric nature of a downtown RTZ. Notice the blocks that are outside the RTZ boundaries. People who live or work in these blocks will either feel too far away from your store — indicated by the large, black dot in the figure — or will be closer to one of your competitor's stores. The pros and cons of locating your store in a downtown area are discussed extensively in Chapter 7.

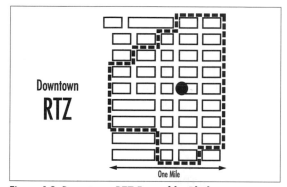

Figure 4.2 Downtown RTZ Formed by Blocks

An Urban Zone

An urban zone consists of the parts of a city or town that surround its core. In a city core, you will find old buildings, poor architecture, narrow streets, and alleys. Here you will find factory buildings, original residential tenements, old homes, railroad yards, and storage places. Many improvements are in disrepair. The area does not reveal its prosperous history and it does not give much indication of an improved future. Certain sections have a heavy population density with a variety of demographic, psychographic, national, and international mixes.

Urban areas are in dire need of redevelopment and revitalization. They can be good for retailing because of the scarcity of goods offered and, often, because of heavy density.

A Suburban Zone

Suburban areas have become independent nodes of activity in the standard metropolitan areas. Many suburban areas have their own downtowns, with thriving commercial and professional activity, where you find prosperous shopping centers, like malls and community centers. You also find office buildings that house corporate headquarters for various companies; professional offices, for attorneys and insurance brokers; and governmental agencies. For instance, Oak Brook, Illinois, a suburb of Chicago, is actually a city by itself. It offers the full array of basic services and products. Its citizens have civic pride and, to a large extent, identify themselves with their city. Also, Coral Gables, Florida, is a complete city within the greater Miami area. If your retail business is in one of those suburban downtowns, you may be part of a suburban RTZ, which is distinct from the

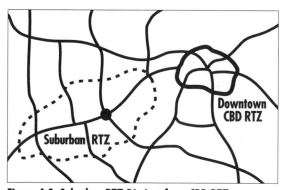

Figure 4.3 Suburban RTZ Distinct from CBD RTZ

city's central business district (CBD). To better understand this concept, look at the illustration in Figure 4.3. The dashed line represents the suburban RTZ that is separate and distinct from the downtown RTZ — indicated by the heavier line and marked CBD.

A Rural Zone

A rural town can be sectioned into city limits, city zones, and the surrounding countryside. The retail gravitation of a rural town varies with its size and vitality. Thus, a rural RTZ tends to be geographically large. This is especially true in the Western portion of the United States, where the percentage of automobile ownership is high, roads are good, and traffic congestion is low. Subsequently, people may drive half an hour or even a whole hour to go to town for essentials — the goods and services needed for living. To get a better sense of how far people of a rural RTZ will travel, look at Figure 4.4. The dashed line represents a rural RTZ that can stretch as far out as 20 miles in one direction. Because of the scarcity of roads in the countryside, some people in a rural RTZ will travel several miles to get to a road leading to the town in which your store is located. A full discussion of trade in small towns and the influence of interstate highways is in Chapter 8.

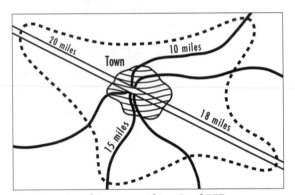

Figure 4.4 Travel Distance within a Rural RTZ

Now that you have a basic knowledge of the various types of retail trading zones and how the different zones impact your business, turn your focus to the way a town connects.

Study the Way Towns and Sections of Towns Connect

As you learned from Chapter 2, a critical part of finding the right location for your retail business involves knowing the importance of the road system of the area you want to serve. Thus, your next step in identifying your trading area is to study the way the towns and sections of towns connect and how these connections will impact your potential customer base.

In many cases, you may find a road web that enwraps an entire state and connects one town to another. A *road web*, or network, is made of radial roads. In fact, towns are usually built along radial roads or at an intersection of radial roads. The livelihood and survival of a small town — and its stores' RTZs — depend upon its linkage to other towns from all directions to connect it to older towns and to the nearest big city. To illustrate the importance of a road web to a small town, look at Figure 4.5. The town labeled "B" will be directly impacted by the roads that lead to and

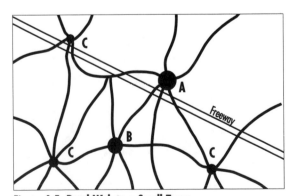

Figure 4.5 Road Web to a Small Town

from the rural towns labeled "C" and the big city labeled "A." In fact, in this situation the RTZs of the various towns will probably overlap.

Of equal importance are the effects of a busy freeway intersection on the radial roads that lead to and from a small town. The RTZ of a small town is greatly changed, expanded, and enhanced by a busy freeway with a full-fledged intersection. In Figure 4.6, look at the cloverleaf-shaped freeway intersection. The most likely locations to study for a retail store are indicated by the large black

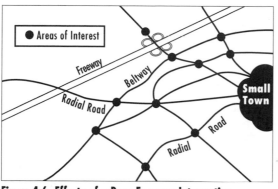

Figure 4.6 Effects of a Busy Freeway Intersection

circles where the radial roads intersect with various beltways around the town. Further, each one is situated along a radial road that serves a central business district. Most freeway drivers will pass by without taking more than a glance at a small town. However, more people will move to, from, and through the town itself because of the freeway than would be the case without the freeway. Consequently, the radial road that goes from the town to the freeway intersection is the most desirable for your store. Obviously, you will have an advantage if you locate your retail business near a busy freeway. Be cautious, however, of RTZs that do not connect.

An RTZ's limits may or may not connect with another RTZ's limits. Whether or not they touch depends upon the physical or human-made barriers and distances. Take a look at Figure 4.7 to understand this concept. In the illustration marked "A," the dot represents the store, and its RTZ is a combination of the town (Roosterville) and its surrounding rural area. In "B," the dot represents the store, and the RTZ's size is quite a bit smaller because it is comprised of only the rural area. In "C," the smallest town in this area has the smallest rural RTZ. In addition, the smaller RTZs on the right don't connect because there is not a true radial road that connects them. The people who live outside these two RTZs do shop somewhere, but they make up a very small percentage of the sales volume at any one location. In short, their business is spread among several RTZs. Also, notice that the major radial road bisects two of the three RTZs. Another interesting fact is that the RTZ marked "A" does not include the entire area of Roosterville. The west side of town does not gravitate toward the center.

After you have determined the type of RTZ your prospective store will serve and studied the connections, or lack thereof, to nearby towns and cities, consider two important RTZ factors — size and shape.

Size Up Your RTZ

The size of your RTZ will be determined by the nature of your business. For example, a commodity business, because it sells goods and services that are popular, easily substituted, and affordable by the majority of consumers, creates a smaller RTZ than a specialty business. Also, the cost of entry into a commodity business is smaller. A specialty business, on the other hand, carries items that are special and needed only once in a while for certain occasions or places. A good example is a grocery store called Byerly's in Minneapolis, Minnesota. With a high level of service and high-quality products, this specialty store caters to a higher income, higher education, and white-collar customer profile. Because fewer people drive farther to buy its specialty goods, its RTZ is larger.

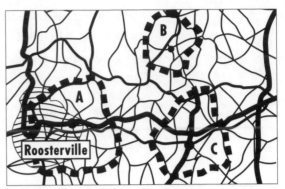

Figure 4.7 Unconnected Retail Trading Zones

Shape Up Your RTZ

An RTZ is never shaped in a geometric way, such as a circle, square, rectangle, or polygon. Instead, if you draw a line outlining your potential RTZ, you will show an area shaped like an amoeba. If a retail location is in a valley, the shape of its RTZ will be an elongated amoeba following the road along the valley. If the area is flat, like in Phoenix, Arizona, the shape of the amoeba might be irregularly round, elliptical, or rectangular. The RTZ, like an amoeba, has a living shape. The amoeba-like shape can be as varied, and as interesting, as the human life it represents. When you look at the RTZ of your prospective business site, realize that it is not a statistical entity, but a behavioral and environmental one. You are dealing with the unpredictability of the human being.

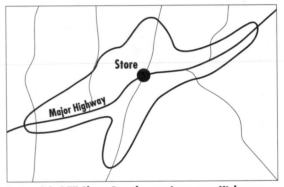

Figure 4.8 RTZ Shape Based on an Important Highway

In Figure 4.8 the shape of the RTZ is elongated, because it is located on an important highway. Also, notice the secondary roads that cause a secondary pull on the RTZ. As other nearby roads serve residents in the area, the RTZ stretches out into a shape that resembles a starfish on a beach. The movements of your customers create the shape of the RTZ of your store.

You will remember from earlier discussions that understanding the road system and road web will give you clues about where your customers are located and how they will arrive at your store.

If your store will be located near an important crossroad, your RTZ will stretch out along each of the important roads, resulting in a configuration that looks like a diamond shape similar to the illustration on the left in Figure 4.9. Further, if the two roads are of equal importance, your RTZ will tend to resemble a slice of bread, as suggested in the shape on the right side of Figure 4.9.

There are other factors will alter the shape of your RTZ, including:

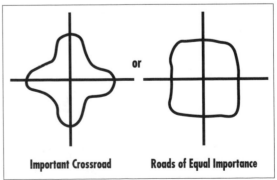

Figure 4.9 RTZ Shapes Based on Road Types

- Additional roads
- Geological formations or other barriers
- A lop-sided mix of zone types

For instance, you may have problems with your customer base if your RTZ has farmland in one sector, single-dwelling residences in another sector, an industrial park in the third sector, and commercial developments in the fourth sector. Your goal, then, is to find a location with a large RTZ that is based on an important intersection of two main (radial) roads.

Obviously, a location with a larger RTZ that includes more people will have a larger retail success as illustrated in Figure 4.10. Notice that the RTZ shape identified as "A" is similar to the RTZ shape identified as "B" since each surrounds an intersection of roads.

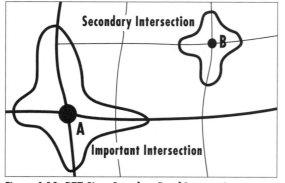

Figure 4.10 RTZ Sizes Based on Road Intersections

The shape in each case is a function of the roads themselves, which pull potential customers in from four directions and draw upon people residing in each of the RTZ's four sectors. "A" is an important intersection because both roads that intersect are important roads — important because they either carry heavy traffic for a fairly long distance or fairly heavy traffic between cities. "B" is part of an area served by a secondary intersection — secondary because the roads crossing by are themselves secondary.

Secondary roads are roads that carry virtually no long-distance traffic and little work traffic. They are narrow, go short distances, are interrupted frequently by stop signs, or do not connect to major traffic generators. Thus, if you have a choice, your best bet will be the location with the larger RTZ. When studying the shape of your potential RTZ, you want to pay attention to not just the intersection of major roads, but also the roads that lead to those intersections.

Whereas an intersection of roads — also called *hubs* — collects people's movements, their *spokes* or radial roads disperse those movements. All developed areas contain a web of hubs and spokes that intertwine each other. If your location is in the center of a hub, as in the five-spoke map at left in Figure 4.11, your RTZ will expand on the spokes, up to a distance determined by the interest gravitation of your business. Interest gravitation is discussed at length in Chapter 2.

If your store is located on one of the spokes, as in the shape at right in Figure 4.11, your RTZ will be smaller because it is fed by just one road. Clearly the location on the left is better for attracting business.

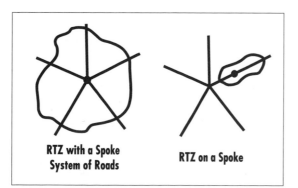

RTZ with a Spoke System of Roads   RTZ on a Spoke

Figure 4.11 Importance of Hubs and Spokes

If a major road at a certain point fans out into secondary traffic channels, then that delta point marks the peak of traffic. Figure 4.12 illustrates the advantage of locating in an RTZ with a delta configuration. As you can see, the best location for your retail store is on the major road just before eastbound traffic reaches the delta and just after westbound traffic leaves the delta, as in the delta complex at left in Figure 4.12. This results in the maximum size for your RTZ. In like manner, if you locate on any of the three spokes of the delta, your RTZ will be smaller, as shown in the delta configuration at right in Figure 4.12. In this case, traffic on the other spokes will elude you.

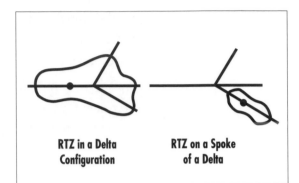

Figure 4.12 Significance of a Delta on an RTZ

Keep in mind, if you choose a location at the edge of a town, you will have a larger geographical RTZ than many RTZs inside the town, but your RTZ will have fewer people in it. You can also learn about your potential RTZ by looking at its grocery stores.

Familiarize Yourself with the Grocery Stores

Some say the best way to get the attention of people is to get them by their stomachs. The manner and frequency in which people purchase food tell the importance of grocery stores for retailing purposes. The grocery store is a place where people go every week — sometimes several times each week — to get supplies. Grocery stores generate the best kind of traffic for your retail business. Take the opportunity to gain vital information about your potential RTZ by examining the number, size, and image of the grocery stores in the area in which you wish to locate.

Grocery stores and superstores are planned with a careful evaluation of demographic elements, including number of people, income, age, and sex. A large number of successful grocery stores in an area form a powerful RTZ. Thus, when planning your retail business, you may want to be under the umbrella of the combined grocery stores' RTZs. On the other hand, if some of the grocery stores feature or duplicate your type of business, such as home video rental, 24-hour photo processing, or selling fruits and vegetables, be very careful of locating near them. Unless your product, price, service, and sales system are special and superior, the grocery store will probably capture the potential sales.

The size of a grocery store will give you an idea of the customer base. It reflects the size of the RTZ it serves. For example, a 10,000 square foot store only serves approximately 15,000 people. A 30,000 square foot store may serve 20,000 to 30,000 people. For comparative purposes, it is easy to measure the size of a grocery store. One easy way involves counting the ceiling tiles, which measure two feet by four feet, or the fluorescent lighting fixtures, which are usually eight feet or twelve feet in length. You will learn about your potential customers by reading a grocery store, too.

Read the Grocery Stores

Grocery stores currently use the barcoding system to control inventory. They manage this system by practicing the "First In, First Out" rule and the "Just-in-Time" policy. In other words, as merchandise is sold, new merchandise is bought accurately and precisely. Consequently, the inventory, look, and layout of a grocery store mirrors the population it serves, especially if the store has been in business for a few years. If you learn how to read a grocery store, you will learn the characteristics of the local market in which you intend to locate your own retail store.

As you examine the number of grocery stores, the type, and the merchandise offered, you will have an accurate picture of the income, ethnic composition, lifestyle, and number of people who gravitate toward that hub. You can read a grocery store by looking at several key factors, including its:

- Exterior appearance
- Interior appearance
- Product offering
- Price positioning

To read the outside appearance, look to see if it is well-maintained. Determine whether the parking lot is sealed, clearly striped, and free of potholes.

- Are there any discarded wrappers and papers flying all over?
- Are the windows plastered with cheaply made posters?
- Is there excess merchandise cluttering the front of the store (except for promotional items)?
- Is the parking lot well illuminated and adequate?

A lack of order and neatness indicates a struggling store and a low median income in the area.

When looking at the interior appearance, look at how clean and orderly it is. A well-maintained grocery store means the store is successful. Also, the number of cash registers will give you an idea of the volume as compared to other grocery stores in the area. Count the number of registers, examine the service layout, and note the number of customers at each register. Do this at various times during the day, night, and week. Sharp merchandising indicates professionalism in management. Clear directional and informational signs reveal inventory organization and a sensitivity toward customers, because the signs make it easier for them to find what they want.

Your next task is to look at the products it offers by checking its departments. You can learn many things about your potential customers' likes and dislikes by observing each department and section within the nearest grocery store. Notice what is there and what is missing. For instance, in the produce section, an abundance of fruits and vegetables means there is a high product turnover — that is, the products are sold and restocked at a high rate. It also indicates a profile of the consumers — individuals with good incomes and a concern for health. In the meat department, selected and expensive fresh cuts indicate a good income and a healthful lifestyle. The presence of a lot of prepackaged chicken, pork, and salted meats indicates lower income.

In the delicatessen, salads, soups, roasted meats, and pasta answer the needs of people with a youthful profile leading sports-oriented lives and of young families with two incomes who have little time to cook. Prepared foods also fit people with active social habits like partying, visiting, and recreating. Further, frozen meals fit people on the go, youthful, with a lack of time but a good income. The number of linear feet of childrens' foods gives an idea of the number of families with children in the store's RTZ. And, the variety and amount of ethnic foods is like a mirror of the ethnic composition of the area. Further, bulk merchandise on pallets indicates that the store caters to lower income groups.

Keep in mind, each grocery store or chain has its special target customer and price positioning. In some cases, the superstores and grocery clubs do not mirror the local RTZ as well as a typical neighborhood grocery store does. The RTZ of these types of stores is geographically very extensive — meaning people will travel from afar to shop there.

You can narrow your research and examine the convenience stores in the same areas. They vary by size and inventory. You want to know whether the business is generated by nearby residents or by long distance traffic and tourists.

Now that you have an idea of the importance of the grocery and convenience stores located in your potential RTZ, make sure you understand the significance of your RTZ's boundaries.

Discover Your RTZ's Boundaries

The process of site selection includes outlining the RTZ of your future location and its competitor stores. If you study the boundaries of other key retail stores' RTZs, you may be in a better position to make the right location decision. For example, a grocery store has a bigger RTZ than a McDonald's; a Wal-Mart has a bigger RTZ than a grocery store. Envision a market with these overlapping boundaries. The best location for your business is the one with the greatest potential number of customers. Thus, the RTZ of your store may be part of the RTZs of three grocery stores, two drugstores, and a community shopping center.

In addition, you can learn about the RTZ of your future retail store by studying the RTZ of a similar store — an *analogue* store — in the same industry. As a franchisee, you should get some information from your franchisor or other franchisees. If you are on your own, pick the best of your competitors in the area and attempt to discover its RTZ boundaries. To discover your RTZ's boundaries, follow these three steps.

- Identify your amoeba.

- Locate the barriers.
- Compute the travel hassle index.

Identify Your Amoeba

Your first step is to identify the area where you intend to open your store. At this point you do not know the exact parcel of land. Take a map with roads that are clearly and completely identifiable. Identify the main roads that link the area to more important areas. Determine whether the population of the area is dense with people who live, work, and move about. Find out whether there are big areas with nothing but forests or mountains and whether there is a network of streets, highways, and freeways. Also, locate the significant public, educational, employment, or health care establishments — all indicators of a healthy and prosperous environment for a retail business.

Locate the Barriers

For your business to deliver goods and services, you must next consider any existing barriers that limit your RTZ. It will not make much difference if your customers will come to your store or if you or your employees will travel to your customers' residences or businesses. You still will have to deal with natural or human-made barriers. Don't think that people will climb mountains or cross rivers to come to your store. First, select an area with a greater population than you think you need. Second, look around you — look at all 365 degrees of the location. Determine whether the people who live in the area can get to your store. To do this, identify the obstacles on a map — a river, an industrial belt, a railroad, a hill, or no roads — and draw a line. The line will form an amoeba; it indicates the boundaries of your future RTZ.

Compute the Travel Hassle Index

Your third step involves determining a travel hassle index by computing your customers' driving times. If you are in retail, you are in the convenience business. Also, if you handle a line of commodity products, people will make decisions based on how long it will take them to get to your facility and then to return to their point of origination. The driving time — the amount of time it takes to drive from a certain point to your store — is an essential component of your business. Your type of business will dictate how many minutes a customer will be willing to travel either by car to most locations or by foot in downtown areas. An RTZ's boundaries correlate with driving time and distance. The boundaries tell you how many minutes and how many miles people must drive or travel to patronize your retail business.

The elements of distance and time translate into a *travel hassle index*. It is more troublesome to drive a longer distance, fight traffic, and cross busy intersections. Consequently, you can draw a curve called a *decay curve* — meaning the farther away your customers, the fewer times they will visit your store. Obviously, the degree of convenience diminishes with the distance.

Another important factor affecting a location is the psychological time or distance your customers perceive. The distance between a retail outlet and an important traffic generator must not only be close, but also must feel close. Psychological distance is not measured by miles nor by minutes; it is a gut feeling. Although this gut feeling is not measurable, it is a real perception. It is like measuring the time in a waiting line — 5 minutes can easily become 20 minutes. In like manner, your customers may only need to travel one mile, but it feels like five miles. Your customers will make decisions based on these perceptions.

For example, suppose you have a medical supply store. Your major source of business is the county hospital that serves the area. If there is a major freeway overpass, a railroad crossing, five stop lights, a power center, and a road that narrows to two lanes between your store and the hospital, the psychological distance is multiplied tenfold. Yet the county hospital may be only one mile away.

Keep in mind, the number of visits that originate closer to a retail store is higher than those visits that originate from distant areas. This decay curve, or decline in numbers, is gradual and measurable through surveys in which you can ask your customers their points of origin or departure. If you ask them how long they travelled to get to the store, the answers may not be accurate due to perception rather than fact. Figure 4.13 illustrates the effect of distance and driving time on the frequency of customer visits. Your goal is to locate in an area that minimizes the driving time and distance of your potential customers.

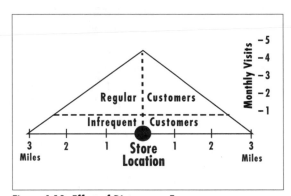

Figure 4.13 **Effect of Distance on Frequency**

To understand this, look at all variables of road structure that slow down and thus, increase driving time. Driving time and distance are conditioned by variables like:

- Topography;
- Road structure;
- The number of lanes; and
- The time of the day (low-peak or high-peak traffic).

People are able to drive more miles in less time when the roads are straight, wide, and flat. This type of RTZ is shown in the upper left corner of Figure 4.14. A similar situation occurs in two-way stretches like the RTZs in the lower left, upper right, and lower right corners of Figure 4.14. With a quadrant layout, people can drive to your store in the same amount of time from all directions, as evidenced in the center RTZ in Figure 4.14.

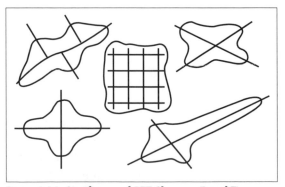

Figure 4.14 **Significance of RTZ Shape on Travel Time**

To further identify the points from where your customers come, you can pinpoint their departure points within your RTZ. Most likely your business is a *two-trip retailer* — customers leave a point to come to your store and then they return to that point. Statistically, trips from a retail store to home represent the highest percentage of retail trips. If people stop at a store while going to work,

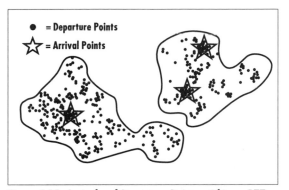

Figure 4.15 Arrival and Departure Points within an RTZ

the trip is called work related. For instance, in Figure 4.15, each dot represents a departure point of customers coming to Blockbuster Video stores, which are indicated by stars. The line enclosing these dots defines the stores' amoeba-like RTZs. The amoeba-like shape of these RTZs can change according to the time of day. Often, an RTZ is larger by day, when it includes commuter traffic, and smaller in the evening, when business comes mostly from areas immediately surrounding the store. Further, take another look at the shape of the RTZ at left in Figure 4.15. This RTZ indicates that a large share of business comes from the east. To maximize a store's customer potential, it is important to find out why something like this happens.

To make sure that your location is the right one for your business, calculate the time it takes to go from your store to the major traffic generators, including residential. Given the importance of time over distance, you should understand how long it takes for your customers to return to the point of departure or to the point of arrival. If it takes too long to get to your store, your customers may refuse to make the trip and start to look for alternatives. This means that your location has to be within an acceptable driving time according to your industry. To see how your location's driving time rates, determine how long will it take for customers to:

- Leave their points of departure;
- Come to your store;
- Purchase the goods or services;
- Use the goods or services; and
- Return to their points of arrival.

The investment in time that you require might be too much for too many. See the discussion on making a time-convenience line and measuring its impact located in Chapter 9. To begin to compute driving times, look at your competitors.

If you are a new entrepreneur, you can study the movements of your competitors' customers. Determine the longest distance from which they are coming, then interpret the figures to arrive at a tentative *opinion of distance*. The opinion of distance is mileage expressed in travel time. When interpreting the data, consider variables like time of day, the barriers that slow traffic, and the topographic layout of the land. The maximum amount of time a competitor's customers are willing to travel to get to that competitor's store is likely to be the same for your future customers when they travel to your store. To compute its customers' driving times, McDonald's used to follow a distance rule of three, five, and seven minutes. In other words, a restaurant's core part of its RTZ was considered to be within a three-minute radius of that store; the secondary part of its RTZ was within three to five minutes away; and the outer area was within five to seven minutes away. The three-, five-, and seven-minute distance changes with a business' type of industry. For instance, apparel stores call for a higher driving time because they are more specialty-oriented than commodity-oriented. Car dealerships may have a 10-, 25-, and 50-mile drive time radius.

Because driving times vary — depending upon the hour of the day and the location and size of the residential areas — you must tally your numbers during

peak business hours. You need to know the hassle your customers go through to get your products or services. Make sure you take your map with you on your drive time study and mark down the time in regular intervals as you drive each route going away from the target store. In Figure 4.16, each of these points — three minutes, six minutes, and nine minutes — helps you compare drive times along different routes. The equidistant time points — technically called *isochrones* — can be connected by lines that show you the locations of the core, secondary, and outer areas of your RTZ in a specific time frame. If

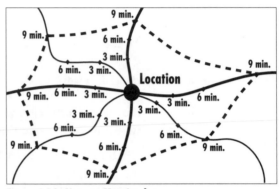

Figure 4.16 How to Map Isochrones

your peak business hours happen during the peak rush hours, then the area literally becomes smaller. In residential neighborhoods, the distance covered will be even shorter. This is reflected by the concave curves in the drive time graph in Figure 4.16. The graph shows the limits (the dashed line) that connects the nine-minute equidistant time points on the various roads that lead to a retail location.

As you plot the driving times on a map, you will begin to see four important boundaries. As illustrated in Figure 4.17, the true RTZ of your store is a combination of three boundaries that are superimposed on each other.

- A nine-minute drive polygon;
- Natural and human-made barriers, also called the barrier ring; and
- The actual RTZ limit line.

The RTZ limit line is determined by conducting an RTZ Survey, which is discussed in the next section. The one-mile circle indicated with the light dashed line in Figure 4.17 helps you to understand these distances. These boundaries surround your store and touch at several points, but they never precisely coincide. Remember, the RTZ amoeba is the most important

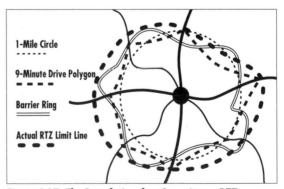

Figure 4.17 The Boundaries that Comprise an RTZ

to your business, since it accurately describes the area that generates between 75 to 80 percent of your business. Also, the nine-minute drive polygon and barrier ring may change when barriers are developed or removed, and drive times are changed by roadwork, alternate routes, and increased traffic. The three steps — identification of your own amoeba, evaluation of the natural human-made barriers, and computation of travel hassle index — must be validated with the actual results of an RTZ survey after the store is open. It is best not to take the survey immediately; rather take a survey after your store has operated for several months.

The Retail Trading Zone Survey

With a properly designed questionnaire, a Retail Trading Zone Survey — also called customer spotting — will reveal how a business functions at a specific location. An RTZ Survey will show:

- The people that live in the RTZ;
- Their demographic profiles;
- The movement of people within the RTZ;
- Who the customers are;
- The areas where the customers gravitate;
- How much business comes from specific grids;
- Grids from which you get no business or little business; and
- The geographic boundaries (distance) beyond which you do not get any business.

You can also use an RTZ Survey to:

- Identify under-served areas.
- Gauge the frequency of visits or use.
- Tally the number of first-time visit customers.
- Understand the relationship to other similar or competitive locations.
- Know your customers' locations relative to your prospective retail store location.
- Determine when other stores, in a franchise or multiple corporate operation, can be placed in a market without adversely impacting the sales of existing stores. (Impact will be discussed at length in Chapter 9.)
- Apply marketing and advertising dollars effectively in your RTZ.

Your findings become relevant when they are validated by the area's demographics; psychographics; daily, monthly, and weekly sales curves; and current business trends of competitive retailers in analogue areas. Depending on your situation, you will have three options for where to complete your RTZ Survey.

If you are planning to open a franchise business, take the survey at the store of another franchisee of the same company, preferably one whose trading area is similar to the area where you plan to locate. If you are planning to open a second store near your original location, use your original store as the site for your RTZ Survey. The findings of your survey will help you check out the new location and improve business at the existing store. If you are not part of a franchise family or do not have an analogue for comparison, then complete the Competitor's Location Analysis located in Chapter 1. You will need to assume and then verify as many factors as you can by studying similar existing stores. If you will be part of a large, established organization, get as much existing customer information as you can.

Some businesses — such as department stores that offer their own credit cards — have key customer information that is readily available in company records. This information is stored electronically and easily identifies what the customers buy, what their preferences are, who they are, where they live, and their gender, age, and ethnic group. For instance, Blockbuster Video has a computer system that identifies the customers of a store and produces an actual map showing where they live. J.C. Penney and Sears have current sales and market penetration data on each ZIP Code in which credit card customers reside that is broken down by specific store and by merchandise line. Because you are not part of a larger operation, you may need to interview customers directly.

To learn more about the customers who make up your prospective RTZ, interview several hundred people in relation to the number of customer visits. In other words, make sure you interview a good sample of customers at each of the peak and low periods of business. The best time to take an RTZ Survey is a time when no special or exceptional market events will occur, like holidays, heavy advertising, promotional campaigns, or new product introductions. You should vary the number of customer interviews based on the average weekly sales patterns. To do this, you must determine the percentage of an average week's sales (in dollars) and transactions (in number of orders) that occur by day for weekdays (Monday through Friday) and weekends (Saturday and Sunday).

- If 25 percent of the store's weekly sales occurs Monday through Friday from 10:00 A.M. to 2:00 P.M., then 25 percent of your customer interviews should be taken Monday through Friday between 10:00 A.M. and 2:00 P.M.
- If eight percent of the weekly business occurs on Saturday and Sunday from 5:00 P.M. to 8:00 P.M., then eight percent of the interviews should be taken during those hours.
- If there is a drive-thru, the interviews should take place at the order board.

In general, if your type of business has relatively even sales per transaction, like a shoe store, then the number of interviews should be based upon the number of transactions. If your business instead has uneven sales per transaction, like a fast-food restaurant that specializes in roasted chicken (low-average sales at lunch and high-average sales at dinner), then base the number of interviews on the average sales per transaction. In this case, divide your survey into two parts — daytime business and nighttime business. You should analyze the results of both separately. Additionally it is important to identify the amount of business that comes from the various parts — also called *grids* — of your RTZ and the boundaries of that RTZ. Look at the length, width, and depth of each grid. The length and width relate to the percentage contributed (capture rate) to the store by the grid. The depth relates to the percentage of business contributed versus the potential dollars available in the grid for that type of business industry. The smaller the grids, the more precise the information. You will be better able to link your customers with specific traffic generators. For instance, you will know that a nearby high school, hospital, Kmart, or apartment complex generates traffic that will pass by your store, which eventually translates into customers. In downtown areas, the grids should be the blocks. In urban and suburban areas, the grids should be one-fourth of a square mile. In rural areas, the grids should be one square mile or bigger.

You can customize your RTZ Survey to discover additional information, such as:

- Perception of products and services
- Frequency of visits
- Impact on other stores
- Distances in the RTZ itself

Your RTZ Survey can be done in one of three ways. You can use a one-question pin map survey to find out the basics — your customers' points of departure and points of arrival. If you prefer, you can go a step further and use a more detailed questionnaire, like the one located at the end of this chapter. Your other option is to pay a market research professional to complete the survey for you. To decide which survey method is best for you, weigh the pros and cons of each. Any of the three studies should be made in a store that has been open for business for a few months to allow the business to establish its presence in the market.

The One-Question Pin Map

For a one-question pin map survey, use a map with various colors that show political subdivisions and areas like parks, airports, shopping centers, and schools. The map must clearly reflect all the streets; the street names must be legible. The map has to take in an area bigger than the estimated size of the RTZ in which you are interested. Remember, you have established the boundaries of your prospective RTZ by identifying the natural and human-made barriers and driving to all the isochrones (equidistant time points). As an example, a map for a typical fast-food restaurant should cover a five-mile radius.

Tape the map onto a hard backing, such as cardboard or poster board and place it on a tripod in your store. Use red pushpins for daytime business and blue pushpins for nighttime business. Assign an employee to invite your customers to put a pushpin on the map. Mark the position of your retail store and draw a one-mile circle to facilitate locating the pushpins. Make sure you leave a wide margin around the map. It is for customers that come from off the map.

At the top of the map, write a clearly legible sign asking one of your survey questions. Use one question per survey. For instance, your first pin map survey question is, "Where are you coming from?" In a second pin map survey the question is, "Where are you going?" In a third pin map survey you will ask, "Where do you live?" Word the questions very simply. People can easily get confused. When finished, you can:

- Check the results with the demographic data that you originally collected when you decided to open your store in that location. Compare the results with the data of each grid of the survey map.
- Draw a line around two-thirds to three-quarters of the pushpins — this marks your primary trading area, or RTZ amoeba.
- Check the number of pushpins, block by block, against the demographics you obtained.
- Determine the main roads or shortcuts customers take.
- Check how many customers travel a long distance.
- Check the distribution of your customers against competitor stores.

You may find that the RTZ extends one mile to the east and five miles to the west. If so, determine why the amoeba is short on one side and stretched out on the other. Your further investigation will help you discover the barriers and interest gravitation.

A More Detailed Questionnaire

If you want more information than a one-question pin map survey can provide, use a more detailed questionnaire for your RTZ Survey. This involves a battery of questions, a trained crew, and your good old pin map. Before making an RTZ Survey, you need to establish the specific purpose of it. Thus, your questionnaire must include questions concerning what you want to discover specifically. This more in-depth RTZ Survey consists of individual interviews of representative customers of a relevant number — perhaps several hundred.

Prepare a questionnaire that helps you understand the real estate characteristics of the location. Ask each respondent no more than twelve questions not including your physical observations, such as the gender, age, and ethnic background of the respondents. A tried and proven format for the questionnaire is located at the end of this chapter for your use. Train your interviewers so they will get clear and truthful answers. When interviewing, tell your interviewers to:

- Be courteous.
- Speak clearly and firmly.
- Interview people in a variety of age and ethnic groups.
- Listen carefully.
- Record their answers carefully on paper.

In preparation for the actual survey, predetermine the time and number of people to be interviewed as a percentage of hourly and daily sales or transactions.

Next, you need to prepare a map like the one used in the pin map study and highlight its major streets and roads. Draw a one-mile square with one-eighth square mile grids; make these grids easily visible on the map. You can number the small squares consecutively for easy identification by the interviewer. In addition, prepare three clear plastic overlays, to indicate:

- Where customers are coming from (their points of departure);
- Where customers are going (their points of arrival); and
- Where the customers live.

Each customer response should be indicated on the map by stick-on paper dots. The dots should be in a variety of colors to signify variables like weekday or weekend; daytime or nighttime; and residence or workplace. Once you have the proper sampling of customers, take a look at the results.

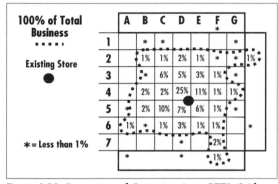

Figure 4.18 Percentage of Customers in an RTZ's Grids

The results of these interviews will reveal the percentage of customers related to a particular grid on your map. These percentages are based on a total of the responses. The percentages will vary and will decrease as the distance the customer must travel increases. Consequently, at the margins of your map, you will have percentages of one percent or less. You will have to decide, given your type of industry, to include or exclude the outer grids with less than one percent. Figure 4.18 includes the grids with one percent. Notice the percentages off-map.

The map in Figure 4.19 gives the percentages related to work and the map in Figure 4.20 shows the percentages related to shopping. Notice the lack of off-map percentages. The maps in these two figures show how an RTZ changes its boundaries according to the single activities your survey has isolated. If you overlap the maps you will find that the boundaries overlap each other. They are the boundaries of the single activities related to specifics like:

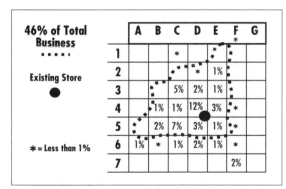

Figure 4.19 Percentage of Work-Related Customers

- The time of day (morning, noon, afternoon, early evening, or late night);
- A product (breakfast, liquor supplies, or tennis balls);
- A service (dry cleaning or photo processing);
- Type of activity (work or recreation);
- Day of the week (Wednesday); and
- Day of the weekend (Sunday).

In the example in Figure 4.19, the RTZ varies from a triangular shape for 46 percent of total business related to work. In Figure 4.20 the RTZ forms a kidney shape for another 17 percent of total business related to shopping.

The questions of the RTZ Survey may concern location, products, store experience, and the profile of the customer. The survey results will become your marketing bible. You will use the information to get more customers to your store, more often, to spend more money. You will find yourself wrestling with questions like:

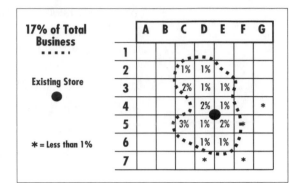

Figure 4.20 Percentage of Shopping-Related Customers

- Why don't I get any customers from Grid 8 C, only half a mile away from my store?

- Why do I get only five customers a week from Grid 7 G, which has a population of 5,000 people?

- Why don't I get more customers from the nearby shopping center?

- Why don't I sell any pink shoes or red tennis balls in Grid 5 A?

- Why do I get a small average check from Grid 3 F?

To better understand the percentages in each grid, you must walk it, drive it, and fly it, as described in Chapter 3. You also want to check the percentage of customers against actual demographics and sales potential data. You will learn essential sales forecasting methods in Chapter 5. Look for the reasons why one grid has more business than another. Perhaps the map shows clusters of customers' homes, apartments, townhouse complexes with young, upbeat single professionals. Further, try to see where the number of customers decreases to less than one percent. Identify the barriers — road problems, mountains, rivers, or strong competition. In another grid you may notice a wide area with no customers.

A physical survey may reveal a forest preserve, an industrial belt, or agricultural fields. In yet another grid you may see a widely scattered number of dots. This could indicate single dwelling, middle income families. Carefully evaluate the results of the RTZ Survey. Question everything and leave no stone unturned. The RTZ Survey will help you run your business in an entrepreneurial way and make money. It will be wise to have a new survey done every couple of years, or after a significant event that has affected your store.

A Professional Market Research Study

A professional market research study should include data collection, the interview, training of the interviewers, customer sampling, computerization and analysis of the data, and visual documentation of the results. Various types of professional surveys are available.

- A marketing module provides the profile of the customer by such factors as age, sex, race, frequency of visits, and usage of competitors.

- An operation module measures the level of customer satisfaction regarding quality, service, cleanliness, and other attributes peculiar to the goods and services you provide.

- A real estate module delineates the size and shape of a business' RTZ and shows trip patterns and activities associated with the customers' visits that you need to understand the dynamics of your store's appeal.

The cost of a professional RTZ Survey varies considerably — $2,500 to $3,500 per survey — according to its scope.

Plan for Success

The RTZ Survey is a prime tool for location purposes as well as your main tool for planning your marketing efforts. In fact, think of your survey as a battle plan to help you get the most business from everyone within your RTZ's boundaries. The customers are already there: get them in!

Now that you know and understand the status of your RTZ, it is time to get to work. Understand the relevance of the findings in relation to your industry: always per grid. With this in mind, you can:

- Plan inside-outside store promotions.
- Offer special products and incentives.
- Target specific grids for special advertising, like using door hangers.
- Advertise in the local newspapers.
- Use full-color newspaper inserts.
- Consider billboards and directional signs.

You should not rest until you get some business from all the grids that have population and activities.

Advice for First-Time Retailers

While precise trading zone information is missing when you are looking for a new location in a market, you need to use your knowledge of other company's RTZ Surveys to make comparisons with similar or competitive analogue stores. The best route is to start your own business after several years of practice and experience, especially with a big company with a well-known success rate. If you do start anew without practical retail experience, then you should:

- Join a local group or chapter of business operators in your industry. This will help you make acquaintances and create contacts you can use to find out information.
- Retain an expert or consultant who has experience and knowledge with more than one company and use that person's familiarity with surveys done by others.
- Negotiate an agreement to conduct a survey at someone else's location — it could be worth the money.

You may have heard the saying that you learn by doing it. In retail, the theoretical-statistical knowledge is not enough — you need to learn the practical knowledge. If you are new to retailing, most likely you are taking or have taken accelerated business courses. Although interesting, all the theory in the world won't make any difference until you put it into practice. In short, you need to learn the business by actually working in it, especially by managing it. In some cases, the only way to learn it is to apply for a job with your best competitor. The practical knowledge of your retail business will help you immensely in the understanding of your location. In an actual store setting, you will experience the customers, you will observe their behavior, you will sense their needs and desires. These are the people that live, work, shop, and recreate around your location.

Two helpful resource tools will help you plan your start-up retail business. *Retail in Detail* is chock-full of practical tips and advice based on the real-life experience of Ronald L. Bond and his wife, who have been retail operators for several years. And, for a general, nuts-and-bolts approach to starting a business for the first time, get a copy of *SmartStart Your (State) Business*, with state-specific regulations, resources, and sample forms. To find out more about these invaluable resources, contact:

The Oasis Press
(800) 228-2275 or *www.oasispress.com*

Chapter Wrap-Up

The very livelihood of your retail business depends upon your thorough understanding of the retail trading zone that you will serve. As you have learned, your best option is to serve a market in an RTZ that encompasses as much of the market as possible. The larger the RTZ, the greater the potential for your business' retail success. As you continue your site selection process, keep in mind the key points for identifying your trading area, including:

- Know what type of zone you will serve and the most important factors for each type.
- Determine the way the towns and sections of towns within the RTZ connect and what these connections mean to getting customers to your store.
- Discover the shape and size of your RTZ to gain keen insights into the dynamics of the way your RTZ can change and how you must adapt your retail business to this ever-changing amoeba-like entity.
- Study the town's grocery stores to give you a clearer picture of the customers who will make up your trading area.
- Understand the boundaries of your potential RTZ by knowing the driving time and distance your customers must travel to get to your store and any natural or human-made barriers that might influence this travel time.

You have your work cut out for you. But if you invest the time now you will reap a big payoff later. The following chapter will give you essential sales forecasting methods to help you continue your search for the location that will properly serve its RTZ and will produce profits.

RTZ Survey Instructions

The Retail Trading Zone (RTZ) Survey is specifically designed to discover an RTZ. You do this by identifying customers' origin and destination points. During the interview the customers tell where they were before arriving at your store. They tell you their origin points and help you classify them according to useful categories, such as home, work, shopping, hotel, recreational activity, church, entertainment event, social, professional appointment, school, or passing through. Customers can also tell you where they are going after leaving the store.

A more precise RTZ Survey could ask for the names of the points. For instance, if there is a big university within walking distance, you want to know how much business you get from it. If there is a community shopping center, find out if it is a Wal-Mart or Kmart, for instance. You want to know how much business these generators will contribute. The question concerning the roads is also important. People have a way of figuring out the best way to get to your store by using shortcuts and, at times, by avoiding the main roads. Finally, the survey indicates the most important areas from which you get a significant amount of business.

With this RTZ Survey, you will see different patterns through the busiest operating hours, different times of the day, weekdays, weekends, and holidays. You will also discover whether the sources of business are concentrated in one or in several places throughout the market. This will indicate varying degrees of penetration. Invariably, a percentage of your business will come from beyond five miles. The survey will give you the reason for such long-distance business.

This survey can also become a marketing survey if you ask additional questions. For instance, you might ask, "Which competitor did you visit during the last month?" You can add other questions about the personal profile of the customer, such as marital status or occupation and the customer's perceptions of pricing, merchandising, inventory availability, and other important matters.

For site selection purposes, keep the survey simple and short. If you ask too many questions, the customer will feel uncomfortable, and the resulting data may not be reliable. When you ask, "How long did it take you to get here?" you may not get an accurate answer in terms of real time. The answer will be more of a perception of time than a fact. However, it is useful to know what customers perceive.

To properly complete each survey, make sure your interviewer has a map of the area — a good visual that indicates the road systems surrounding the store. Remember, these questions are a sample representation to help you get key RTZ data. Feel free to add or delete questions, if necessary.

RTZ Survey

[Show interviewee the map and point to it.]

Where were you before coming to the store? [Mark the nearest intersection on the map.]

☐ Home ☐ School ☐ Recreational activity
☐ Work ☐ Passing through ☐ Hotel
☐ Shopping ☐ Social ☐ Church
☐ Entertainment ☐ Professional appointment ☐ Other [specify]: _____

Which road did you take to come here? _____

Where will you be going after you leave this store? [Mark the nearest intersection on the map.]

☐ Home ☐ School ☐ Recreational activity
☐ Work ☐ Passing through ☐ Hotel
☐ Shopping ☐ Social ☐ Church
☐ Entertainment ☐ Professional appointment ☐ Other [specify]: _____

Please indicate on the map where you live. [Mark the nearest intersection.]

If applicable, please indicate on the map where you work. [Mark the nearest intersection.]

How much did you spend today? _____

How many people in your party today? _____

How did you get here?   ☐ By car   ☐ On foot   ☐ By bus   ☐ Other [specify]: _____

How long did it take you to get here?

☐ 3 minutes ☐ 5 minutes ☐ 7 minutes
☐ 10 minutes ☐ 12 minutes ☐ 15 minutes
☐ 20 minutes ☐ 25 minutes ☐ 30 minutes or more

Please indicate your age group:

☐ 10–14 ☐ 20–24 ☐ 30–34 ☐ 45–54 ☐ 60–65
☐ 15–19 ☐ 25–29 ☐ 35–44 ☐ 55–59 ☐ Over 65

Is this your first visit here?   ☐ Yes   ☐ No

If not, how often do you come?   _____ per week   _____ per month   _____ per year

Physical Observations [Do not ask interviewee.]

Date: _____   Day of the week: _____   Time of day: _____

Location of interview: _____

☐ Male ☐ Latin-Hispanic ☐ African-American ☐ Native-American
☐ Female ☐ Asian ☐ White ☐ Other [specify]: _____

Chapter 5

Forecast Your Store's Sales

In retail site selection, the correct forecasting of your store's future sales is a matter of life or death to your business. Inevitably, you will face hard costs, such as real estate, construction, equipment, interior decoration, furniture, and computers. In addition, you may be responsible for soft costs, such as zoning, professional fees, training, and personnel relocation. Only with an accurate projection of sales will you be able to determine the right amount to invest to produce the needed return on investment (ROI). You may be confident that you have the skill and talent to open your retail business, but are not thrilled at the idea of attempting to predict the future via complicated mathematical methods. In response to these real business concerns, this chapter gives you various ways to estimate your store's future sales. You will learn how to evaluate similar stores — also called *analogues* — in the area in which you are interested to help you estimate the sales potential for your future store. To use the analogue concept to forecast sales, you can use the following five methods:

- An analogue study
- An analogue rating system
- An hourly sales analysis
- A success model
- A market share approach

These five sales forecasting methods should be used independent of one another. However, your best bet is to take the time to use all five methods to give you a more accurate picture of your store's sales potential in relation to existing analogues. To help you use these methods, corresponding worksheets are located in Appendix C to help you identify the important and relevant site factors to achieve the maximum sales potential at your new store.

Also, the more complex sales forecasting methods included in this chapter will give you an idea of what the bigger retail establishments use, like grocery stores and department stores. Once you have gathered your critical data regarding the sales forecast of your prospective store, you will learn how to adjust your sales projections to achieve an equilibrium between your store's sales, market share, costs, and profits. In short, knowing your future sales will help you know the amount to invest to get the profits you want.

To gain a better understanding of the sales forecasting process, consider the similarities between methods of projecting sales and the real estate appraisal process.

Understand the Analogue Concept

When you buy a home, empty parcel, commercial building, or other real estate property, you want to make sure that you will pay the right price. To know the fair and reasonable price, you will contract a certified real estate appraiser. As a result, an appraisal of the property will not come up with an absolute, indisputable value, but with an *opinion of value*. This opinion of value will be part of a formal written report that will contain information about the property itself, its market, and rationale for the evaluation. The appraiser's conclusions must be supported by:

- Truthful and relevant data concerning actual transactions;
- The analysis of various similar properties; and
- Reasoning that uses facts and figures.

Further, an appraiser will produce at least three figures of property values by using three different methods, including:

- The market approach, which is based upon historical transactions;
- The income approach, which is based upon the income that the property produces or may produce; and
- The cost approach, which is based upon the costs of replacing the improvements.

At this point, the appraiser will not average the final figures, but will weigh them. The final opinion of value is not the result of averages, but the result of the study's rationale.

When forecasting your store's future sales, you will use a similar approach. You will examine different ways of looking at existing analogue stores and of projecting your opinion of sales volume. Your sales projections will be based upon the evidence, not upon a mathematical average of data.

This is not a theoretical approach. It is the study of stores already in operation. You will compare, compare, compare to see what exists in actual stores so you can project your future sales.

The study of analogue stores, whether from a same chain or a competitor, is a way of forecasting the sales of a new location. If you want to project the sales of your proposed facility in its new location, carefully examine what is happening in similar stores or in competitive stores in the area, or in an area that is similar in demographics, density, and other characteristics. Competitive stores in the area in which you are interested — no matter how large or small — are definitely analogues. Similar stores are analogues if they are similar in significant ways. For example, if they carry merchandise that harmonizes with yours — their baseball cards harmonize with your toys — or if their customer profiles are similar to yours. Additionally, the compilation of analogue data must be from stores in the same social, demographic, and economic parts of a city. In short, they must be analogue stores in analogue areas. To locate your store's analogue, look at the nearest area to the RTZ in which you want to locate.

Most often the adjacent areas offer analogue characteristics. For example, in an area west of Chicago, Illinois, analogues are found in the areas between the east and west tollways to Lake Street to the north. Near Los Angeles, California, analogues are obvious in the San Fernando Valley. In Atlanta, Georgia, there are abundant analogues in the areas between I-75 and I-85 to the north. Notice the four locations in Figure 5.1. They are similar or analogous in various ways. As you can see, the similarity of the locations relates to their locations near a central business district (CBD). They are located at intersections of radial roads and beltways. They are all part of the southwest part of the RTZ of the city. The individual RTZs of Store 1 and Store 2 are analogous to each other, each being located along the same ring around the CBD. The RTZs of Store 3 and Store 4, being suburban areas with fairly new construction, are more analogous to each other than to Store 1 and Store 2, which are denser and housed in older construction.

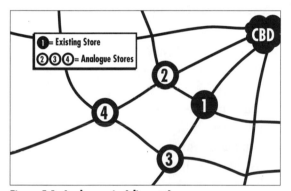

Figure 5.1 Analogues in Adjacent Areas

Method 1 – Study Your Analogues

The first method to forecast your store's sales involves a careful analogue study in which you try to obtain four types of information, including the:

- Type and density of the demographics and psychographics within your projected retail trading zone;
- Physical site characteristics;
- Type and size of the facility; and
- Sales in absolute dollars and trends, through the day, week, month, and year.

Evaluate the similarities and dissimilarities of your store and its analogue stores to arrive at an opinion of sales volume. To accomplish this, you must begin an analogue study. In your analogue study you might find similarities in:

- Demographics, such as socioeconomic status, ethnic profile, and lifestyle profile;
- Types of traffic;
- Industries, schools, and colleges;
- Commercial developments;
- Single and high-density developments;
- Professional buildings;
- Health care institutions;
- Military bases; and
- Recreational areas.

At times, you may need to study the history of the area to understand the dissimilarities. For instance, you may find a beautiful, prosperous residential area adjacent to a dilapidated area. From your further research, you may conclude that military service personnel used to live a short distance from the stately homes of prosperous society members. This type of dramatic difference will occur when the absence of zoning regulations allows for a variety of developments in the same areas, like in Houston, Texas.

To formulate an opinion of how successful an analogue is in your industry, look at the location and the facilities with a critical eye. Determine whether the analogue's location is better or larger than what you have in mind for your retail business. Also, look at its accessibility and visibility — can customers easily access and identify the facility? You will learn more about accessibility and visibility as key site requirements in Chapter 6. In addition, you can evaluate the analogue's facility by looking for tell-tale signs of a business' success, like:

- How well the landscaping is manicured;
- How attractively displayed is the merchandise; and
- Whether the employees are available, courteous, and competent.

Use the Analogue Study Worksheet located in Appendix C. This worksheet will help you gather pertinent data that will identify clear-cut traffic generators and will help you with the sales forecast for your new store.

Method 2 – Rate Your Analogues

The second method for forecasting sales available to you is the analogue rating system — a judgmental and statistical method to compare various characteristics of one or more retail stores. Using this method, you can rate your prospective location against the existing locations of the top three analogue stores. By using a simple analogue rating system, you can determine which of each store's characteristics are the most important sales generators. To use this method, you must have first completed the RTZ Survey from Chapter 4. Remember, the main goal of your RTZ Survey is to reveal the sources of your potential customers. For instance, a survey of an entrepreneur interested in opening a drugstore may reveal that ten percent of its potential customers comes from a hospital a mile away. In like manner, a fast-food restaurant may find out that 15 percent of its customers are maintenance employees that come from a nearby airport. Once you have this data, you can use the analogue rating system to rank the importance of the main factors that will contribute to your store's sales.

If you are a franchisee of a progressive company, most likely you can get results of formal analyses of existing stores. If you are an individual entrepreneur, you must use the knowledge you gain from this book to improve your comparison and evaluation skills. For example, in your evaluations, you can rate the relevance of factors like:

- Residential
- Employment
- Shopping patterns
- RTZ size and density
- Population
- Visibility
- Accessibility
- Facility attractiveness
- Income

For your convenience, use the Analogue Rating Score Sheet in Appendix C. After you have completed the score sheet, you will have an idea of which factors are better or worse by the total amount of points for each store. The rating factors will allow you to formulate an opinion of sales volume, just like the way an appraiser formulates an opinion of value for a property.

Method 3 – Analyze Your Analogues' Hourly Sales

Another method to forecast your store's future sales involves familiarizing yourself with the hourly sales patterns of your top three analogue stores. The hourly sales analysis will help you understand the peak and low hours for sales for both weekdays and weekends. In fact, the hourly sales analysis is like taking the pulse of a business — you can analyze the health of a store by the fluctuations in sales that occur each business day. However, there are businesses that don't lend themselves to this kind of sales estimate method. Retail businesses that deal with ready money — cash or charge — are more suited for this kind of hourly sales comparison. For example, if you will operate a restaurant, convenience store, or grocery store, you will benefit from an hourly sales analysis.

An hourly sales analysis for businesses like travel agencies, financial planning or accounting firms, or home decorating shops will not help you predict sales because the customers' visits cannot be tied to any day, time, or season.

Even if you have the results of a formal RTZ Survey, you still need to know why and when you reach peak hours. You also want to know whether your business is reinforced by other businesses in this area, and whether there is any interdependence.

To begin your analysis, construct daily and weekly sales curves based on an average, nonholiday season. To illustrate the concept of an hourly sales analysis, look at Figure 5.2. This hourly sales analysis illustrates a typical sales chart that shows the sales per hour throughout a normal business day. Notice the two sales peaks — the primary peak occurs around 2:00 P.M. and the secondary peak occurs about 7:00 P.M. Based on these two main sales peaks, you are likely to see corresponding sales lows, or valleys. As you can see in Figure 5.2, the first low is about 4:00 P.M. and the second low begins to drop off after 9:00 P.M. A retail business may have one of more of these peaks, depending on its type of industry and the nature of its RTZ. The charts for the other four weekdays are likely to be similar, but the curves change substantially during the weekends.

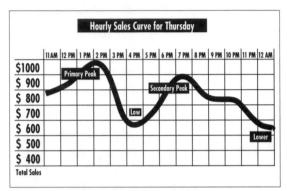

Figure 5.2 Weekday Hourly Sales Analysis

Saturdays, Sundays, and holidays have peculiar curves. Compare the hourly sales analysis for a Saturday as illustrated in Figure 5.3. Notice that the sales curve for a Saturday will normally be higher than a weekday, but sales activity is more uniform and steady. Similarly, a Sunday will show drastic sales peaks in the afternoon and evening, and then sales will vanish rapidly to near-zero at night. In like manner, a holiday, depending on which one it is and the time of year, has its own interesting sales curves.

The hourly sales curve is also heavily conditioned by the type of RTZ you will serve. For instance, the businesses on Broadway in Manhattan, New York, will have higher than average sales curves with higher than average peaks. On Wall Street in New York, the peaks

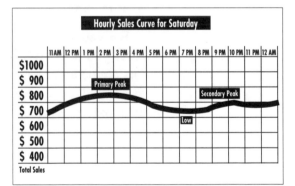

Figure 5.3 Weekend Hourly Sales Analysis

literally will go through the roof in the middle of the day and then slow down to nothing later in the day. Now that you have an idea of what an hourly sales analysis and its corresponding sales curves look like, it is time for you to plot the sales of an analogue store.

The next step of your hourly sales analysis is to "camp" outside your analogue store and begin charting and evaluating the foot traffic going into the store during each hour it is open. For example, in Tokyo, Japan, marketing analysts for McDonald's stood at the corner of a planned store and literally counted all the people that passed by the door of the future site to compute potential sales curves. The same method was used in Manhattan in front of a Chock Full o'

Nuts and a Nathan's Famous Coney Island Hot Dogs. You can use the Hourly Sales Analysis Worksheet located in Appendix C to help you identify key sales curves. You will also need to spend time in the existing analogue stores to be able to see and analyze the customers. Your objective here is to find out all you can about the people who contribute to your peak sales — what they look like, what they ask for, how much they spend, and where these customers come from. Do they come from:

- The college next door
- The Wal-Mart two blocks away
- The regional shopping center
- The office park half a mile away
- Home
- Work

After you have tracked the hourly sales of your analogue stores, go to your prospective site and visualize the future number and kind of people to project your store's future sales. For instance, if you noticed a high sales peak at 12:45 P.M. in Analogue Store 1, find out the reason for the peak. The reason may be a huge telephone office building across the street, full of employees with changing shifts. So, if your business will not cater to this type of customer — full-time employees that need to take lunchbreaks within walking distance — most likely your business will not have the same sales peak of 12:45 P.M. You must analyze the sales hour by hour to know whether your business' sales curves will be similar to the analogue stores in the area.

To help you make sense of your hourly sales analyses for your prospective store and your analogue stores, compare the various traffic generators. In short, find out what pulls in customers to an analogue store and your store. You can create a simple listing, like the one below, to help you.

Analogue Store	**Your Store**
3 grocery stores	1 grocery store
5 office buildings	0 office buildings
1 regional mall	1 community shopping center
5,000 residences within one-quarter mile	1 residential park (300 tenants)

You now can see the difference — it will be reflected in the hourly sales. If the projected sales, hour by hour, make sense, your total projection will also make sense. If the parts are more correct, then the sum of the parts will be more correct. It is like building a house — brick by brick.

Once you have analyzed the sales for one or more weeks, you can project the sales over a one-year period. But this is not that simple. You will need to talk to your accountant. Each month has a different number of days. Some months have, at certain times throughout a year, five Sundays, four Mondays, or four

Fridays. Your accountant will help you use a system called the *chart of accounts* — a system by which each quarter is divided into 13 comparable weeks. It is nothing but a succession of periods (not months) that make up four and five weeks alternatively. There are three periods per quarter, each period with 13 weeks (four weeks, five weeks, four weeks). All the periods end with a Sunday.

Using the chart of accounts system, suppose you estimated the sales of the first week of the first period. The sales of that week, based upon your analysis of analogue stores, represent 2.4 percent of your yearly sales. Using this system, you will be able to mathematically compute the yearly sales; of course, you will need to make adjustments to them according to your analogue research and your educated judgment. For more details on this process, contact your accountant.

Method 4 – Use a Success Model

The success model is another judgmental tool you can use to compare analogues to help you predict your store's sales. A success model is a list of characteristics and measures that are ideal for a location and specific to the type of retail business. The success model allows you to look at existing similar or competitive businesses from all sides. It is not flatly predictable, and you cannot put exact numbers to it, but the success characteristics will have an effect on sales.

Do not look for a perfect success model. Instead, look at actual situations and competitive businesses. Don't start from a prototype model, which is abstract, intellectual, and nonexistent. Instead, start with existing businesses, both analogous and competitive. Identify the most relevant characteristics and include them in your success model. To help you study these characteristics, use the Success Model Worksheet located in Appendix C. Use the Success Model Worksheet to learn the characteristics of the location you have tentatively chosen and as a basis of comparison with competitors.

You will have to develop your own model that is specifically geared to your type of industry — convenience store, shoe store, beauty salon, liquor store, toy store, hardware, flower shop, or whatever. For instance, if you plan to open your hardware store, your model should include the rate of growth of local residential, professional, and commercial new construction. Look at all aspects of an existing retailer of goods and services. Make comparisons by giving each factor a score. At the end of your evaluation you will end up with a total score and a total of those factors that are present and those that are absent. Apply those ratios and give your opinion of sales volume without using any mathematical calculations. Keep in mind, the relationship between factors and sales is not absolute. For instance, a gas station generates a certain amount of sales based upon a traffic count of 80,000 cars per day. But, the sales are also generated by the fact that the station is located on a far corner of a four-way intersection with full signal lights and also by the fact that the service is superior. The factors-to-sales relationship is behavioral and environmental, not mathematical. Remember, human behavior cannot be measured and predicted — but it can be guessed.

Method 5 – Determine Your Market Share

The process of determining your market share is another method to forecast the sales of your new store. To properly forecast your store's future sales, you will compare the results of this method with the results of the other four methods so you can reach an opinion of sales volume.

To start, you need to know the dollars spent per capita in your industry per year in your market. For example, suppose that you are in the floral gift business. The market has 100,000 people. Each person spends an average of $30 per year to buy flowers. The market — also called a standard metropolitan area (SMA) — has five retail florists. The average volume per store is $600,000. To determine your market share, you will need the:

- Population in the SMA;
- Dollars spent in your industry per capita, per age group, per income group, and per year in the SMA;
- Population in your projected RTZ;
- Dollars spent per capita, per age group, per income group, and per year in your projected RTZ;
- Number of competitors in the SMA;
- Number of competitors in the RTZ;
- Whether the per capita expenditures are increasing or decreasing;
- The number of people per store in the SMA; and
- The number of people in the RTZ.

To get this industry market share data, talk to people in the same business, join a business association, or hire the assistance of consultants. Further, you can get industry expenditure data per capita from the economic census published every five years by the Business Division of the U.S. Census Bureau. Some states have their own statistics. For instance, California issues a *State Taxable Retail Sales Report*, which you can find in public and college libraries.

When you have collected all information, you can calculate important ratios, such as people per store in an SMA or people per store in your RTZ. From these findings you can determine the average store's sales volume, and then arrive at your opinion of your probable share of sales volume. Market share research gives you not only the dollars spent per person, but also per age group. For instance, you might find that 25- to 30-year-olds are the biggest purchasers of your goods or services. They spend $200 a year, while 45-year-olds and over spend only $75 a year.

Market share percentage information is provided by companies that specialize in specific industries. For instance, The NPD Group, Crest Division, offers market share data for the restaurant industry, and Paul Kagan Associates provides market share data for the home video rental industry. Refer to Appendix B for more information.

Theoretical Statistical Methods

For the mathematically-minded, several complex theoretical statistical methods exist that can be used to forecast a store's future sales. The three primary statistical methods are:

- The regression model
- The gravity model
- Reilly's Law

It might interest you to know that these are the main theoretical statistical methods used by larger retail centers, such as standard grocery stores, junior department stores, and department stores like Sears and Macy's. These statistical methods can also be used for large chains of small retailers like Color Tile, Dunkin' Donuts, Pearle Vision, and Blockbuster. However, the collection and computerization of data require great expense for personnel, equipment, time, and travel. For the average retailer these systems are probably not essential, but it won't hurt you to become familiar with the principles upon which they are based.

The Regression Model

The regression model is a mathematical equation that relates the sales of a store to one or more variables in respect to actual sales performance. The regression model begins with the variable that has the highest correlation with sales. Each step calls for another variable and a variable of a variable. Variables can include:

- Parking spaces within 200 feet of a store
- Number of competitors within one-half mile
- Population within one mile
- Median income within one mile
- Competing stores within one-quarter mile
- Visibility

Then, the importance of each variable is rated. This theory assumes that sales are positively related to the population within certain mile radiuses. These models use multiple combinations of variables with ratings like "better" or "worse" in the equation. An equation with too many variables and variables of variables will certainly result in a mathematically impressive, but unreliable estimate of sales. Regardless of its mathematical accuracy, this theoretical statistical method has several downsides.

Although the regression model provides a discipline for a market analyst to follow, look at some of its many downfalls. It is very expensive to build and difficult to construct a regression model. Furthermore, it requires knowledgeable personnel, equipment, and systems that are continually kept up to date. Another downside to the regression model is the way the data can be misinterpreted. For instance, an analyst might interpret factors too conservatively and out of context. Usually, an analyst does not want to get into trouble by forecasting sales that are too high and unrealistic. So the predictions are normally low, and they discourage business owners and managers from making sensible marketing decisions.

Finally, it is difficult to include all existing and future market situations — the results will almost always be incomplete and one-sided. The regression model might indicate that you have the right type and number of demographics around the area, but the interest gravitation might be toward the opposite direction from which you intend to locate your store. Consequently, your location is not within the flow of interest and your sales will be lower.

The Gravity Model

The gravity model, developed by market researcher David Huff, utilizes the gravitational notion that claims consumer attraction to a shopping center is directly proportional to the size of a retail center and inversely proportional to a customer's distance from a center. In other words, customers want better shopping; they will be attracted to a shopping center in proportion to the degree of convenience and attraction it offers.

Huff uses complicated formulas to project future sales based upon assumptions and probabilities. The gravity model simultaneously takes into account distance and competitive effectiveness. As the distance from a store increases, the percentage of the people who come to a store becomes lower — also known as the decay curve. In this case, gravity indicates power attraction, which is composed of:

- The distance between the stores
- Their size
- Their image or degree of attractiveness

The gravity model assigns a weight of attractiveness outside and inside, considers the number of square feet and sales space, and comes up with a variety of assumptions of type and quality of operations.

To understand this model, think of what happens when a store is remodeled and expanded. For example, when facilities are remodeled at McDonald's, sales increases follow and, at times, the increases are very high. People like new and inviting places. Further, the gravity model can be used to forecast sales within the same company; for example, one can easily compare a Sears store with a Sears store. Also, the model can be used to compare similar competitors, such as Kmart, Target, and Wal-Mart. On a smaller scale, the model applies to fast-food restaurants like Burger King and McDonald's, and to beauty salons, instant print shops, and many others.

Using a gravity model to forecast sales requires an experienced, mature analyst who will not only create mathematical models, but will be able to make experienced judgments. The theoretical assumptions do not take into consideration factual entrepreneurial skills, market conditions, competitive forces, consumption patterns, and marketing activities.

Reilly's Law

In 1929, William J. Reilly, a noted market analyst, invented an instructive technique called the law of retail gravitation. The law of retail gravitation originally was used to compare the degree of business attractiveness that single towns have in respect to each other. The law uses a formula to measure that pulling force. Suppose you want to calculate the mileage from Town A to Town B. To do so, use this formula:

$$\text{Mileage from Town A to Town B} = 1 + \sqrt{\frac{\text{Population of Town B}}{\text{Population of Town A}}}$$

Today's analysts use Reilly's Law to analyze the sales potential of retail stores. Instead of towns you can think of retail centers and apply the same rationale. Reilly's Law shows that people normally go to the biggest and best places they can travel to more conveniently. For instance, an analyst may start by looking at the population of rural towns. A town with 40,000 people will have twice the pulling force — meaning people will travel from two times the distance as a town of 10,000. If the towns are 30 miles apart, the breaking point is 20 miles from the smaller town and 10 miles from the bigger town.

Recent findings, however, show that this formula should be applied to retail centers with a grain of salt and a lot of experience. When applying this law to retail centers, for instance, the size of the total square footage — and also the square footage of major tenants — become the factors in the formulas. Distance should be in miles or in time depending upon which is more relevant in the specific case. Although Reilly's Law has merit, it is like calculating the velocity and direction of a soccer ball in a vacuum versus its velocity and direction during a hurricane. Great inaccuracies will occur when other factors of equal importance are ignored.

Adjust Your Sales Projections

Once you have used all or some of the five analogue methods readily available to you to estimate sales volume, you can look at the negative factors and attempt to calculate the sales dollars lost as a result. For instance, when exiting from a site, you cannot make a left turn on the road — this may cost you five percent of your business. Or the parking lot is full during peak sales hours and you observe some cars leave as they realize there is no space — this may cost you another five percent of your business.

You need to force yourself to look at the positive and negative sales generators to know if your site is the right one for your retail business.

From your original estimate of sales, subtract the dollars you will lose because of the prospective location's problems. One of the main negative factors that can influence your store's future sales is time — or more specifically, the amount of time it will take to actually open your store. It is possible that from the time you project the sales of your retail business, two or three years will go by before you will open its doors. This is particularly true when free standing buildings and new shopping centers are involved. If you are dealing with in-line or storefront locations that are part of an existing strip center, delays may still occur; but it may be a matter of months, not years. If you have to modify the building structure, you may have a long waiting time. There are many reasons for such time delays, including real estate availability, construction problems, local zoning jurisdictions, and environmental requirements.

Other key factors to consider include:

- Economic or physical market conditions — maybe the economy of the city or area is declining due to local or national conditions.
- New competitors entering your market and impinging on your RTZ will impact your sales.
- Physical conditions like road construction will make it difficult and dangerous for your customers to come to your store.
- New centers of attraction, like a huge mall under construction that will be adjacent to your retail store may cause an increase in your sales estimates.
- Seasons and events, such as tourism and celebrations, indicate sales trends that will influence your sales.

To come up with a yearly estimate, look at your weekly sales volume totals. You can use four steps to accomplish this. In the existing analogue store:

- Find out what percentage of the quarterly volume or the period volume the particular week represents.
- Calculate the quarterly or period volume.
- Determine the percentage of the yearly volume that quarter or period represents.
- Calculate the yearly volume in the new store.

Balance the Factors to Achieve Maximum Profits

A retail business must develop, evolve, and increase year after year. Retail sales will never remain flat for a long time — they either go up or they go down. As a retailer, your main goal is to achieve the highest possible market share in the standard metropolitan area that you are interested in serving. Market share consists of the revenues with respect to the total dollars available for a particular industry. Market share not only guarantees profits, but also survival and long-term success. Market share is the best offense and defense against competition; it guarantees repeat business and customer allegiance.

You can achieve a deeper market share with more stores. However, you must consider the sales that will be taken away from your existing stores. For example, you must look at the amount of market penetration — or the number of people sponsoring a business as a percentage of the local retail trading zone — to determine whether the existing store can afford to lose customers and revenues to allow for new stores. You must consider the balance between what is gained and what is lost at each store. For an in-depth discussion of market penetration, see Chapter 9.

Consider the Highest and Best Use Potential

To get a better idea of the balance factors you must consider when deciding to open a new or additional store, look at the real estate characteristics of the commercial parcel of land. A fundamental law in real estate is that the value of a parcel of land is directly proportional to its highest and best use potential. In other words, your intended use of the property must create the highest possible return on that investment. So your existing store's profit and loss statement should show enough profits at the bottom line to justify the occupancy costs called for by the market value of the real estate. The law of supply and demand dictates the value of the land, and it helps resolve the dilemma between penetration and profits.

The balance between sales, market share, costs, and profits will tell you whether or not you should:

- Open a retail store;
- Continue in a certain location;
- Tear down your existing facility and build a new one; or
- Lease out space to a different business with a higher potential for profits and better ability to pay the current occupancy prices.

With your sales estimate, you can create a break-even point statement to help you know the right occupancy percentage. Then, you can relate that occupancy cost to the highest and best use of the property you are considering. When you look at the relation between the occupancy cost and the highest and best use of the property, you will also have to consider the type of business as a factor that will influence your ROI.

Each retail business has a different degree of profitability. For instance, suppose you want to open a dry cleaning business on Wilshire Boulevard in Los Angeles, California. To open your business, your sales predictions must show a per square foot ROI equivalent to what the office buildings, department stores, and highly priced specialty stores already located on Wilshire Boulevard are producing.

Even if the site has all the characteristics that will make it a great location — the right consumer profile for the dry cleaning business, excellent visibility, a dense RTZ, and an excellent median income — you must determine whether this is the best use of this property. Your eagerness to have a location in a prestigious area like Wilshire Boulevard has to be tempered by the fact that the excellent RTZ will not produce a sales volume with an ROI to make it profitable for you.

You can evaluate a site's ROI by using your pro forma statements. Talk to your accountant or other financial representative to learn how to use the pro forma statements to help you make the right decision.

You can also estimate property value to determine whether the site will bring you the highest ROI by examining the:

- General economy of the area;
- Economy of the particular section of town;
- Position of the location in respect to growth areas;
- Retail buying power of the residents;
- Employment status and industry diversification;
- Building permit trends for new construction and remodeling;
- Commercial bank lending trends;
- Sufficiency of utilities and their trends;
- Size of the land and its physical characteristics;
- Condition and function of structures on the proposed property;
- Residential, professional, industrial, and retail vacancies; and
- Zoning.

An analysis of data, sales, leases, and offers to buy or sell similar commercial properties will also give you an idea of the site's present or potential use.

Two helpful sources of data include:

- *Percentage Leases,* published and revised periodically by the National Institute of Real Estate Brokers of the National Association of Real Estate Boards; and
- *The Dollars and Cents of Shopping Centers,* published and revised by the Urban Land Institute.

From these sources you can learn the normal range of profits, costs, sales, payroll, and controllable and noncontrollable expenses according to your type of industry.

Chapter Wrap-Up

To guarantee your future store's survival and success, you must take the time to estimate your future sales. When you know the amount of income your store will generate, you will be able to know the amount of money you must put up-front to get started and the money you will need to prosper and grow. You can get accurate sales forecast data by an apple to apple comparison — like real estate appraisers do when they determine their opinions of value of real estate properties. Remember, you must compare, compare, compare the relevant and important site characteristics for each analogue store you study. Then, look at how your store's characteristics fare against these analogues.

Your goal is to choose the location that will maximize your profits with a minimum amount of overall investment. These comparisons can be done via five sales forecasting methods. Keep in mind, you need a fairly accurate estimate of future sales. To get the most accurate estimate, use all five methods to determine an opinion of sales volume. After you have gathered your analogue data, make sure you look at your site's negative factors and adjust your earlier sales projections to know if you have a healthy balance of site pros and cons, and whether your business is suited for the highest and best use of the site. Doing these things will help you avoid big mistakes and help you keep your future store alive and prosperous.

Once you have your sales forecasts, you will be one step closer to the best location for your retail business. Next, you will want to take a closer look at your proposed location and specific site factors that will make your location decision the right one for your business.

Chapter 6

Consider Essential Location Factors

When it comes to choosing the right location, there is always more than meets the eye — until the eye looks again. What can at first glance appear to be a plus may turn out, upon close inspection, to be a drawback. For example, heavy traffic is a good thing, unless it is nonstop heavy traffic. The area may look poor for a store location, yet it may be excellent. A multitude of factors contribute to the total quality of a location. When looking for the right location for your retail business, you must consider essential location factors, including:

- Visibility
- Accessibility
- Regional exposure
- High density
- Growth
- Operational convenience
- Safety and security
- Adequate parking

One negative factor alone can annihilate all other positive factors. Visibility, regional exposure, and density will mean nothing if accessibility is poor. For instance, one of the best locations in the world is the Statue of Liberty in the New York Harbor. It is the epitome of visibility and recognizability. It is perfect except for one thing — you need to swim to get to it. To choose the right location, consider it in the context of the above essential location factors. Density may provide the demand for your goods and services, but if people cannot get to your facilities — that is, if you do not welcome them — they will feel rejected.

When you see a retail business struggling and on the verge of bankruptcy, it is not because the location didn't have people with a median income of $32,000 or that the age group was 40–45 instead of 35–45. These subtleties are important, but they are relative. The real reason for low sales is that the location lacks one or more of the essential location factors. This chapter highlights these important location factors and gives you practical advice on how to look for them in various types of properties. In addition, you are given tips to:

- Gain the attention of impulse buyers.
- Add or expand a drive-thru business, providing the convenience for today's fast-paced customers.
- Understand the challenge and the potential of a home-delivery business.

Your first consideration will be whether your proposed site is accessible and visible.

Make Sure It Is Visible and Accessible

Visibility and accessibility are the top essential factors of the right location — which means you will want to put your store where the people are. For maximum visibility, consider a site that your customers can see from as far away as possible; it takes time for a driver to make decisions. In addition, a successful location will have excellent accessibility — meaning easy, ample, and clearly marked entrance-exits from both directions of traffic. Your store will be accessible if a large number of people are able to move safely and easily into your parking lot and into your store.

Your Best Choice – A Far Corner

The best location is a *far corner* of a main road that intersects a secondary road, if it has access from both roads and there are no median dividers on either road. This location is very strong on visibility and accessibility. Figure 6.1 shows a location that was planned to maximize its potential for accessibility. The minimum frontage allows for two driveways as shown in Figure 6.1. Each driveway should accommodate two cars — one entering and one exiting. The minimum width in front should be 125 feet; anything less will cause a loss of sales and will hamper future business growth. The higher the speed limit on the main road, the more frontage is needed. As for the main road itself, it is important that it be a long-range route that accesses a freeway, passes over or under any railroad tracks, and does not dead end.

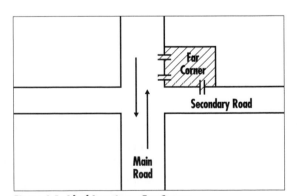

Figure 6.1 Ideal Location – Far Corner

Notice the two full-size entrance-exits on the main road that welcome incoming motorists from the main road and assure safe departures — even during peak traffic periods. Further, the entrance-exit on the secondary road is set back far enough from the corner to prevent blockage of departing cars when traffic stacks up at the busy intersection. To learn more about the importance of user-friendly entrance-exits, refer to the parking section later in this chapter. This type of location will give you a chance to make your store highly visible and capture the traffic most likely to yield a flow of customers — northbound traffic on the main road and both eastbound and westbound traffic on the secondary road.

Drivers will have plenty of time to spot your location, decide they want to visit your store, and maneuver to get there. Before you jump at the chance to locate your retail business on a far corner lot, consider traffic control issues. If you take another look at Figure 6.1, you will notice that all four roads are clear of obstructions.

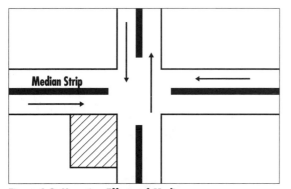

Figure 6.2 Negative Effects of Medians

Now compare the same location as illustrated in Figure 6.2. In this case, raised median strips on the four arms of this intersection may make traffic safer for your noncustomers, but it discourages many of your customers and guarantees that your sales volume will fall short of your retail trading zone's potential. Access to your store is dramatically reduced by median strips. With the barriers up, a near corner lot is a better location if it has a right-of-way opening onto a secondary road. However, keep in mind that the near corner location tends to be blocked at its main road exit because cars are stopped by the red light ahead.

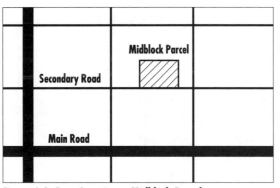

Figure 6.3 Poor Location – Midblock Parcel

Figure 6.3 shows a parcel in the middle of a block on a secondary street. This is a typical low-volume location. Accessibility and visibility are limited and, because of the secondary road, it will have fewer daily eye impressions. Also, its RTZ is much smaller in comparison to a location on one of two main roads.

Your Second Best Choice – Next to a Far Corner

The second best location is a parcel *next to a far corner* that faces a main road if it has a right-of-way behind the corner property that leads to the secondary road. As Figure 6.4 shows, this location will provide adequate accessibility and visibility even if a median strip on the main road exists. However, without the right-of-way to the secondary road, the property is less desirable. An additional access to and from the secondary road will help a lot. In addition, an exit onto the secondary road provides a measure of safety and ease that customers will remember next time they are tempted to visit.

In Figure 6.4, notice that the secondary road entrance-exit provides another opportunity for signage to make your store even more visible. Some retailers consider this kind of location better than the far corner lot shown in Figure 6.1 because it has more parking and car movement is easier.

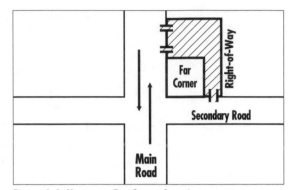

Figure 6.4 Next to a Far Corner Location

Avoid a Location Inside a Curve

To gain maximum visibility and accessibility, avoid locations on curves — especially on the inside of curves — as shown in Figure 6.5. A location on a curve on a descending or ascending road can spell disaster. Your store's visibility to approaching cars is greatly reduced. Also, customers emerging from your location onto a curve are taking their lives into their hands due to the traffic hazard. In addition, the increased speed of traffic due to gravity or acceleration makes it difficult and dangerous to turn into the property.

Also, avoid a location on any incline, no matter how slight. Once drivers see your business, they will have to react instantly and prepare for a sudden turn. By the time most of them have noticed your store, they will have bypassed you. Just as important as avoiding a location on the inside of a curve, you will want to opt for a location on level ground.

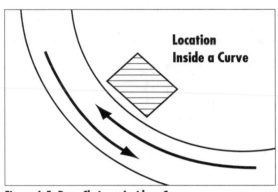

Figure 6.5 Poor Choice – Inside a Curve

Opt for a Level Location

Do not build your retail store on a parcel that is noticeably above the road level. Many drivers simply resent having to climb a hill to get to your store. On the same token, avoid building your store on a parcel that is lower than the road level. Some drivers will find this an unwelcome thrill and will encounter serious hazards when they reemerge onto the major road due to the disadvantage of going uphill and lack of visibility of approaching traffic.

Some retailers opt for a location on a service road because of cheaper rents and overall lower costs. Service roads — roads that are parallel to main roads, with access that may or may not have stoplights — cause both visibility and accessibility problems. A location on a service road will be recessed; hence, its visibility will be reduced. The best free standing retail location is at an intersection of a service road and a crosslateral road. Retail businesses on a service road located in the middle of a long block are inconvenient to customers.

Avoid these locations, particularly when there is a long string of buildings. Your store will become lost among them. Further, if a service road is a one-way road, then you will lose substantial potential sales.

Avoid Locating on a One-Way Road

Avoid a location on a one-way road even if you are at the corner with a secondary two-way road. You will be able to serve only a fraction of your potential

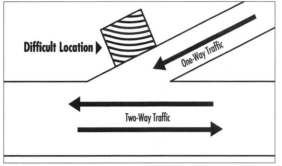

Figure 6.6 Difficulties with a One-Way Road

customers. One-way roads can create other accessibility and visibility problems as Figure 6.6 illustrates.

This site becomes a difficult location because it is accessible only along a one-way road that forces drivers to make an angled turn onto the main road. In this case, a potential customer may have difficulty finding the one-way road itself. Because this location is difficult to get to, most drivers don't want to bother. Your best bet is to avoid these tempting sites created by the angled convergence of streets.

Steer Clear of Dead Ends

Always avoid locations on any street that dead ends. A *no-outlet dead end* is the worst of all, but the T-intersection shown in Figure 6.7 is effectively a dead end.

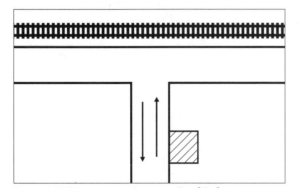

Figure 6.7 T-Intersection Acts as a Dead End

You may think that you will lose customers from only one direction; in reality, you will lose customers from all four directions.

As shown in Figure 6.7, even if a road continues over or under railroad tracks, the tracks themselves make the intersection a part-time dead end. By the way, a street running along railroad tracks tends to be a very poor retail street because retail stores are located only on one side and they are interspersed with other land uses — like used car lots, truck depots, kennels, and nurseries.

Don't Rely on Top-of-Mind Awareness Only

Some retailers excuse the lack of accessibility and visibility at their locations because they rely on their customers' top-of-mind awareness. *Top-of-mind awareness* is a marketing concept that says if people are asked which store they prefer in your industry, they will mention your store first. Let the retailer beware! Top-of-mind awareness will not fill enough customers into your store to make it profitable. Also, if your store is difficult to access, advertising and promotions will not help. You must couple the top essential location factors — that is, accessibility and visibility — with top-of-mind awareness to pull in customers and keep them coming back for more.

Accessibility and visibility in fact will bring them in; top-of-mind awareness will keep them loyal. You will find more minuses to avoid than pluses to look for in site comparisons. Think in terms of accessibility alone, and you will quickly eliminate several possible locations.

Locations for Commodity and Specialty Products

Commodity products are those that are purchased frequently with minimum effort, and the cost of entry (goods production) is reasonably low. Groceries, fast foods, and gas are commodity products. Impulse goods fall into this category, as well. The essential characteristics of a location for commodity products is high convenience, so it requires high visibility and accessibility.

Specialty products are unique products. Customers will put forth special effort to obtain them. A refrigerator, diamond ring, and sport car are quality items and are expensive. If necessary, people will drive long distances and search for the site, rather than be attracted by the site, to buy them. If you are in a specialty business, do not make the mistake of relying on the fact that customers will come to you. The characteristics of a specialty store should remain the same as for the commodity store, high visibility and accessibility. The convenience factor remains supreme.

Choose a Spot with Regional Exposure

To understand the importance of regional exposure, consider the influence of the regional road — also known as radial and quadrant roads. A regional road:

- Is wider than a neighborhood road;
- Carries a lot of traffic;
- Has rather constant traffic through all hours of the day and night;
- Is well illuminated at night;
- Carries more work and long-distance traffic than living traffic;
- Connects various city towns and nodes;
- Allows drivers to cover more distance in a shorter time;
- Has commercial activity on both sides and is well established; and
- Has rather expensive real estate prices.

For the right amount of regional exposure, choose a site that is located on radial or quadrant roads that carry local and long-distance traffic and are busy and alive during most of a 24-hour day.

Stay Away from In-Between Areas

In-between areas are areas that people pass through but don't have a reason to stop. People who drive the in-between areas have one thought in mind — to get through that section as fast as possible to get to the next point of activity in which they are interested. Also, people drive an in-between area with their feet pressed on the accelerators at speeds that may exceed the posted limits. These in-between areas can be recognized by the:

- Lack of traffic generators
- Design of the road itself

- Presence of medians
- High speed limit
- The lack of road intersections

Whatever the reason, if you establish a location in an in-between area, you will have to work extra hard to pull in your customers. The traffic and demographics of the area might be excellent; however, cars will not stop. Even excellent visibility will not suffice.

Choose the Right Side of the Street

Based on different traffic patterns and customer needs, one side of the street may be more important to your business. You will need to know the dynamics of the retail trading zone and the shopping patterns of your customers to know which side is the right side for your retail business. Consider whether your store is better suited for people on their way to work or people traveling to accomplish their daily tasks. For instance, a Pizza Hut is more oriented toward dinner, so customers can pick up a pizza on their way home. Therefore, a Pizza Hut is better located on the way home.

A retail business like Blockbuster Video, however, may be located on either side. A Blockbuster's customers may pick up a video on the way home, but many come to the store from home after they have had dinner. Further, a Dunkin' Donuts — which offers a quick breakfast alternative — is better suited on the going-to-work side. Remember, people will avoid anything that forces them to make a detour. Particularly, drivers with children in their cars will be wary of any sudden and difficult traffic movements.

Don't locate on the side where there is not other commercial activity. You will be tempted by the availability of the land; however, people will gravitate toward the active side.

Look at climate variables also. Determine whether the sunny or shady side is better for your customers. In northern climates, businesses favor the sunny side of the street. The difference is perceived in winter when pedestrians avoid cold, shady sidewalks — an obvious occurrence in New York City. On the other hand, in El Paso, Texas, retailers tend to line up on the shady side of the street to avoid the hot and scorching desert sun.

Avoid an Inside Parcel

For maximum regional exposure, you will want to avoid a location on an inside parcel. Although most locations in a commercial block are *inside parcels*, as opposed to locations on corners, these locations can be undesirable.

As a merchant or service provider, you cannot expect to do the volume of business you can do at a good location. Cars will zoom by at sustained speeds, contrasted with the slower speeds at intersections. By the time drivers have noticed your business on an inside parcel, they have accelerated to the point that it is too late for them to remember that you probably have something they have been looking for, decide to shop for it now, or cut across traffic or jam on the brakes and swerve to enter your lot.

In this case, impulse shopping by motorists is virtually out of the question. Thus, you will be restricted mostly to customers who make a point of coming to your store. They will have to know right where you are and how to get there safely. Inside parcels are especially undesirable if there are median strips on the main road, as shown in Figure 6.8.

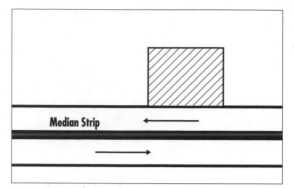

Figure 6.8 Inside Parcel with Restricted Access

Avoid Near Corners and Swing Corners

To select a spot with high regional exposure, you must avoid a location on a near corner and a swing corner. *Near corner* lots tend to be attractive to retailers looking for good locations. In fact, they are more attractive to retailers than they are to customers. A retailer may think that a busy intersection means a busy store. However, a near corner location is less visible than the far corner because drivers' views are partly blocked by cars ahead of them in midblock. By the time they notice a near corner location, drivers are already accelerating to get through the green or yellow light. The location next to the near corner has none of the advantages of the location next to the far corner in Figure 6.2, but it does have an advantage over the near corner location with respect to access, if it has a very wide frontage and easement to the secondary road.

Additionally, the worst situation for a near corner location is at a signal where a significant amount of traffic turns right onto another thoroughfare — also called a *swing corner*. The store marked "A" in Figure 6.9 shows a near corner/ swing corner. You can see that the near corner/ swing corner also has a negative effect on a far corner location because it diverts a major share of traffic away from it. The near corner/swing corner location tends to be blocked at its main road exit much of the time and at its secondary road exit some of the time. The location adjacent to the near corner, indicated by a "B" in the figure, is effectively blocked as well, unless it has an adequate entrance-exit from and onto the swing street as shown in Figure 6.9. The adjacent location in this case is better than the near corner since it is accessible from the secondary road at times when the near corner location is completely blocked.

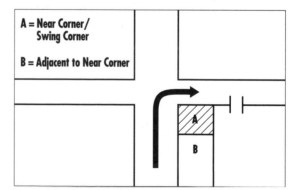

Figure 6.9 Negative Effects of a Swing Corner

Stay Away from Irregular Properties

Irregular properties have all kinds of shapes, including triangular shapes. Although they do not have four 90-degree angles, you will find some irregular properties with excellent visibility and accessibility. If you find the one you like, get a certified survey of it to find out the easements and restrictions that will affect your future building and parking layout. Suppose you need 50,000 square feet of property. Your irregular property is 50,000 square feet but:

- You will lose a great amount of square footage, which can be used only for landscaping.
- The prototype of your building will have to be substantially redesigned.
- The entrance-exits will need to be repositioned.
- The inside sales area, service area, and storage area will need to be changed.
- If you have equipment or production machinery, it may have to be partly redesigned and repositioned.

All of the above will delay your project, cost you more money, and may lessen your operation's efficiency. An irregular property may also force you to construct your building with a side or even the back of your store to the main road. Thus, while convenient, an irregular property is not desirable.

Target an Area of High Density

High density of the population is vital regardless of the perfect demographics and lifestyles that may fit your business. In areas where there is a lack of community-wide economic development, there is opportunity for today's retailers because of the dense demographics. People in the communities crave new and exciting things. For example, the day after the Watts' riots, a McDonald's executive decided to establish a new facility there in Watts. The density was high; the executive was convinced that there was a clear need for a new, modern McDonald's store. As a result, the restaurant was built on Century Boulevard and has been successful since its opening day. Density plus need created the success.

Density in a given geographical area can be vertical or horizontal. Vertical density can be found in Manhattan, New York; near the north side of Chicago, Illinois; and in downtown Pittsburgh, Pennsylvania due to the number of high-rise apartment buildings. Horizontal density can be found in Phoenix, Arizona; on the north side of Atlanta, Georgia; and in Ft. Lauderdale, Florida due to the sprawling ranch-house style developments.

An RTZ with vertical density will have smaller limits; an RTZ with horizontal density will have larger limits. You may have the same amount of people in both RTZs but what makes the difference is getting to your store. In Manhattan, people will walk to your store. In Phoenix, people will drive to your store and therefore they will face a higher degree of inconvenience. This results in lower sales volumes in horizontal density RTZs than in vertical density RTZs. However, high density is the universal remedy, the panacea that cures all sales volume problems.

Secure an Area with Growth

In Chapter 3, you found several suggestions of what to look for when you analyze an area, including apparent growth. At McDonald's, planners used to practice a favorite exercise that involved counting the new swimming pools and the parcels under construction, from a view above in a helicopter. In addition, they would drive a city and count the construction cranes against the sky. These simple exercises are effective ways to determine whether the area in which you are interested is growing and developing economically. Your goal is to secure an area with growth.

When you start your business, you intend to make your future with it. This will happen only if you will be able to offer your goods and services to more and more people. Growth must be obvious now, with potential for future growth. If you look at areas with only potential growth, it may never happen. Make sure enough demographics exist now to run your business profitably today.

Assure Operational Convenience

In retail, your goods and services should be convenient to your customers. At times, convenience is more important to your customers than the quality and price of your merchandise. Convenience covers an infinity of shortcomings in retail; it can transform a poor location into a viable one. For instance, suppose your restaurant has a kitchen layout that has a production line that runs left to right. So, you put an entrance to the left to avoid any disruption to your operation. Now your location has no front entrance; instead you offer two back entrances, which are inconvenient to your customers.

Customers don't care about your operations problem — whether it be in the production lines, storage, or delivery systems. They demand that the visit to your retail business be convenient and trouble-free. Also, internal operations, organizational, managerial, and financial problems are not your customers' concerns. You must look for ways to make coming to your business convenient for your customers instead of yourself.

You will find many customers are lazy — they will not move an extra foot, they will not make an extra turn, they will not wait an extra minute in line, and they will not compromise. To make your retail business operationally convenient, you may have to lease more parking spaces, buy another cash register, hire another service representative, buy an improved copy machine, or change a policy. The understanding of convenience, particularly in this era, is the greatest opportunity for all businesses, not just retailers. Take Nordstrom department store, for example. If you need a pair of shirts before getting on a plane for a long trip, it will ship the shirts overnight to your destination. And, if you purchase an automobile in Japan, a few weeks following your purchase, your car salesperson will pay you a follow-up visit to your home to see how your car is doing.

Make It Safe and Secure

Safety and security are essential attributes of a good location, specifically important for shopping centers, downtown storefronts, and free standing buildings. To tackle safety and security issues for your retail business, make sure your store is well illuminated. Although electricity is expensive, more light will encourage more people to come to your business more often. Consequently, more light will minimize accidents and crime and will maximize sales. You need to think of lighting as an investment, not an expense.

Take a look at the areas around your proposed store that are more isolated to make sure you have the highest candle power there. For maximum candle power, use white lights (metal haloid), specifically 1,000-watt bulbs on 30-foot poles. The minimum standard is two foot-candles; with proper placement of lights you should achieve better than eight foot-candles. Although some people prefer yellow lights (high-pressure sodium) because they are less costly, they will discolor and bleach out your building and signs. They will provide sufficient light, but will give a perception of darkness and closeness.

Make Parking a Priority

Your retail business' parking needs must to be foremost in your mind when considering a location, since a significant number of your customers will arrive by car. People expect to be welcomed by your business; hence, the least you can do is to offer them an easy, comfortable way to park. Thus, welcome your customers in your parking lot as you would inside your store. Although nobody ever claimed to prefer a certain store over all others simply because the parking experience was good, a bad parking experience will cloud your customers' views of your store as a good shopping experience — and it will color their decisions on where to shop next time.

Know Your Customers' Parking Habits

Your customers will follow certain norms of behavior when it comes to parking. They will:

- Park near an entrance at a distance of no more than 100 feet.
- Be reluctant to walk, regardless of the climatic conditions.
- Seek a well-lit area at night.
- Refuse to park in remote or dark areas or on the side of a building.
- Refuse to park in the back, because it is too far away from the front entrance and they are simply fearful.

Some retailers have parking layouts that are dangerous, too tight, or insufficient for their business needs. Don't make the same mistakes that many retailers do by relying on off-premises spots, such as on the street or on adjacent lots of shopping centers, office buildings, and churches.

Customers tend to avoid parking on the street or on off-lot spaces. Furthermore, it is risky because you cannot count on the use of somebody else's property for any extended period. Also, people simply do not want to walk that far. In addition, if you choose a building right at the front property line, as shown in Figure 6.10, you will force your customers to park on the side and in the back. As a rule, customers like to park near the front door and will do so if they can.

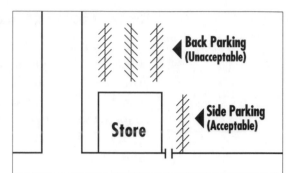

Figure 6.10 Side Parking versus Back Parking

To more fully understand your customers' parking needs, consider your parking lot's *setback*, or the acceptable distance (in feet) a customer will walk from a parking spot to the entrance of a store.

As seen in Figure 6.11, customers will gladly walk 50 feet to get to your store, they will have no problem with 100 feet, and they will tolerate 150 feet. If you ask your customers to walk more than 150 feet, you risk losing them, or at the very least, earning their displeasure. Rest assured, your customers will blame their sore feet and fears of mugging on you.

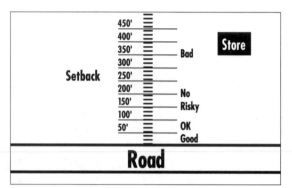

Figure 6.11 Significance of Parking Lot Setback

Create a Safe and Convenient Lot

The quality and quantity of parking is as important as the quality and quantity of your products. Make sure that the pavement is smooth, with clearly marked lines and directional arrows. Use illuminated entrance-exit signs. Keep the height of the outlying curbs to six inches. If adjacent to other parking areas, design your driveway to coincide with adjoining driveways. If your store is on a shopping center pad, make sure you surround your parcel with a raised cement curb that allows good accessibility to the other stores.

You need to have well-disciplined traffic in your lot. The traffic should flow in both directions. If that is not possible, then you need clearly marked pylon signs. There will always be someone coming from the other side of the lot.

Try to find a location that allows both left turns and right turns from your parking lot. Just as important as accessibility is the opposite side of the coin — the ease and safety of leaving your store. If leaving your store is hazardous or inconvenient, an otherwise happy customer might not want to come back.

You will find a "no left turn" sign restrictive to your business, especially if the left turns are barred for a good reason, such as flow of traffic. In Figure 6.12 a good reason for the ban is the median strip on the main road. Remember, median strips are enemies of good retail business.

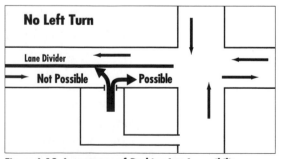

Figure 6.12 Importance of Parking Lot Accessibility

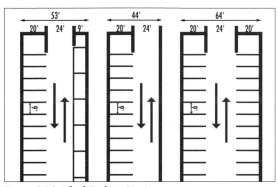

Figure 6.13 Ideal Parking Lot Layouts

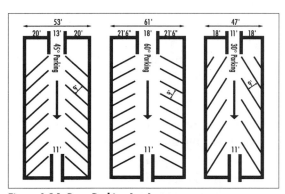

Figure 6.14 Poor Parking Lot Layouts

The best parking layout offers 90-degree parking with driveways of 24 or 25 feet in width. Figure 6.13 shows three layouts for 90-degree parking, each with a 24-foot driveway. In this illustration, notice the geometric designs of the parking spaces and rows. This best parking layout avoids slanted parking. Customers hate slanted parking. With slanted parking, accidents can occur easily and often. Yet, retailers continue to offer this kind of parking. Don't be fooled by thinking slanted parking will require less space and possibly a narrower driveway because a slanted car intrudes less into the driving lane than a car of the same size parked at a 90-degree angle.

Figure 6.14 shows you three common slanted parking lot designs. Compare the 53-foot width of the layout at far left in Figure 6.14 with the layout of equal width (53 feet) in Figure 6.13. The figure with slanted spaces shows twelve usable parking spaces, plus two unusable ones. The figure with 90-degree spaces shows 15 usable spaces. Also, notice the narrow driveways of the slanted lots, which provide more opportunities for scraped fenders and give drivers cramped feelings when they enter or exit. In addition to these many considerations, your parking lot must have enough spaces for the sales volume of your store.

Plan for Enough Spaces

To estimate the correct number of parking spaces for your business, start from the premise that more parking will produce more business. Then, tailor the number of spaces to easily accommodate the peak hours of the week. To help you, contact the local city hall of the city in which you wish to locate your retail business. A city hall usually has requirements for the number of parking spaces you must have versus the gross floor area of your building per 1,000 square feet. For instance, a business with a 9,000 gross floor area will need at least nine parking spaces per 1,000 square feet. This official requirement may be insufficient for you.

You may have to study the parking turnover per hour per space and compute the number of spaces your business needs. If you are a start-up business, look at existing or similar (analogue) competitive businesses to figure out the highest hourly sales, average check, number of persons per car, and minutes needed per car. Use the Hourly Sales Analysis Worksheet in Appendix C and other important analogue study methods discussed in Chapter 5 to help you. Pay attention to present neighboring businesses and future possibilities. You must assess, for instance, the nature of their activity to determine whether they require intense parking, which could eventually smother your own business.

Keep in mind, you want your business to grow and you intend to enjoy the business during the highest peaks of the year, either because of a change in season, a special event, or other trend. So don't be too conservative with your estimates — in the long run, you are better served, as are your customers, to have one more space rather than one less. Also, create a feeling of confidence in your customers that, when they come to patronize your business, they will find a parking space. You know how irritating it is to have to drive away. Other important parking precepts to consider include:

- One acre in a square or rectangular shape will give you more parking spaces than one acre in the shape of a circle, rhomboid, or triangle.
- If a large number of your customers shop with their children, easy and convenient parking is essential.
- In cold climates, ramps and descents are very dangerous to negotiate because of snow and ice, so you will need an area on which to pile snow in the winter.
- Parking for your employees must be away from the building at all times.

Design User-Friendly Entrance-Exits

Before you make your location decision, you need to match the entrance-exit accessibility with the hours in which you will get most of your business. Remember, if your customers feel that it is risky to get into your location, you can be sure that they will not come back. Try to avoid a location that is served by only one entrance-exit or, worse yet, a single lane that is used both for entrance and exit. Your analysis of traffic entrance-exit accessibility may change your mind regarding a particular site. For example, you may observe that the 12:15 P.M. heavy traffic does not allow accessibility to and from the main road; at 12:18 P.M. the traffic clears; at 12:20 P.M. the traffic resumes; and at 12:23 P.M. the traffic clears. You may learn that 60 percent of the time your business is not accessible. Refer to the Traffic Count Example from Chapter 2 to help you.

When planning for your entrance-exits, consider the posted speed limits in the area in which you wish to locate. Because you want to make accessibility, visibility, and easy entrance-exit a top priority, know the effects of speed on a driver's vision. As speed increases, a driver's concentration increases. The vision cone is longer and narrower with faster speeds. On the contrary, when driving slower, the cone becomes shorter and wider, as illustrated in Figure 6.15. In fact, researchers J. R. Hamilton and Louis L. Thurstone found that the focusing point of the eyes lies approximately 600 feet ahead at the speed of 25 miles per hour. The focusing point becomes 1,200 feet with a speed of 45 miles per hour. Because speed does not allow a driver to distinguish objects clearly, at 40 miles per hour the closest point of sharp vision is about 80 feet ahead of the car. At 60 miles an hour

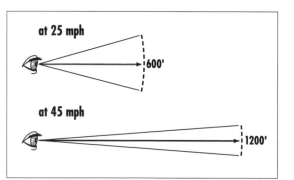

Figure 6.15 Effects of Speed on the Vision Cone

a driver sees only the details within 110 to 1,400 feet ahead of the car and within a cone of 40 degrees. As driving speed increases, a driver's perception of space and speed deteriorates and his or her judgment becomes more dependent on visual benchmarks.

Another study found that a driver moving at 30 miles per hour has a reaction time of ten seconds. This means a driver will travel about 500 feet before he or she can respond to a street sign, situation, or event and come to a stop. The gas station business uses a rule of thumb to determine the reaction time for visibility: seeing the sign, two seconds; checking the gas gage, two seconds; breaking, two seconds; turning into the station, two seconds; total, eight seconds. The lesson: easy traffic access and clearly marked entrance-exits mean better business.

Consider Your Business' Impact on Traffic

When you consider a new location, you must assess the impact your business will have on the traffic in the area. Specifically, you need to determine whether your business will create traffic hazards on the roads that allow access to your store. In becoming aware of the traffic safety issues you may face, familiarize yourself with the two important terms: diverted traffic and generated traffic.

- *Diverted traffic* is the traffic that already exists for its own sake and reason; you can expect some of this traffic to enter your parking lot and sponsor your business.

- *Generated traffic* is the traffic created by the magnetic force of your business alone. The traffic that passes by your store from home, shopping, and workplaces is augmented by generated traffic.

The amount of generated traffic your business creates may be a concern to local zoning authorities who try to keep traffic at a safe level. For instance, if your business generates a percentage of new traffic, zoning officials will evaluate the degree of danger that results. When requested by the various zoning and administrative bodies, you may need to provide information like:

- Number of hourly sales at your business;
- Dollar sales per hour of your business;
- Number and kind of traffic generators;
- Traffic counts;
- Inbound and outbound traffic from your site;
- The role of secondary arteries; and
- Your judgment of safety.

City and county regulatory agencies often require detailed studies concerning environmental impact produced by traffic. Several companies specialize in traffic analysis. One company that can help is Barton-Aschman Associates. Refer to Appendix B for more information.

Try to Capture Impulse Shoppers

If you are in retail, you will benefit from *impulse shoppers*. You have the ability to influence people by creating in them a sudden inclination or impulse to leave traffic and head into your store. A number of factors can generate this compelling force in a potential customer, including:

- An awareness of a special need that surfaces when a person sees that your store can satisfy that need;
- A feeling of time pressure that tells a person to take advantage of an opportunity that becomes unexpectedly available;
- A strong curiosity caused by the external look of a business in terms of design originality, desirability, attractiveness, and ease of access;
- A sense of safety coupled with attractiveness, like an island of light that illuminates your facility at night and catches a person's eye;
- The nature of the road, such as long-distance transient roads with very diverse traffic; and
- The time of day, such as morning traffic that impacts sales at a doughnut shop on the way to work.

Your location and facility must create an emotional response powerful enough to cause an impulsive reaction. For instance, you need a sign that can be noticed, not just read. In fact, your sign doesn't need to be legible, but it must be recognizable. To bring home this point, consider the familiar Golden Arches — recognizable from both near and far. Additionally, you will need to position yourself (the right location) to ensure that your store is distinct and separate from the other retail businesses in the area. Just blending in with other retailers, or with the landscaping or other buildings is not enough to create impulse. People must notice your business just like you would notice a famous movie star. The personality and noticeability of your business must cause a passerby to take a second look.

Your retail business presence must be bold and proud with no hints of timidity or second thought. If your business is buried away — surrounded by buildings, bushes, and trees — you will not enjoy much impulse business. In addition, you may have to increase your marketing and advertising substantially because people cannot see you. Your facility advertises your business. Particularly when you are new in a market, your location assures a double function:

- To exercise your business; and
- To act as a billboard in the marketplace.

Any device that makes your place recognizable from a distance adds to your visibility. McDonald's founder, Ray Kroc, learned the importance of visibility when he displayed an American flag in front of each McDonald's store. The visibility of McDonald's benefited greatly from this move. For instance, in Manhattan, New York, the McDonald's storefronts were lined up with hundreds of other stores along Broadway, First Street, Third Street, and so on. A big, beautiful flag was hung over the front of each McDonald's store, prominently projecting over the busy sidewalk. The noticeability of their stores increased 100 percent.

Visibility becomes a key issue when your store is located in a busy downtown area. Consider the story of the McDonald's franchisee who opened a storefront location in downtown Cincinnati, Ohio — one street behind the main square. The store was located on the ground floor of a four-story building. The visibility of the store was so poor that the store's operator decided to attach a horizontal pole to the fourth floor with a giant American flag extending over much of the street. You can guess that the entire city knew where the downtown store was located. In addition, make sure your location is situated to allow enough time for impulse shoppers to access your store.

When considering a location, look at the lanes of traffic to determine the time your customers may need to access your store. For instance, the right lane is the least apt to create impulse — visibility to the right will be hampered by trees, bushes, landscape berms, and buildings near the front property line. People will not see your facility or your sign until they are too close to it. At that point it is too late and surely too dangerous to make a turn. Your visibility is much better from the inside lane. Looking to the right, a customer can see several yards ahead. Also, your visibility to the left is excellent from both the inside and outside lane; however, that advantage is diminished by the fact that the effort to turn left is difficult and drastic. Keep in mind, the reaction time a driver needs to see an object and respond to it is:

- Eight seconds on a two-lane road;
- Ten seconds on a four-lane road; and
- Twelve seconds or more on freeways.

You can increase your chance of capturing impulse shoppers by locating in a high-traffic area. Common sense tells you the importance of the number of visual impressions and the potential business caused by impulse. If 100,000 people see your business in ten minutes, it is better than if 500 people see it in the same amount of time.

Cater to the Carryout Crowd

Today's fast-food restaurants have three types of business, including:

- Dine-in customers
- Carryout customers
- Drive-thru customers

Because each customer type is based on a different buying mood, each needs special handling. If you are a restaurant owner, you realize that the three types of customers are different from each other.

- A dine-in customer looks for a pleasant experience.
- A carryout customer looks for efficiency and for an easy, spill-proof way to hand carry the food.
- A drive-thru customer demands efficiency, speed, accuracy, and reliable packaging.

For some businesses, carryout customers represents the biggest percentage of sales and this percentage is increasing in absolute terms. During the next ten years, meals prepared to be eaten at home will offer the greatest potential for growth. If you want to cater to the carryout crowd, you may want to consider a drive-thru.

The drive-thru concept has become an ordinary mode of dispensing products and services in today's fast-paced society. A drive-thru meets the demands of customers on the go — it is pure convenience. Customers do not like to walk an extra foot nor make an extra move. They willingly trade quality for convenience. They know that the food later will be cold and taste stale, but they still want it that way.

Believe it or not, McDonald's opposed the drive-thru concept for almost 20 years. McDonald's founders preferred that customers eat their hamburgers and french fries while the food was still hot. They felt that food carried out of the restaurant would be cold, shriveled, and would not taste right. In the early 1970s, a regional vice-president had the courage to open a drive-thru in Texas to make it possible for troops at a nearby military base to come to McDonald's and have a quick lunch. These military personnel would not need to change their uniforms if they stayed in their cars. The McDonald's in that location was a tremendous success; it marked the beginning of the drive-thru explosion. Even though the drive-thru concept had its beginnings in the fast-food industry, today you can find drive-thrus in banks, grocery stores, liquor stores, dry cleaners, video stores, photo processing shops, and coffee shops.

Some retailers prefer that customers come inside their stores and admire properly displayed merchandise. However, a great percentage of people prefer not to get out of their cars. Figure 6.16 shows an excellent example of a well-planned drive-thru. If you intend to have a drive-thru, consider some suggestions about the layout. First, the stacking lane should accommodate seven to ten cars. It is a function of the depth of the parcel. Second, the minimum drive-thru curve should be a 15-foot radius. Third, the ordering board and speakers should be two or three car lengths behind the customer in the car who is picking up his or

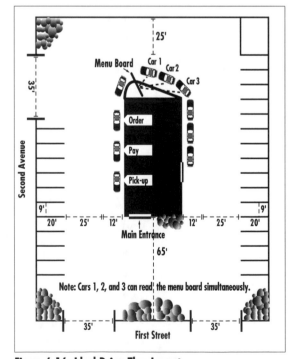

Figure 6.16 Ideal Drive-Thru Layout

her merchandise. Fourth, the tilt of the ordering board is dictated by visibility from the two cars next in line. They must be able to read the board while waiting. Fifth, the size of the menu lettering should be no less than 1 1/2 inches.

To manage the service of a drive-thru you must pay close attention to details. For instance, keep track of your service time per order. The average service time will tell you about the quality of your management at your drive-thru, particularly at peak sales times.

Advice for Home-Delivery Locations

Another option for running a retail business in today's fast-paced world is home delivery. Some home-delivery retailers profit from this type of business, including some pizza restaurants, carpet cleaning services, catering services, rental services, packing and shipping services, and florists. If you are considering a home-delivery business, consider the pros and cons of operating costs. Compare a regular store with a home-delivery store.

Generally, you can expect a home-delivery store to have:

- Lower sales
- Higher payroll
- Higher vehicle costs for delivery
- Lower repair and maintenance
- Lower utilities
- Similar water and sewer costs
- Lower security costs
- Higher telephone and fax costs
- Lower rents
- Similar rental equipment
- Lower depreciation
- Similar license fees

Thus, the business economics — that is, the ratio of expenses versus sales — of a home-delivery retailer requires that the base facility have:

- Lower occupancy and operational costs;
- Storage space for merchandise; and
- Sufficient workspace for assembly and preparation of products for delivery.

Also, the average sale per order of a home-delivery retailer must be higher than that of the nondelivery retailer to justify the cost of delivery. To accomplish this, you may have to add a delivery charge to each order. However, when you add these charges, make sure you don't upset the balance of competitive value. If you do decide that a home-delivery business is right for you, make sure your location will be right for a home-delivery business.

A home-delivery location should have excellent visibility, with a prominent building or facade and clearly distinguishable signs. Often, signs may be the primary appeal to customers. You can increase the efficiency of your signs by displaying your delivery vehicles conspicuously in parking areas when they are not in use. Even in delivery-only facilities, a percentage of business is done inside the facility to order services or pick up products. Thus, make sure parking is readily available and sufficient to take care of walk-in customers as well as delivery vehicles. Further, don't locate in an isolated area, such as an industrial park or run-down area on the edge of town. Rather, locate near or adjacent to locations with strong traffic generators. Of course, a retail trading zone (RTZ) with the right demographics and psychographics is required for the same reasons that a nondelivery retailer needs one.

An RTZ with a high population density is essential for home-delivery retailers. The size of the RTZ depends upon the areas that can be driven by the deliverers. For instance, if the roads are wide, the area is flat, and no barriers exist, such as rivers or hills, then the RTZ will be larger. Although, due to the importance of delivery time, a home-delivery business' RTZ will be smaller than a nondelivery business' RTZ. This happens because the RTZ shrinks during peak traffic time due to slower traffic delivery time. In addition, as a home-delivery business, your RTZ may not include the 15 to 20 percent of transient business enjoyed by nondelivery retailers.

A recent debate has ensued in the fast-food industry over the desirability of adding home delivery as a service. Some businesses have succeeded in this home-delivery concept — take Pizza Hut, for example. Although, you should note that home delivery will not increase the size of your RTZ or increase the frequency of orders. Before you decide home delivery is the final remedy to flat sales, consider some important variables. You will have added costs because you must:

- Add to the land and building you already occupy.
- Acquire computer facilities for order taking.
- Pay your delivery drivers adequately for the use of their cars and the cost of insurance.

Together with the serious possibility of traffic accidents and related lawsuits, a home-delivery venture seems uncertain. You may achieve greater penetration in the market you serve, but profits are not guaranteed. Typically, the retail industries that have customized their existing facilities for home delivery have most often experienced losses.

Chapter Wrap-Up

No matter which way you look at it, your retail business is highly dependent upon the traffic — or potential customers — that passes by your store. To capture the most customers, you must consider yourself a high-traffic retailer.

The location requirements for high-traffic retailers are much the same as for other retailers, but amplified. Retailers like Color Tile, Pearle Vision, Walgreen's, Ace Hardware, Blockbuster Video, Wendy's, and Pollo Tropical are considered high-traffic retailers. Especially when operating in a free standing facility, they must go for the best location in the best available set of circumstances regarding traffic, access, and parking.

As a high-traffic retailer, you must make sure the location you ultimately choose has many, if not all, of the essential location factors discussed in this chapter. To recap, you must:

- Make the visibility and accessibility of your store a top priority.
- Select a site with heavy regional exposure.
- Situate your business in an area of high density.
- Target an area that has current and potential growth.
- Make your store operationally convenient to your customers.
- Design your facility with customers' safety and security first in mind.
- Create convenient, user-friendly parking situations for your customers.
- Know the importance of impulse shoppers and plan your facility with these key customers in mind.
- Plan a top-notch drive-thru, if applicable to your business.
- Deliver high-quality service and products if you will operate a home-delivery business.

In short, design your retail business to accommodate your customers. If you integrate the essential location factors into your retail business' site, you will gain the confidence of your customers — and probably the confidence of your competitors' customers. Before you make your decision, however, take a look at the various urban and rural retail location options discussed in the next two chapters.

Notes

Chapter 7

Evaluate Urban Location Options

By this point, you will have formed a good idea of what to look for in the right location for your retail business. In fact, as you have read through the first six chapters, you have probably been formulating an opinion of whether a metropolitan or suburban area is better suited for your business. This chapter will highlight the many city retail environments available to retailers and will provide you with the advantages and disadvantages of choosing:

- The downtown of a big city;
- One of the many types of shopping centers, including free standing, in-line, and end cap; or
- A mall, outlet mall, or supermall as part of a cluster of businesses.

After you have considered the pros and cons of metropolitan location options, you can move on to Chapter 8 to explore your rural site options. For now, take a close look at the many opportunities of locating in a downtown.

Familiarize Yourself with the Downtown

When you consider whether or not to locate in a downtown area, get to know both the origin and current status of the downtown of the city in which you want to locate. A city's downtown area — also called the *central business district* (CBD) will typically mark the origin of the city. In many cases, downtowns are near major bodies of water; they were natural transportation harbors for people and goods. Also, the downtown supplied most of the goods required by the community, and most of the commercial activity was transacted downtown. As a city grew, its downtown expanded by constructing more buildings. For many decades a city's downtown represented the heart and pride of the community.

Today, some CBDs are alive and prosperous, like the Loop in Chicago, Illinois. Even though in the Chicago standard metropolitan area (SMA) other major trade areas exist, such as the Woodfield and Oak Brook areas, the downtown continues to pull people because of general interest, including:

- Culture
- Government
- History
- Retail
- Professional activity
- Hotels
- Conventions
- Entertainment
- Tourism

If you are interested in a site downtown, you will need to study and rank these activities. Then, simply add up all the government buildings, department stores, office buildings, and theatres to determine which activities are the heaviest pullers. Usually, you can find several big department stores and many miscellaneous retailers that are located in high-rise buildings. There are also industrial buildings for all kinds of manufacturing. An active downtown acts as a magnet that attracts and unifies an entire city. Other CBDs are partly active, like in Dallas, Texas. The activity happens mostly during the day. At night, many sidewalks are rolled up and empty. Safety becomes an important factor that reduces the activity during the nonbusiness hours.

You can gain key insights when you look at a downtown's current trends. For example, history tells of the erosion of the downtown's pulling power after World War II, based on the new attraction of suburban areas. These suburban areas became homes to commercial-professional-industrial centers. Also, people craved the more open and airy suburban areas; the convenience of car transportation made this shift possible. In fact, this trend of breaking away from a city's downtown has caused entire SMAs to divide into areas that are self-sustaining. As a result, an SMA in most cases is fragmented into subcenters that generate their own interest gravitation. For instance, the SMA of Chicago, Illinois, includes Oak Brook, Shaumburg, Skokie, and Elmhurst. The SMA of Los Angeles, California, includes Hollywood, Santa Monica, Santa Ana, and many other subcenters. However, there is a strong movement currently to return to downtown — bringing back commercial, professional, and cultural activities. Today you will see more residential apartments and townhouses being built there. However, if you are considering a location in a CBD, do not proceed if you detect negative trends like vacancies in various blocks, office buildings, department stores, and retail shops.

Know the Downtown's Access and Pull

Before you select the area of the CBD in which you intend to locate your retail outlet, you need to assess the pulling power of the downtown. The retail pull of the downtown is due to the complementary nature and diversity of the businesses located there. For example, commodity businesses intermingle with specialty businesses. Often you find more specialty stores downtown. All these generators form a cumulative attraction; as a result, the CBD continues to be the heart of an entire city.

In the CBD, the pull of a traffic generator causes movement. The wind, or interest gravitation, flows between certain stops and destinations, including:

- Transportation-parking hubs and retailing hubs;
- Major retailers and minor complementary-diversified retailers;
- Retail hubs and workcenters;
- Government buildings, courthouses, banks, and insurance offices;
- Transportation-parking hubs and workcenters, tourist attractions, and entertainment centers; and
- High-density residential areas and workplaces.

If your retail business is placed outside the flow of those currents, it will have shorter hours of operation, high and low sales peaks, and deep lulls of activity.

The degree of the pulling power of the downtown will affect the adjacent and related RTZs in other parts of the city. Some purchasing power will be transferred to and from downtown. Some people refer to this as *leakage* — meaning not all dollars are spent in one place.

The downtown has one large RTZ of the entire city and many RTZs within the CBD. To illustrate this point, look at Figure 7.1 and Figure 7.2. In the first figure, notice that the entire city has its own RTZ that is separate from the many RTZs that exist within the city's CBD, as shown in the second figure. The first (city) RTZ is produced by the movement of people to and from it. This movement is

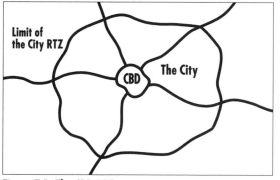

Figure 7.1 The CBD RTZ

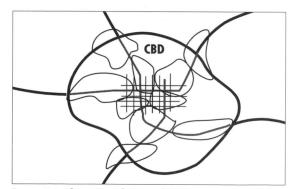

Figure 7.2 The CBD with Several RTZs

caused by people who come downtown from outlying suburban areas via cars, buses, trains, and tramways. They come from a huge area of a 10-, 20-, or 30-mile radius. In fact, millions of Americans have daily access to CBDs by bus or train. So, to find out more about your potential customers, go to the city transportation offices or other jurisdictions and get public transportation schedules. These offices can also give you the number of routes, runs, and passengers. You want a chunk of this business. Thus, you will want to examine:

- The most important entrance-exits;
- The peak hours;
- Directions in which people will scatter;
- The streets used most often — the ones with the strongest wind;
- Obstacles to people's movements;
- The block that benefits from the wind the most; and
- The difference between people movement on weekends and holidays.

The analysis of the mode of transportation is very important in the downtown areas and in most cities outside the United States, particularly in Europe, Asia, and South America. An RTZ Survey of a retail business in Dublin, Ireland, found that 40 percent of the customers came by public transportation, 30 percent by bicycle, 10 percent by motorcycle, and 20 percent by foot — but none by car. This type of traffic made the RTZ huge, but extremely irregular in shape. The traffic came from the north, south, and west of the store. The store faced east, on an important road, and the RTZ ended exactly in the middle of that road. The dividing island was the boundary.

In the United States, people usually do not live in downtown areas. Some exceptions to this rule exist. For instance, people live in Manhattan, New York, and Chicago, Illinois, but even in those urban areas there are different and distinct kinds of RTZs. Some people will live in suburban areas and work downtown as illustrated in Figure 7.3. Using Dallas, Texas, as an example, this figure shows that nearly half of the downtown employees live outside the LBJ Beltway.

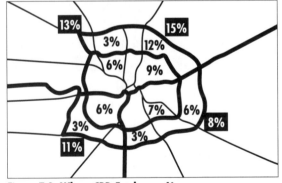

Figure 7.3 Where CBD Employees Live

As you can see from Figure 7.2, the CBD itself contains a series of RTZs that are geographically small, independent of each other, and overlapping each other. These RTZs are based on a *time-convenience line* — their limits are the equidistant time points from your stores. Also, these RTZs are almost totally comprised of foot traffic. People will not walk more than five blocks and no more than five or six minutes for retail purposes. Hence, an RTZ within a CBD is formed by a few high-rise buildings that immediately surround the retailer from all sides, as shown in Figure 7.4. The people of the city become more mobile by the presence of escalators, elevators, and crosswalks — whether they be underground passages like in Toronto, Canada, or overhead walkways like in Minneapolis, Minnesota. If you are interested in a downtown location, you will want a clear picture of the people who live and visit it.

When you look downtown, you must realize the presence of two different populations:

- Residents
- Transients

Downtown residents have a special consumer profile and lifestyle. In general, they are upper-class, well-educated professionals, and are often single and mobile. They are rather young and they live active social and cultural lives. A downtown RTZ may also consist of transients — people who come to visit the town because of interests, work, and tourism, like artistic and cultural attractions. They come for transportation, food, gifts, entertainment, and recreation. The easier the access from outlying areas, the more prosperous the downtown.

Weigh the Pros and Cons of Operating Downtown

Obviously, you must weigh the upsides and downsides of running a retail store in a CBD. For instance, a downtown has fewer activity hours and days than suburban areas. As a downtown retailer, you can expect customers to patronize your store 52 weekends and 12 or more national holidays each year, plus additional holidays for special groups and local occasions. Thus, you can count on a business calendar year of about 250 days. If you locate in a state in which there are *blue laws* — laws that regulate work, commerce, and amusements on Sundays — downtown activity is further curtailed. In addition, you must consider that each day, activity may start as late as 10:00 A.M. and end at 6:00 P.M. — when people rush to catch a train or bus or head to a parking area. If the downtown has residents, the business fluctuations through the day and year may be less dramatic, but the pattern remains the same. Further, business downtown can be affected by transportation problems that result from employee strikes and poor weather.

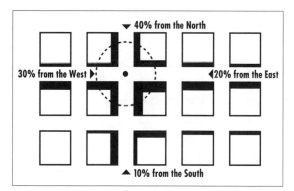

Figure 7.4 Percentage of People from City's Perimeter

No matter what downtown retail business you are in, you will experience peak sales hours based on the needs of the people who work downtown. You can count on your business having many customers at the same time during peak hours; these customers will be pressed for time. The profits you generate at peak hours are very important to you. Customers have a high degree of sensitivity during high-peak hours, and you can lose many of them very easily. Hence, your operation must be exceptional during these business peaks. It requires outstanding sales skills, efficiency, and personality. Your equipment must function to perfection and you must have a preselected, preorganized, and perfectly displayed inventory. Your employees must be well trained and strategically placed throughout your store in the areas of the busiest activity. Additionally, you must place the right number of cash registers to ensure a fast and efficient checkout. You are best served to use multiple checkout stands because one meandering line is slow.

If you locate downtown, you will cater to customers on the go. To get a better idea of your customers, consider their routines as they run against the clock. In the morning, people rush to work, coming from all areas of the city. By the time they reach downtown, many of them are late. People will rush in front of your store, unless they have forgotten some essential items. Around noon, they normally have 30 minutes to one hour as a lunchbreak. By the time they leave their workplaces and reach the sidewalks, 15 or 20 minutes will have expired. Now they have a very short time left to shop. Besides, they must catch a bite to eat somewhere. In the evening, people have to leave on time to beat rush hour traffic, or to take the 5:45 P.M. bus or the 5:59 P.M. train. These people don't have time for impulse shopping. Consequently, fast, courteous, and efficient service is essential for any retail business downtown. The type of operation is very different downtown compared to suburban stores.

If you look at locations that do not have high-peak hours, you may be able to run them well from an operational standpoint, but such locations are not likely to work. Most likely you will not see enough foot traffic that is needed to support your store. Also, watch out for areas that do not have strong peak hours. They are areas located outside the wind — the flow that connects strong traffic generators.

In a downtown location, your retail business' profitability is directly correlated to sales, occupancy costs, and labor costs. Thus, as a downtown retailer, you must use the premises for the maximum available hours and days. You can take a rule-of-thumb census of the office building population that is in your RTZ. To accomplish this, contact your local chapter of the Building Owners and Managers Association (BOMA). BOMA is a national organization that gives occupancy guidelines for office buildings. BOMA recognizes a ratio of one person for every 200 square feet of workspace. This applies mostly to newer buildings. In older buildings, the ratio is much lower; for instance, it might be one person for every 100 square feet of workspace. You can follow a seven-step method to calculate occupancy.

- Pace the outside frontage and depth of the building. A pace is approximately five feet.
- Count the number of floors.
- Calculate the gross square footage.
- Subtract the floors that don't contain working people, such as basements and utility floors.
- Subtract the space dedicated to lobbies, elevator space, and corridors — usually 10–15 percent.
- Divide the total square footage by the number of people per 100 square feet.

- Verify the results by interviewing the local real estate firms with information about vacancies in the area and talking to building management.

Although your estimate need not be completely accurate, a reasonable estimate is all you need. Generally, the relationship of the net rentable square feet to the gross square feet is about 75 percent. This information is a good substitute for the actual count of the employees entering and exiting a building. If you have decided that a downtown location is right for your business, next you will need to consider what floor of a building will suit your needs.

Consider the Ground Floor

Ground floor locations are suitable for tenants that can afford high rent, architectural and permit fees, construction costs, and other charges connected with opening a store downtown. If you are considering a ground floor location, you should have high:

- Average sales volumes;
- Customer density;
- Availability of square footage; and
- Availability of additional space above, below, or in back of your store.

Because your potential sales are directly proportional to the number of daily visual impressions, your ground floor location must have the highest degree of visibility and recognizability. With this in mind, you will want to place your store on the busiest corner, or, if the store is in-line, then you will want a place as close as possible to the busiest corner from where people — especially pedestrians — can see and recognize your store. For a more detailed discussion of in-line locations, refer to the discussion later in this chapter. Some tenants, such as tie shops and trinket boutiques can maintain their operations with a reduced frontage opening into an expanded interior, or even a narrow front matched by an interior of limited square footage.

You can evaluate the degree of exposure a ground floor location can have on the foot and vehicle traffic of the area. To accomplish this, do an informal survey by standing on the store's nearest corner to take pedestrian and traffic counts. If the exposure is insufficient, rethink the location.

Compare Underground and Second Floor Locations

The extremely high-priced real estate downtown makes it logical, at times, to consider an underground location. For example, restaurants located on New York City's Wall Street face a real challenge in serving people at lunch. This challenge is a result of the thousands of people who flood the sidewalks at noon as they descend from the surrounding skyscrapers. In addition, if you are in the restaurant business you need to offer instant service; hence, your retail business needs a big kitchen, many cash registers, and adequate seating. An underground location offers you sufficient space with an affordable rent. Because your downtown location relies on customers on lunch breaks, 75 percent of your daily sales are seen in three hours — typically 11:00 A.M. to 2:00 P.M. Keep in mind, though, you must work to make an underground location attractive and appealing to your customers. Nobody likes to go into a cellar. Thus, your store's architectural design of the entrance becomes extremely important. The entrance must be open, wide, and very well lit; it must also have appealing decorative touches.

Take the McDonald's located underground in Hong Kong as an example. The entrance features mirrors, light wood, plants, and flowers. When a customer enters the restaurant, it is like entering an outdoor garden with patio furniture. The architecture removes the feeling of enclosure and oppression. In Toronto and Montreal, Canada, and in Tokyo, Japan, a whole world of retailing, services, and transportation exists underground. It is like a second downtown with the same type of people pull and movement.

Because of the more affordable rents, a second floor location may be a better option for your business. However, only a strong, specialized retailer can survive alone on a second floor. The presence of mobile escalators will help your accessibility, but not enough to appeal to many. The best case for second floor retailing can be found in downtown Minneapolis, Minnesota, where several miles of enclosed corridors go from one building to another — crossing places of work and retail areas with bridges. The cumulative attraction is strong, even though the total activity hours are fewer than at the street level.

Beware of Downtown Pedestrian Malls

Several cities have downtown pedestrian malls — separate foot traffic malls designed with sidewalks, landscaping, benches, and kiosks. However, be cautious about locating in a pedestrian mall. Although well-known businesses will continue to prosper in these locations, a new business may not be well received. Americans are car people; they don't like to walk and they don't like public transportation. Also, parking is usually too far away.

Don't Try to Be the Exception

In certain downtown areas, there are situations where the essential location factors like accessibility and visibility become irrelevant. In other words, the retail businesses in these areas are thriving, yet the location doesn't have any of the essential location factors. For example, in Miami, Florida, there is a Pollo Tropical restaurant located in the back of a building, on a very small lot, with poor accessibility and visibility. When you see it, you know that it should not be there, but that restaurant has the highest volume in the chain. The reason for the business' success is a compressed demand for goods and services. In these types of areas of compression, there is no distinction between office buildings, residential quarters, and workplaces. Thus, the types of traffic are totally commingled.

- Public transportation joins local traffic.

- Transient traffic from all parts of the city gathers at the center and from there fans out into suburban areas.
- All kinds of pedestrians roam the sidewalks.
- The area bustles with life, work, and commerce.

A retail business in an area of compressed demand is normally successful. Customers are more prone to suffer long waiting lines, large crowds, noise, and discomfort. They simply appreciate the convenience. Demographics and lifestyle data in this case are not relevant. The sheer sum of people and activities creates sales volumes. Although these businesses are the exceptions to the rule, never think that your business will be the exception. Always plan for the best possible location — even in a highly compressed area. There is always a possibility that a competitor will spend more money and build a bigger and better facility than yours. No matter which type of downtown location you choose, make sure your store tempts potential customers by its overall appeal.

Make Your Store Appealing

The outside of your store should look very attractive. Downtown retailers are lined up in a row, one next to another. Their individual image tends to wane and merge with all the others. Your business must stand out despite the architectural and signage controls. Your store will need large windows, adequate lighting, clean signs, and contrasting construction material on its facade to broadcast your presence there. Also, the inside decor must maximize the sense of space and light. Bring the outdoor look indoors. Bright lights should be clearly visible from the outside through windows with clear glass. Tinted glass may protect from the sun, but it will prevent people from seeing and appreciating your merchandise. Further, your store should offer an island of relief from traffic, crowds, dust, and even noise. Design the interior of your storefront to allow for partitions and different floor levels to prevent it from looking like a glorified corridor.

You must also choose the street that best fits the character of your business. Downtown streets are classified into certain types, including:

- Aristocratic, high-rise office building streets, with very specialized and highly priced tenants, such as Tiffany, Gucci, large department stores, and financial institutions;
- Popular streets with retail stores that sell goods necessary for living and working, such as grocery stores, bookstores, hardware stores, and drugstores;
- Tourist streets with historical landmarks, museums, art galleries, music centers, art centers; and
- Night-life streets.

To decide on which street to locate your business, first, define it as a specialty or commodity; and second, look at the demographics and psychographics of the customers presently patronizing the stores. For example, if you are in the dry cleaning business, you may not want to locate near a Gucci store on the most expensive street in town. You must ask yourself, "Will I be able to meet my pro forma profitably? Will I be able to produce the sales that will allow satisfactory earnings before interest, taxes, depreciation, and amortization (EBITDA)? The lesson here is to pick your street accordingly.

Another factor you must consider is the restrictive ordinances regarding signs over downtown storefronts. Because the signs must be a uniform size, color, and position, your sign will tend to disappear with all the others. Look for creative ways to avoid blending in. For example, a Blockbuster Video in downtown Chicago, Illinois, used its big, tall windows to place additional signs inside the store that faced the windows. Coupled with the fact that the store was located on a corner with inside signs facing both streets, its visibility became excellent due to the lowered eye level for pedestrians and drivers.

If a downtown location doesn't seem right for your retail business, you may want to explore your shopping center location options.

Explore a Location in a Shopping Center

You may find locating in a metropolitan shopping center is a better option for your type of retail business. When looking at shopping centers, understand these three types:

- The community shopping center
- The neighborhood center
- The strip center

Typically, a *community shopping center* with one or two junior department stores has an RTZ that overlaps three to five neighborhood shopping centers. Usually, a *neighborhood shopping center* includes a grocery store, a drugstore, and several retailers. In turn, a neighborhood shopping center's RTZ overlaps small *strip centers* — centers with small shops of five or more tenants. Before you decide to locate your business in one of these shopping centers, determine the effects of other centers on the area in which you wish to locate.

All shopping centers compete with each other. At times, they are located unfavorably in respect to each other. For instance, the wind or interest gravitation is strong between a community center and a neighborhood shopping center, but if a strip center is located outside the wind, it must rely on its own power alone. Also, some strips are hidden in the back or on secondary roads; typically, you will find an abundance of strip centers in relationship to the demand. Determine whether there are any new proposed commercial developments in the area.

If you find that a new center will open, try to learn what will happen to existing centers. If you choose to proceed with securing a location in a shopping center, you must choose the shopping center category that is best for you.

Choose between Free Standing, In-Line, or End Cap

You have three possible retail store categories from which to choose, including:

- Free standing, which is separate and detached from other structures;
- In-line, which is adjacent to other stores, like in a strip center; or
- End cap, which is at either end of a strip center.

End cap stores tend to produce more volume than in-line stores. Sometimes a shopping center's arrangement makes both end caps desirable locations, but usually one of the end caps is a better location than the other because it is:

- More visible to oncoming traffic;
- First seen when entering a shopping center's parking lot; or
- Less obscured by trees, berms, or other features.

Also, an end cap location offers you the possibility of improving the outside look; thus, enhancing your image. A free standing store in front of a center is in the best marketing position, but the economics of your business may make the improvement costs and rent unaffordable.

If you choose an in-line store, then your business will become one of many. If you decide on an in-line location, make your store's identification and noticeability a top priority. Many shopping centers are developed with the notion of equal treatment of tenants and a uniform design for all. Figure 7.5 gives you an example of the strip center in which every tenant, with the possible exception of the primary end cap tenant, achieves total anonymity. Assuming that the main road is a two-way road, the occupant of the secondary end cap is no better off than any one of the in-line stores. The primary end cap store near the street corner may not have an advantage either, if the store doesn't allow signage or access on the secondary road. The in-line stores in this strip center have definitely had their visibility and distinction stripped away.

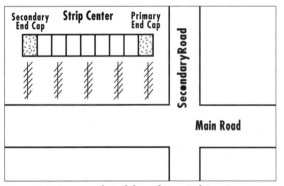

Figure 7.5 Decreased Visibility of Non-End Cap Stores

Each tenant store must identify or diversify itself to attract the attention of the customer. The theory that "once people know about your store they will seek you out" is not correct. You must be where people are already and where people can notice you, right in front of their eyes. Remember, customers are accustomed to and prefer convenience.

There are times, however, in which your retail store can be located right in the middle, with the shopping center carrying your own architectural theme. Your store then will dominate all other retailers. People may even refer to the shopping center by your business'

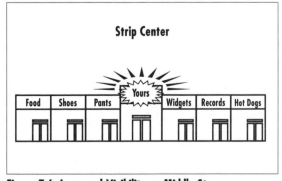

Figure 7.6 Increased Visibility as Middle Store

name. Figure 7.6 shows how your store can become the focal point and magnet of a strip center. Actually, your distinction becomes a benefit to the other tenants, who will sell more hot dogs, widgets, pants, shoes, and food because people are attracted by your store's perceived beacon. Two other types of strip centers exist and each is preferable to a long building. You may want to consider:

- A U-shaped structure or
- An L-shaped structure

Take a look at the U-shaped structure in Figure 7.7. The short arms of both structures extend toward the main road, partially enclosing a common parking area. The end cap stores are clearly the most noticeable and dominant of all the stores in this strip center. The end cap on the long arm of an L-shaped structure has little advantage over the in-line stores. In the case of the U-shaped structure, the two end caps may have equal visibility, but in Figure 7.7, the end cap at left is clearly preferable to the end cap at right. It is more noticeable to oncoming traffic because it is closer to the main road and is not partially hidden by trees and bushes. Both end caps are positioned so they may present display windows that face the front and the side of the store to enhance the merchandising of the

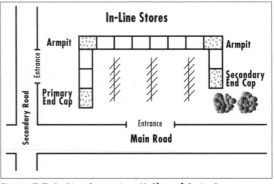

Figure 7.7 In-Line Stores in a U-Shaped Strip Center

products and make the store about as visible to the passing traffic as a free standing structure. Also, if the center is U-shaped or L-shaped, avoid locating in the armpit or the elbows because these spaces are hidden; thus visibility and recognizability are severely hampered.

The tenants in a strip center are about equal in retail pull. However, in the bigger shopping centers, you need to find out about their *anchor* stores — grocery stores, drugstores, junior department stores, and others. You need to know whether their specialty and marketing strategies are highly recognized and whether you can expect them to pull for you. This is important, particularly for new units under construction of which you intend to be part. If you intend on becoming part of a strip center, make sure to:

- Analyze the type of anchor.
- Plan your opening after the anchor is in operation.
- Study the total tenant mix and see whether locating in this center will have a synergistic effect that will benefit your business.

Determine the Potential for Retail Synergy

Consider the case when diverse and not directly competitive stores are gathered in a cluster. As an individual retailer, you must determine whether you will gain or lose by joining a cluster of businesses. For example, some tenants will piggyback on the strength of others. This tends to create a lower average sales level for all stores in the cluster. In some cases, the best tenants will not be able to achieve their peak volumes. Take a mall food court as an example. Even if the total cluster is successful, the individual retailers may continue to struggle because of diluted sales, very high rents and charges, long labor hours, and a plethora of other problems. If your business' image is strong because of your business formula or because you belong to an established franchise, you will have to decide whether joining other competitors with lesser gravity will strengthen your identity. Consider Blockbuster Video, which has a very good and profitable business formula. The costs are low, the sales are high, the profits are great, and the top-of-mind awareness is excellent. Locating next to or near a Blockbuster store may strengthen your business' identity.

Typically, when you join a cluster of stores, the layout includes mutual entrance-exits. So you must look at factors like how you will be located as far as prominence and convenience to your customers. Also, the uniform architecture, design, and layout will take away some of your unique features and your individuality will be diluted. In the mind of a consumer, the image of each tenant may blend in with the other stores' images. Your business will be automatically compared with all the others. You are just one of them — not Number One. Further, you will not be totally free to operate. It will be difficult to follow high standards and motivate the other tenants to do the same. For example, you may find it difficult to convince all tenants to join promotional-advertising campaigns. Also, as a part of a cluster of businesses, you must consider the effects of certain daily tasks on the other retailers, like:

- How to time deliveries;
- How to use the parking area;
- How to dispose of trash; and
- How to manage the common area maintenance.

If you decide to join a retail cluster, you can locate yourself in a manner that will safeguard your distinct individuality. See to it that your store is:

- First at the entrance of the cluster;
- Separate and distinct from the others to some degree; and
- Unique, with your regular facilities, color scheme, style, and signage not reduced or modified in any way.

In other words, make arrangements to ensure that you could continue to operate well, regardless of the other businesses in the cluster. There are three kinds of business clusters to consider:

- Diverse, or unrelated;
- Complementary; and
- Directly competitive.

The one that will be of most interest to you is the complementary business cluster. Pay attention to the businesses that have natural affinities with yours, especially if you intend to join a cluster. For instance, a women's apparel business should be close to the right tenant mix — like jewelry stores, beauty salons, and furniture stores — that draws the store's target customers. Further, look at the synergistic effect that a noncompetitive store can offer your business.

- Grocery stores, which bring in customers once a week or more often benefit fast-food locations greatly.
- Drugstores benefit by the presence of hospitals, clinics, and physicians' office complexes.
- Toy stores benefit those stores that aim at children's other needs, such as books, clothing, shoes, and collectibles, plus stores that attract parents.
- Sporting goods stores have an affinity for casual clothing shops as well as bicycle shops and stores that specialize in outdoor activities, such as fishing gear, hunting equipment, and camping supplies.

You must assess the marketing strength of your business and then decide either to exploit the strength of nearby tenants or to be the magnet that will cause other tenants to benefit from your store's pulling power. Tenants like Wal-Mart tend to locate separately, and they create their own market. However, if you follow their lead, you will not always be guaranteed additional business. Some of their product lines may compete with yours.

If a cluster is formed only by direct competitors (hamburgers or tacos or pizza or chicken), then the RTZ does not necessarily expand in size. Customers will have the choice of replacing the objects of their demand — it may be a taco for lunch instead of a hamburger. If the cluster is formed by diverse, but complementary tenants — furniture and appliances, florists and gift shops, women's apparel and jewelry — both the size and depth of the RTZ will increase because they will attract a greater variety of demands. There will be an additional purchase, rather than a substitution, such as a dress and a necklace, a bouquet of roses and a greeting card, and a jacket and pair of shoes.

Landscaped Commercial Areas

Many cities have passed ordinances requiring the beautification of large areas of commercial land with trees and bushes suited to the local climate. Shopping centers are immersed in a forest of vegetation with signs and awnings at the same height as the foliage. Both stores and customers can be lost in this recreational setting. If you decide to join the other tenants in such landscaped centers, you must realize that these amenities may not be the best for your retail business. Customers must exert themselves to find your business. You can lose the pulling power of the daily visual impressions from passers-by as well as the impulse business. The loss is less for specialty stores. As a part of a center, you will have to create visual attraction with large, eye-catching window displays with signs, color, and possibly moving lights, making your store more visible at the driving and walking eye-level, below the tree branches. Be sure to explore all available alternatives in other parts of the market, as well.

Evaluate the Pros and Cons of Shopping Centers

You can also consider the pulling power of the shopping center compared to the one across the street and others within a one to one- and one-half mile radius — which is the estimated core of your future RTZ.

Assess the relative strength of the shopping center in relationship to the RTZ that it serves. Analysis of vacancies will give you a clue. Remember that shopping center developers are likely to build shopping centers in excellent as well as in poor locations. You don't want to open your retail store in a secondary shopping center, only to find out you must compete with a bigger and better one across the street or within a short distance.

In addition, evaluate the shopping center from the main corner of the street. Look for things like:

- What people see while driving;
- The most prominent wing;
- The obstacles to visibility and accessibility;
- Whether the layout is a labyrinth that will puzzle people and make them drive in a maze to reach the front of the stores;
- Where you should locate for the first and best impression in the center;
- The free standing buildings in the front of the center, and whether too many of them block visibility or contribute to your business;
- Whether developers will try to build more *outparcels* — parcels of land around the perimeter of a mall or shopping center; and
- Whether the owner can allow other tenants to build in front of your store.

You can also determine the line of visibility by checking what is recorded in the title report, which allows or disallows buildings to be constructed.

You will also want to familiarize yourself with the center's architectural design. Architectural features give a location more noticeability. Thus, study the columns, porches, roof lines, and triangular or curved accents on the facade. Try to locate where such architectural features are, but don't locate behind columns, arches, or anything else that might obscure your store. Avoid any recessed footage because it will hide your store. In addition, don't locate in the back of an existing structure; you will be a mystery tenant. Remember, don't expect people to walk extra steps to come to your store.

Ask Critical Questions

Before you commit yourself to a lease, you will want to know the answers to many important questions. Some of the questions you must answer yourself, such as "Can I live with the hours of operation of the center?" and "How can I expand in the future?" Think about these questions at the beginning and negotiate options and rights-of-first-refusal now. You will have to direct some of your questions to the leasing manager, owner, or developer. Make sure the owner of the center isn't just interested in filling space that hasn't been renting out easily. The quality of the tenants may be less than desirable. You do not want to be used as a filler. Determine what kinds of promotions you can run independently versus the ones organized by the shopping center's merchants association. In addition, meet with the owner and learn about the shopping center's rules on signage, lighting, parking, traffic, and zoning. To begin, you can ask:

- What kinds of signs are allowed?
- What are the restrictions on color and height for signs?

You must think of ways you can devise a sign that will make your store more noticeable, yet stay within the center's restrictions.

Further, determine whether wide windows are allowed. Pedestrians must be able to see inside your store. Thus, the windows should be the maximum size. In fact, once a potential customer enters your store, he or she should not experience any surprise other than, "It is nicer than I thought." Of course, your store should have excellent inside and outside lighting. When you look at exterior lighting needs and restrictions, look for yourself to see whether the center is well lit during the evening. Ask yourself whether the light poles on the parking lot are adequate. If not, determine whether you need to add more lighting or more floodlights. Also, when looking at lighting needs, make sure your store's frontage isn't in a shadow. You will need excellent lighting, traffic, and parking.

Observe the traffic that connects paths for pedestrians and cars among the various tenants in the center including the anchors that generally have more pedestrian activity. In addition, analyze the parking needs of the other tenants. The tenants around your space may need a lot of parking. For instance, a Chinese restaurant requires a normal number of spaces. However, if it has banquet facilities to serve parties, weddings, and large group meetings, it will use the majority of the parking lot for long hours. Any adjacent retailer, including you, will suffer greatly. Further, consider your business' future deliveries. Determine whether they can take place in an area that is easily supervised and controlled without interfering with the customer traffic and the inside service.

As discussed in Chapter 3, make sure you understand the zoning issues — specifically the restrictions that may affect your business if located in a shopping center. Zoning restrictions often prevent a retailer with a standard architectural format from carrying out plans to build a free standing building. Also, at times, a retailer's development doesn't represent the highest and best use potential of the land. Remember, the profitability of your operation will be affected by:

- High rents;
- Percentage rents based upon sales levels (with percentage rent leases);
- Common area maintenance charges;
- Shorter lease terms and higher depreciation per year; and
- Restrictions imposed by the shopping center's bylaws.

Your goal is to seek low rents, high parking ratios, maximum exposure, excellent traffic, livable costs, and the highest possible sales. If your business offers services — not products — such as a barber, beauty shop, travel agency, or shoe repair shop, you may have to settle for a secondary location because of lower rents. However, you should have clear and visible directional signage.

Discover the Benefits of Malls, Supermalls, and Outlet Malls

Your evaluation of other metropolitan location options may lead you to consider locating in a mall. In 1995, malls attracted $300 billion in retail sales. Currently, you have three types of malls from which to choose, including:

- Regional malls
- Super-regional malls
- Outlet malls

A *regional mall* offers a wide selection of general merchandise, apparel, and home furnishings as well as a range of services, and recreational facilities. It is built around one or two full-line department stores of not less than 100,000 square feet each. A *super-regional mall* — or more commonly, a *supermall* — provides an extensive variety of general merchandise, home furnishings, services, and recreational facilities, but on a much larger scale. It is built around three or four major department stores of not less than 100,000 square feet each.

Today's malls and supermalls are ordinarily enclosed with proper heating and air conditioning systems. These structures are usually surrounded by outlots or outparcels with free standing retailers and professional office complexes. Most often, the inside of a mall has two levels, served by multilevel parking areas. The exterior architectural design emphasizes either the main entrances to the mall itself or the entrances into the anchor department stores. The interior design tries to equalize the retail importance of the two levels. The architecture influences people to follow certain straight or meandering paths to expose them to more shops and more merchandise. As a mall tenant, you will depend heavily on the life of the entire mall. Even if you are part of a well-known franchise operation, your store's pulling power will depend on the traffic generated by the mall itself. The selection of a location in a mall starts from the selection of the mall itself.

Keep Up-to-Date on Mall Trends

The aging of regional malls will cause changes to happen, often very big changes. These once-popular malls begin to look worn and unattractive. As a result, people go somewhere else to shop. To avoid getting into a bad situation, you need to choose the best mall in the area, using the analogue study methods from Chapter 5. In short, you must compare the mall in which you are interested with other malls. Then, considering the local and regional trends, project its future potential for increased sales. Malls have been experiencing a strategic change. The leases signed in the 1970s and 1980s are now expiring; there are too many malls; and the competition among them is very keen. According to the *Directory of Major Malls*, the number of leases coming up for renewal is now greater than the number of leases available during the peak years of mall construction. Stores are being downsized, allowing for more tenants with a broader variety of products. Some chains operate with multiple formats.

Developers, in the heat of competition, created a mall saturation in some markets. The value of a mall is not increasing automatically any longer. Also, the evolution in retailing forces changes of tenants, as well as tenants that redefine themselves. As an example, consider the trend among teenage mall shoppers, who comprise a great number of overall mall customers.

Teenagers are deserting the malls for the more hip and trendy developments, like New York's East Village and Boston's Feneuil Hall. You may start to see more specialized single-category tenants, discounters, and others that offer good and less expensive merchandise, without the glamour of the department stores. New types of tenants — like grocery stores and entertainment centers — will be added. Many enclosed malls may be reduced or eliminated, due to the expensive maintenance of the common areas.

Over the next five to ten years, hundreds of malls will need renovation and repositioning. The changes will not only consist of new and different tenants, but of new construction, new parking layouts, and new entrance-exists. The convenience of accessibility will call for more outside direct access from the parking areas to the stores. Select the malls that are the most prosperous and, as an alternative, recently renovated malls. Verify the sales trends since the renovation was completed.

Consider a New Breed – Outlet Malls

Outlet malls are an attempt to diversify from the classic mall format. Outlet malls are built in outer areas of cities and at important freeway intersections, central to a number of towns all around. The tenants are discounters and they tend to carry brand-name merchandise. Their prices are lower than in big cities due to the elimination of go-betweens and the sale of seconds. These stores have a vast inventory. The merchandise is predominantly apparel and clothing. The parking is very different from regular malls. Tenants have parking adjacent to their stores. An outlet mall on a somewhat grander scale is referred to as a *power center*. A power center is a huge retail complex that features discount centers, superstores, food stores, and other mass merchandisers. A good example of a popular power center is Sawgrass Mills Mall in Sunrise, Florida. Become familiar with this term in your site selection search.

Outlet malls and power centers are so new that it is difficult to say how they will perform in the long run. Use all the criteria you have learned so far in this book to select your location in an outlet mall. Basically, their customers make fewer trips, but they buy a lot of merchandise per trip.

Meet with Your Lessor or Developer

If you intend to locate your retail business in a mall, supermall, or outlet mall, this is the information you must have.

- Determine the gross leasable area of the mall, and of all the department stores.
- Find out whether there are too many or too few retailers in relationship to the total square footage of the mall.
- Find out if the mall is being expanded and where the best location will be once the expansion or remodeling is completed.
- Discover the average sales per square foot of the mall and department stores and how these figures compare with the nearest malls.
- Know what kind of signs you can have and how you can clearly differentiate yourself with signage.
- Find out if you can place your sign in other parts of the mall.
- Estimate the number of business hours in a yearly period.
- Check the blue laws in your state.
- Research the restrictions in the mall's bylaws that will affect your operation in the future.

Often, your lessor or developer can help you obtain this information.

Do-It-Yourself Mall Research

Before meeting with your lessor or developer, you will need to obtain some vital information — regarding square footage, tenant mix, types of pedestrian traffic, and mall levels — on your own. Start by checking the square footage of direct and indirect competitors. For instance, determine the number of apparel stores, shoe stores, and restaurants. In some cases, developers under financial strain may fill space with tenants selling the same or similar merchandise.

You need to know the ideal amount of square footage that fits your industry to discover the area with the best assembly of tenants that will complement your business — also known as the right *tenant mix*. Further, you can graph the pedestrian counts at various points, such as at the exterior entrances, interior corners, and along the corridors near department stores. In addition, evaluate whether the developer succeeded in equalizing the attraction and pull of the mall levels. Sometimes, one level may be more relevant than the other. So, find out which level has the promotional activities, such as antique car shows, florist displays, and toy fairs.

Take Some Helpful Advice on Mall Areas

To find the right location in a mall, study its configuration. Start by examining the exterior architecture. Find out the locations of the main entrance-exits. Some malls emphasize — through architectural design — the entrances into department stores. Others emphasize the entrances into the general mall area.

For retailers, general mall entrances are most relevant. The design is also very important concerning the frontage of your own store. Make sure your store has big, tall, and wide windows so that customers can see inside. Actually, it would be better to just have wide doorways and not to have windows at all because they are barriers. Do not erect any barriers. Just let the customers rush in. In other words, your store should feel like an extension of the mall corridor. Other important tips to follow when selecting a mall location, include:

- Avoid recessed frontages.
- Find a frontage that protrudes.
- Avoid dead end corridors.
- Look for a location near the interior entrances to department stores that are not recessed.
- Avoid areas out of the main stream of traffic, such as the extreme point of the wings and corridors that lead to secondary entrances.
- Go where the people traffic is.
- Avoid a location with kiosks that are directly in front of your store.
- Try to locate near tenant stores that will complement your business.
- Make sure your deliveries can be made conveniently, and you have adequate storage for them.

Figure 7.8 illustrates some of the points raised about good and bad mall locations. The good locations, marked "A," are all either near the interior entrance to an anchor department store, in the major passages, or interposed between major magnets in the mall. All have excellent visibility and accessibility in both directions. In these locations you can catch many people coming and going. Locations marked "B" are out of the main flow of people traffic, in recessed areas, or hidden behind kiosks.

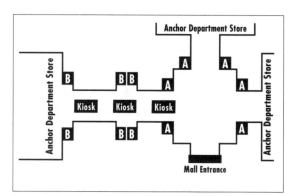

Figure 7.8 Good versus Poor Mall Locations

If you are a food retailer, you have to decide between locating individually or being part of a food court. Often a mall's bylaws will give you only one choice. If you choose to be part of a food court, you may have to consider offering a modified menu due to the lack of space for storage and equipment. Hence, your sales may be lower, and so will your profits. As part of a food court, you should occupy the space that has more relevance and noticeability — the protruding corner, the first spot upon the entrance, or the bulls-eye of the lineup with the best exposure.

It is easier to operate in a mall because of fixed hours, relatively steady business trends through the days, and more predictability from season to season. But, before you decide to locate in a mall, remember that your business can easily get lost among all other businesses, and you do not have the capacity nor the freedom to promote yourself effectively.

Know the Ins and Outs of Mall Outparcels

Malls need to be strategically located to fully take advantage of the highway and freeway systems. Because a mall's retail trading zone includes hundreds of thousands of people, the coordination and discipline of the traffic flow is the key to the success of a mall. Generally, a mall is built between the centers of an ellipsis with a peripheral road and several radiuses leading to multilevel parking lots. The frontage on the peripheral road is developed for commercial, professional, and hospitality purposes.

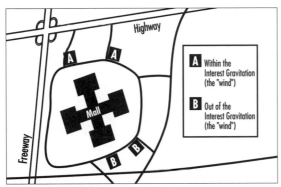

Figure 7.9 Significance of Wind on an Outparcel

The importance of each property or outparcel around the perimeter depends upon its being a corner or an inside lot. However, its real importance is dictated by the intensity of the flow of traffic or interest gravitation to and from the mall and to and from the main highway accesses. Your business must be within this flow. If it is located on a lot in the back, your business may not survive, due to the high rent. Figure 7.9 shows the importance of locating in an outparcel that is within the wind.

If your business has two formats — free standing or in-line — you will have to make the decision to go inside or outside a mall. Some people have even decided to open two stores — one in-line store inside and one free standing location outside. There is a great risk involved, of course. If you decide to place your business outside, you may miss your customers both in their coming and going, and also while they are inside the mall. If you are on an outparcel, plan your business to serve primarily the surrounding RTZ outside of the mall and secondarily, the mall itself. The majority of your customers should come from the surrounding traffic generators and a minority from the mall itself.

Chapter Wrap-Up

To recap, you must weigh the many advantages and disadvantages of choosing a location in a metropolitan area. When looking downtown, remember to look at its origins and trends, its degree of vitality, and access and pull, and whether to choose a ground floor, underground, or second floor site. Also, as a downtown retailer your business must cater to the fast-paced lunch crowds of the people who work there.

When evaluating shopping centers, compare the different types — free standing, in-line, and end cap — to know which type best suits your business. You can get critical information on these shopping centers from developers, brokers, and other retailers; this information may help you determine the benefits of operating in a center that may or may not provide a retail synergistic effect on your operation.

On the other hand, you might be leaning toward a location in a mall, supermall, or outlet mall. As a potential mall tenant, you now know how to do mall research and keep updated on mall trends, and follow essential tips for operating in a mall.

If your search for the right location takes you to a suburban area, you will find the advice in the following chapter especially helpful.

Chapter 8

Discover Rural Site Options

In the previous chapter, you explored the opportunities for successful locations in metropolitan areas. Although most of this book has focused on areas where you can target customers on a 24-hour basis, there are other options available to you. This chapter will direct your attention to retail possibilities beyond the reach of metropolitan areas — out there where the requirements are sometimes looser and where the rules are significantly different.

In your search for the best location for your retail business, you will have three nonmetropolitan site options. The first option involves a newly rediscovered entity — the small town. The second option runs along the freeways and highways that comprise the Interstate system. The third option is the captive-shopper facility — which may be far from a city's central business district (CBD). Your first step is to focus your attention on the endless possibilities a small town offers.

Grasp the Value of a Small Town

A small town is a population center that does not belong to any standard metropolitan area (SMA) and is geographically separate from major cities. For instance, Mankato, Minnesota, is separate from major cities like Rochester and Minneapolis-St. Paul. In Pennsylvania, Lebanon is separate from Harrisburg. Visalia, California, is separate from Fresno — a major city in Central California. However, there are still smaller towns like Bardstown, Kentucky;

Cartersville, Georgia; and Okeechobee, Florida. The population of small towns can vary from 6,000 to 75,000. Rand McNally has a listing of towns it considers small — with populations between 5,000 and 30,000. The listing contains about 1,400 towns located outside SMAs.

The key components of a small town are:

- A core area within the city limits and under city jurisdiction;
- A city zone, which includes the perimeter surrounding the city limits and is occupied by residential, suburban, and industrial developments; and
- A retail trading zone (RTZ) that takes in all the countryside where the population's interest gravitates toward the city.

The true size of the market in a small town should include the population of the core area, city zone, and surrounding RTZ. Usually, demographic data gives you the city limits population only. For example, a city of 8,000 might have a city zone of 3,000 and a surrounding RTZ population of 40,000. This provides you, as a retailer, a potential market of 51,000 people. Before you make a decision to locate your retail business in a small town, make sure you have studied its overall layout — as described in Chapter 2.

Study the Town's Layout and Its RTZ

Your analysis of the geographical distribution of various small towns will give you an idea of their hierarchies based on the road systems of the area. To better understand the hierarchical distinction of small towns, Figure 8.1 illustrates the

hierarchical interest gravitation among small towns. Notice that the larger the town, the farther it reaches to pull in virtually everyone — visitors, shoppers, workers, recreationers, and salespersons. In some areas, you will observe where the RTZs of two small towns meet. To understand how this happens, think of two small towns — one with 15,000 people in its city limit and the other one with 5,000 people. They are 20 miles apart, connected to each other by a road that carries mostly local traffic. Where does the RTZ of the bigger town end and the RTZ of the small town start? Since traffic is heavier near the respective towns and

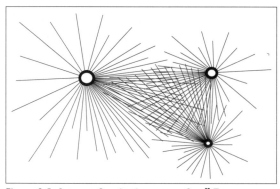

Figure 8.1 Interest Gravitation among Small Towns

it diminishes as the distance increases, the towns' RTZs become tangential at the point on the road in which the number of cars, going in opposite directions, becomes equal. Some towns are more central than others. If you want to locate your store in Findlay, Ohio, you will notice that Findlay is actually a hub where seven highways and roads meet, including U.S. Route 35 — the long-distance connection between Toledo and Dayton. Around Findlay you will find Upper Sandusky, Bluffton, Ottawa, North Baltimore, and several other small towns — although Findlay is the heart of the hub. To the northeast, a smaller town, Tiffin, Ohio, functions as a subhub of still smaller towns.

Your next step is to study the geographic area of the state in which the small town is located. Carefully examine the confluence of radial roads, the quadrant roads according to the cardinal points, and the radial roads overlaying the grids of your prospective RTZ. Refer back to Chapter 2 for tips on how to study a city's road system. In addition, look for long-distance highways that cut across the radial and grid configurations. You do this to make sure the town has adequate service to the nearest interstate freeways and highways. If the town is close to a big city — 45 minutes away or less — then allow for some money transfer (leakage). People will spend some money in the big city. You can take your analysis one step further by visually identifying the bigger towns also called *planet communities* — and the less important ones, the *satellite communities*. Once you understand the strategic importance of the small town in respect to satellite communities, then you should compare the statistical information available. The analogue study methods, as thoroughly described in Chapter 5, work wonders when you use them for small towns. You can use the various towns as analogues among themselves and find out which is the best. If you already have a retail business in one town, then you can compare your town with the town in which you intend to open another store. For an in-depth discussion of opening a second, third, or fourth store, see Chapter 9.

See for Yourself

Any assessment of a small town in which you are interested in doing business must be done by you. To gather the pertinent information for your retail business, you must drive the town yourself. As you drive through the small town, check its radial roads and quadrant roads and count the town blocks from each end of the town. Then, count the blocks with relevant activity, such as commercial, professional, academic, and manufacturing activities. You don't want to locate near empty agricultural fields. Your best bet is to locate in an area that has stores and offices in a cluster that measures ten blocks long and five blocks wide. Continue your assessment by driving through the core area, city zone, and outlying RTZ, which includes the balance of the county.

Because a small town is separate and distinct, it is possible to identify its RTZ by using the distribution map of the local subscription newspaper. All subscription newspapers have distribution maps. For instance, Logansport, Indiana, has a newspaper called the *Logansport Pharos-Tribune*, which has a distribution of 18,000. This newspaper is distributed in town as well as in the satellite towns of Georgetown, Anoka, New Waverly, Walton, and Metea. People in those towns buy the newspaper because their interest gravitates toward Logansport. The line that encloses all those towns is the RTZ of Logansport. You can gain knowledge of your prospective RTZ in metropolitan areas in the same manner. Remember, a newspaper's distribution area may overlap another newspaper's area.

Also, when determining your small town's RTZ, look at its grocery stores. As detailed in Chapter 4, the number and size of the grocery stores of a small town will clearly tell you the makeup of the town and how many people actually live there. A small town's major grocery store (15,000 square feet) caters to about 10,000 people. To calculate the total RTZ of the town, make a survey of all the grocery stores in town and calculate total square footage. An accurate assessment of a small town will also include a look at its own downtown, other retail centers, and your competition.

Consider the pull, or lack thereof, of the small town's downtown area. Look for signs of rehabilitation, remodeling, and growth. Determine whether it has a problem with vacancies. In addition, locate any additional commercial centers, other than the downtown itself. Find out whether there is a mall on the outskirts of town. A mall in a small town might offer an excellent potential for retailing — usually a mall is a real magnet and draws people from miles around. Wal-Mart understands this market possibility. It acts as a mall in the mall's absence.

Finally, examine your competition. Evaluate your competitors' facilities — how new, clean, and attractive are they? Check to see if these businesses are prospering or declining. In addition to your drive through the small town, you will want to pick up critical information from the town's key resources.

Size Up Your Small Town

To approach a town's key contact people, use the helpful tips and strategies on gathering information via city and community leaders from Chapter 3. But first, acquaint yourself with the small town by using a simple tool — the Yellow Pages. Although the Yellow Pages for a small town is usually quite small, it can help you find hotels and motels — which you need to study — and other potential sources of business, such as recreational areas, tourist resorts, and national parks. You need to separately research all information concerning colleges and military bases. For a more detailed discussion on these other potential business locations, refer to the discussion on captive-shopper locations at the end of this chapter. Once you have a good idea of the key contacts and sources of business, set up interviews with:

- Presidents or managers of the local banks
- Editors of the local newspaper
- Presidents of the largest industries
- Elementary school and high school principals
- Managers of the major supermarkets
- The director of the local hospital

In your interviews, try to determine:

- The total bank deposits in town
- The kinds of loans that are made by banks
- Trends in local employment
- The kind of industrial base and whether it is diversified or not
- The presence or absence of unions

- The permanent or cyclical nature of employment
- Labor conditions
- The percentage of high school graduates that remain in town
- The size and importance of the hospital

For instance, if you have an interview set up with the director of the local hospital, you may want to ask questions like:

- How many beds does the hospital have?
- What is the availability of doctors?
- Are they specialists?
- If so, do they attract people from a greater distance?
- What is the percentage of bed occupancies?

As an example, Monroe, Wisconsin, with a population of 10,200 has a hospital with 500 beds. Many people come from surrounding cities and states to have their ailments cured. Patients, relatives, visitors, and medical personnel contribute greatly to the economy of Monroe.

You can learn crucial information from the town's planning department. Here you can find out any known changes to major activities, such as a military base closure, an industry downsizing, or a plant expansion. Find out whether there are any exceptional trade shows, fairs, or recreational events. And, if agriculture is the main economic base, then determine whether there is a flow of population through the seasons — such as migrant workers during the harvest time of the local agricultural products.

There is a difference if the town is a county government seat. The obvious indication is the presence of a stately building with the characteristic town square, with commemorative monuments, retail shops, restaurants, and parking. County offices will bring in many people to do things like:

- Pay taxes
- Apply for construction permits
- Settle legal disputes
- Apply for marriage licenses

To learn more about the demographic makeup of small towns, a good source of information is the *Editor & Publisher Market Guide*, published by Editor & Publisher Association. The annually updated guide covers all towns that publish a subscription daily newspaper and belong to the Editor & Publisher Association. For more information on this helpful guide, refer to Appendix B.

Since you know the characteristics of your retail business and its requirements for the purpose of expanding, you can set certain parameters for yourself, such as:

- The total RTZ population must be at least 35,000 people.
- The total bank deposit in town should be at least $80 million.

- The floor space of grocery stores should be at least 120,000 square feet.
- The minimum retail sales should be $300 million per year.
- The general merchandise dollar should be at least $50 million.
- There must be a Kmart, Wal-Mart, or equivalent retailer.
- The downtown should have no less than 30 blocks of active businesses.

One thing is for certain, if you locate in a small town you can use the monotony factor for your benefit.

Play the Monotony Game

The *monotony factor* says that where ordinarily there is not much new in a small town, the coming of well-known, attractive, and interesting businesses will grab the attention of its people. If there is a new place, product, or service that small town residents know is available in big cities, they will try it. In fact, franchise experience in small towns has been gratifying. Although, interestingly enough, there was a time when planners of McDonald's were not willing to locate in towns with less than 35,000 people. So planners experimented with a scaled-down facility called Mini-Mac, which were opened in towns like Cartersville, Georgia; Clinton, Iowa; and Presque Isle, Maine. With the monotony factor working in their favor, these stores' sales were excellent — to the point that Ray Kroc, the chairman, immediately ordered a remodeling of the Mini-Macs into full-scale McDonald's facilities.

Consider a Suburban Town Center

A new retail trend is developing in smaller downtowns, especially in suburban cities. Malls constructed on the edge of town took away much retail business from the central business district (CBD). Yet in affluent, dense towns with an historical integrity, there is a movement toward refurbishing and upgrading town square buildings and attracting national retail chains into the lineup. You will see this trend well developed in suburban towns, such as Winter Park, Florida; Santa Monica, California; and Evanston, Illinois. The renewed interest in the suburban town center is the result of several factors.

First, people still feel the romance of shopping in their favorite town. Second, people find it more convenient to shop in a suburban downtown than to drive to a mall, wrestle with traffic, and search for a parking space in an oversized parking lot or multilevel parking structure. A suburban downtown is less congested than a big city's downtown, and shopping hours are generally longer. Although this may seem similar to the pedestrian mall concept, in the revitalized downtown you still have car traffic and parking. If you are considering a location in a suburban town center, make sure your products or services will fill the needs of the people who live in the town.

Typically, local merchants have a devoted clientele, but they lack the variety of offerings that a retail chain brings. In like manner, you can benefit from the magnetic pull of such widely recognized stores as the Gap, William-Sonoma, and the Body Shop — all of which are beginning to appear, along with other stores belonging to regional and national retail chains, in renewed suburban downtowns. Consider placing your store in a suburban downtown if:

- The demographics spell affluence.
- Well-known local merchants remain relatively prosperous even after the opening of a mall on the edge of town.
- Several buildings are being renovated, and the entire town center is marked for revitalization.
- The cost of renovation will be affordable enough to make it economical for your store to operate at a profit, even though the sales may be lower than at a mall, where the rent is higher.
- Amenities, such as landscaping, trees, benches, sidewalks, and fountains, are in place to make shopping inviting and fun, similar to European shopping districts where the movement of crowds is entertaining.
- Convenient parking is available, either on the street or immediately behind the retailers' shops.

If a location in a small town doesn't seem right for you, explore the possibility of establishing your retail operation along an important freeway.

Explore Interstate Options

Americans are spurred by the unshakable urge of the road. The number of summer vacationers these days is setting a record. The nation's hotels and motels are reporting the highest occupancy rates since the 1980s. Travel agencies have enjoyed a 35 to 70 percent higher booking rate than previous summers. The United States Travel Data Center recorded 230 million trips by Americans for 1994 — the highest ever. As a retail business, you may want to look into catering to travelers — an ever-increasing market potential you can look forward to. To capture these travelers, you must carefully examine the Interstate system.

When you look at a map of the United States, you will see big blue lines that crisscross all states in all directions. These blue lines indicate the Interstate system. The Interstate system, officially established in 1956, makes it possible for Americans to cover great distances in a shorter time. In fact, today's Interstate system is used for living, recreation, work, and visiting. Because of this constant flow of people, think of the Interstate system as a separate and different market that has its own retailing needs.

The Interstate system is a series of retail trading zones that are obviously elongated, and varied by size and density. These RTZs overlap and strengthen the local RTZs. Often they double the pulling power of the local RTZ — which means that a retailer who serves the Interstate system will not impact retailers serving just the local market. For instance, when you examine the Interstate system in Nashville, Tennessee, you will see that the three interstates (I-65, I-40, and I-24) crisscross each other, forming a stellar configuration from the center.

The dynamic RTZ of these six traffic streams is a net addition to the local RTZs. Further, in Cheyenne, Wyoming, the traffic system of I-80 and I-25 greatly enhances the potential of the local RTZ, because of the long-distance traffic.

If you are interested in locating your retail business in a city along a main interstate, evaluate each city in respect to the existing traffic aggregate — that is, the combination of living, work, and long-distance traffic. In between cities, the Interstate system creates its own RTZ via its interaction with local roads. Often you will not find a city or town — only businesses that support the needs of the travelers.

Cater to Travelers' Needs

The Interstate system carries business travelers, industrial travelers, salespeople, repairpeople on their routes, men and women going to work, and others with fixed purposes. All of them are destination-oriented, and their principal aim on a highway is to travel quickly to their destination points. A minority of travelers is leisure-oriented. They move at a slower pace and make more stops for a variety of reasons. They are typically older and more upscale than the former group.

The characteristics of households that compose the vacation-oriented travelers market indicate that they are mobile, affluent, and family-oriented groups. Their median income tends to be somewhat greater than the national average. On their auto travels, an average of three persons travels together in the same vehicle. Further, more than half of all family vacationers have youngsters in their households. When traveling, they are interested in visibility, accessibility, familiarity, and service. In other words, travelers:

- Want to see the store or have clear directions to it;
- Want easy access both off and on highway exits, plus convenient locations not far off from the Interstate — meaning not more than one mile;
- Prefer known establishments, but they notice new and attractive additions; and
- Want it to be efficient, courteous, and clean.

In addition, when considering a location on the Interstate, pay close attention to the need for parking and access. Retail businesses that serve Interstate customers must have parking for cars, small trucks, big trucks, and buses. People, after having driven miles and miles of freeways, will reject your business if they are forced to look for parking away from your premises. Travelers like to be aware of upcoming facilities ahead of time. While billboards may look cumbersome and ugly, they seem to perform a vital function for travelers. The truth is travelers want to see signs.

Locate at a Good Intersection

Your overall goal is to find a location near an important freeway intersection. Each freeway intersection has its special characteristics and the retailers there offer corresponding types of services. As a retailer located at a key freeway intersection you may:

- Serve only long-distance travelers.
- Serve travelers at a cluster of small towns.
- Cater to trucks and buses by providing mechanical services, food, lodging, clothing, gifts, and local products.
- Serve also a medium-sized city where the freeway represents the major link to the outside world — for instance, I-65 serving Lafayette, Indiana, or I-75 serving Tifton, Georgia.
- Supply information such as tourist maps, directions, promotional brochures, or offer message centers, telephones, and faxes.
- Offer emergency needs like pharmaceutical drugs and medical assistance.

You can spot key freeway intersections by analyzing carefully psychological-physical distances. Interstate travel is conditioned by *psychological-physical distance* — meaning people feel the distance and the fatigue. So, there is a point in which they look for a place to stop — or more commonly referred to as a pit stop. The time period that most generally elapses between pit stops is one hour and 45 minutes. When analyzing the Interstate, you need to choose the intersection that more naturally fills travelers' needs — refueling for autos, and resting, restroom, and food breaks for people and their pets. Take Buttonwillow, California, for instance. It is located along I-5 in the 387-mile stretch between Los Angeles and San Francisco. The psychological-physical distance calls for at least two stops. So if you are traveling to San Francisco, the first natural stop from Los Angeles is Buttonwillow, which has a near-zero residential population. Despite the near-zero population, a McDonald's was opened in Buttonwillow, and the sales were higher than the national average. Eventually the area developed and now there is a sizable cluster of service, retail, and hospitality businesses. Another example is Mauston, Wisconsin. The distance from Chicago, Illinois, to Minneapolis-St. Paul, Minnesota, is 410 miles. Mauston is halfway between these two major cities. Because there is a natural need to stop, you will find all kinds of retail businesses there. And, yet another example is found in Barstow, California. Along I-15 from Los Angeles to Las Vegas, a 272-mile stretch, Barstow offers a refreshing pause to all types of travelers; thus, the need for goods and services is great.

When trying to locate near an important freeway intersection, consider travelers' needs as they both arrive at and depart from their destination points. The last stop after leaving a city and the first stop before entering a city have a particular significance to travelers. As they come to a city, they want to prepare themselves; as they leave, they want to prepare themselves for the long trip ahead. Thus, the need for goods and services is great. In addition, freeway intersections with radial roads and important quadrant roads belong to the local RTZ. These intersections have additional attraction power of their own because they add long-distance Interstate traffic to the local traffic. To get a better idea of your store's sales potential, assess the Interstate intersection in relation to local roads and respective communities.

Project Your Store's Sales Potential

Usually the Interstate freeways are located away from towns; they usually pass on the outskirts or a few miles from them. You need to understand the movement of people to and from the towns; so take a separate car count for both directions. If the intersection is already well developed with several businesses, much of the Interstate traffic will stay there. Also, you can look at the critical time-distance factors. This analysis will give you an inkling of the psychological conditions of the travelers, such as the stages or degree of fatigue or boredom. From your analysis, you can learn:

- The distance from the major point of departure and the major point of arrival;
- The driving time between the points; and
- The driving time from the intersection to the same points.

To project the sales of your store you also need to take the traffic count on and off the Interstate. However, you will need to identify the different types of vehicles, knowing that the different types carry different types of customers that will contribute differently to your business. For example, cars and vans are good for gas stations; buses are good for fruit-gift shops; vans with families are good for hotels and motels; and trucks are good for restaurants because truck drivers typically have hearty appetites.

A traffic count on the Interstate is only meaningful when the traffic is in the mood to exit. If you are located outside those in-the-mood-to-exit points, the traffic count is meaningless. In other words, you must be able to identify the passing-through-only segments of the Interstate to avoid them, even though the traffic count is very high. For example, in Chicago, there is a service island bridge over I-294 near the O'Hare Airport. Retail business in that service island is minimal even though the traffic count is nearly 500,000 cars per day — despite its easy entrance-exits. The traffic there is strictly transitional — far away from its point of departure and far away from its point of arrival. Instead, if you have single- or multiple-head traffic in the mood to exit — even if you have a low traffic count — you will be able to serve a greater percentage of it. An example of this is Limon, Colorado, where gas stations, several kinds of retailers, restaurants, motels, and truck stops form a small city of their own.

Remember, the key to finding the right location, whether it be in a shopping center or along the Interstate, is to compare, compare, compare. With this thought in mind, to predict your hourly business curve, take the customer count of one or more of existing direct and indirect competitors. In addition, you can glean useful information from the managers of local motels. These individuals can tell you the occupancy-vacancy variations based on the seasons or special events, like deer hunting and skiing, that attract a variety of people.

Be Cautious of Truck and Bus Traffic

When you think of the Interstate, you might naturally think of truckers and bus travelers as a main source of business. Truck and bus travelers gravitate toward natural intermediate points between hubs, based on their needs to stop. To prove this, you will find an abundance of truck stops, with restaurants, fuel pumps, repair shops, and some small retailers. However, before you consider one of these locations, proceed with caution.

In general, it is expensive for a retailer, whether in a fast-food establishment, convenience store, or motel, to cater to truck drivers. Trucks take up a lot of space; thus, there is a need for extra parking. Further, the entrance-exits must be wide, and the pavement must meet highway quality standards and requires extensive maintenance. A retail facility that caters to truck and bus traffic must provide telephone booths, information-management boards, larger restrooms — and sometimes, showers, washing machines, trash disposal containers, and other amenities. Keep in mind, the number of customers from trucks is few but, on the other hand, buses will provide many potential customers. You may also want to explore the possibilities of locating on a tollway.

Consider a Spot on a Tollway

The U.S. tollway authority — the International Bridge, Tunnel and Turnpike Association — realizes travelers have a variety of needs, and the tollway service islands, if done properly, can be profitable business centers. Similar to the retail location options along the Interstate, a tollway's service islands are full of potential retail customers. In fact, the distribution of the service islands on the tollway system is normally regular — one every so many miles. However, if an island is near a tollway entrance-exit from and to major population centers, the business is more active. Look for stores that are complimentary with each other, not only competitive. For instance, consider stores like restaurants, gift shops, juice and espresso counters, and stores offering travel items, local fashion, and native agricultural products. A diversified mix will invite the customer to "rest" longer and to spend more money.

Toll systems throughout the United States are regulated by governmental or paragovernmental bodies. The services offered on the tollways are bid out to private companies. Successful retail bidders are confronted with an array of regulations and limitations in their operations, plus hefty financial obligations and short-term leases.

Your Store on Wheels

A retailer who is unsure of the viability of a particular location may first try to set up his or her retail operation in a temporary store — or trailer on wheels. This might be a logical and practical move if you want to serve customers while your permanent store is under construction, while your store is being remodeled, and during special temporary events, like county fairs, city celebrations, sports events, and conventions.

Before you make your decision, consider some helpful tips. First, you need to design and build a trailer that will meet all the proper codes, will have a sturdy structure, and will not cost an arm and a leg. Also, you will need a person in charge who understands your business operation. This individual would be responsible for visiting special events sites, negotiating the lease agreements, working with event organizers to get utilities and provide access, hiring a qualified driver to move your store on wheels from one city to another, and renting a space for storing it during times of nonuse and during the winter. To set up your store on wheels, this person needs to hire local workers to set up the trailer properly and to install a safe platform with steps. In addition, you will need:

- A trailer for the merchandise (restaurants will need a refrigerated van);
- A trailer with power generating equipment; and
- A trailer with restrooms that have proper containers for refuse.

Besides all of these logistics issues, you must carefully prepare a business plan that projects sales, costs, and especially dead time devoted to moving the trailer from one place to another, storage, and nonuse time. Project the payroll and maintenance costs carefully, several tires can blow up along the way!

Locate Captive Shoppers

There are many types of retail locations that do not fit into any of the categories so far discussed in chapters 7 nor 8. They are different from locations normally associated with the downtown, small town, shopping center, mall, or Interstate system. These retail locations are referred to as captive-shopper locations because they cater to customers that are already there. In other words, these customers don't have to travel from afar to get your goods or services. Some captive-shopper locations include:

- Office shops
- Seasonal recreational shops
- Travel facilities
- Military bases
- National parks

You might want to explore the possibilities of locating in a captive shopper location. To begin, you will have to do some brainstorming to identify the right area for your type of product or service. For example, if you are in the food business, you may want to look at institutions like schools, colleges, hospitals, and stadiums. These institutions can prove profitable, especially if you can negotiate an exclusive agreement; thus, locking out the competition. Gifts, flowers, books, magazines, and novelty items usually sell well at hospitals. Schools and colleges have needs for books and writing materials, and photocopying and other services that students may want to have on campus. Your best bet is to contact the respective authorities to explore available opportunities.

Office Shops

Office shops — often gift shops and sometimes drugstores or other retail establishments — are located at the entrances of office buildings. To be successful, the location must be visible, within the main entrance-exit flow of the employees and visitors. Some office buildings contain thousands of workers. You will be faced with the typical dilemma of high rent and small space; high peak hours and a small service area; and quantity of merchandise and small storage areas. Do it right — fill your shop with light. Use big glass windows — let your customers look in. Courtesy and service efficiency will work for you. Be ready when the customers are there.

Seasonal Recreational Shops

You may want to look into a seasonal recreational location, say at a beach resort or ski resort. For example, consider the many retailing opportunities in Aspen, Colorado; Virginia Beach, Virginia; or the Ozarks in Missouri. These businesses are open only a few months of the year, yet they may do very good business during those few months. Before you jump into planning for this type of facility, make sure you weigh both the advantages and disadvantages.

Seasonal recreational areas command very high rents, have a high break-even point, and have a high degree of risk. Your business must take place within a short time — say 12 to 16 weeks — and produce high profits. This calls for spacious facilities capable of welcoming several customers at the same time. Retail businesses well suited as seasonal shops include:

- Coffee shops
- Gift shops
- Bars and entertainment spots
- Sporting goods shops
- Seasonal apparel

Keep in mind, during the off-season months the facility will be boarded up — which may create losses as well as maintenance problems. To determine the feasibility of this type of location for your retail business, work out your pro forma statements. Given the sales and investment, you should have a profit percentage similar to stores open year-round.

Travel Facilities

You may also want to consider establishing your retail operation in one of the many types of travel facilities. The retail potential for airports is very promising. Today's trend is for airport authorities to create retail malls that include a variety of merchants. Because airports belong to political jurisdictions like cities and counties, you must submit a bid to the governing body to be able to lease retail space. Keep in mind, an airport location has the same criteria as a location in a mall. Your best bet is a visible location between the main waiting area and the security check points. Other good locations are in the proximity of security check points, close to gates with the greatest number of seats, and up to half way down a concourse — never locate beyond the half-way point of a concourse.

The hub and spoke system in larger airports creates a special situation. The planes take off and land in bunches; consequently, there are periods of excess traffic followed by deserted periods. In international airports, there are often sterile areas to which foreign passengers are confined while waiting to catch flights to other destinations. Here you have a captive market. A retail shop in the baggage claim area, near the car rental counters, is never desirable.

Your prices and your profit margins should be higher due to the higher percentage rents. Also, you will encounter logistic problems, such as storage, delivery points, security clearance, and parking for your employees — all of which can be negotiated. If you are interested in researching an airport location, a good starting source is the American Association of Airport Executives. See Appendix A for contact information.

Railroad stations, bus depots, harbor terminals, freeway truck stops, and tollway islands all have facilities addressed to the needs and whims of travelers. Transportation companies, like Greyhound, usually control and operate the shops, counters, and booths in their terminals, but they may grant franchises, also. Contact these authorities directly.

Military Bases

Military personnel are a big customer group that you may be interested in serving. In fact, more and more, all branches of the U.S. military are allowing private retailers to locate in their commissaries and on their bases. As a retailer located on a military base, you can provide troops, their families, and military pensioners with excellent merchandise at lower prices compared to retail stores not located on military bases. Before you make a decision, make sure you weigh the pros and cons. First, base commanders have the authority to approve the merchants. Because all contracts have a long list of conditions and restrictions, you may lose your independence in terms of pricing and in the goods you offer. For more information on operating your private retail business on a military base, contact the American Logistics Association or one of the specific branch information centers. Refer to Appendix A for more information.

National Parks

Another option you may want to consider is a location in one of the U.S. national parks. In fact, due to an increasing awareness by the National Park Service that visitors need a better welcome and a better service, park officials are more open to the presence of retail businesses than ever before. In the past, contracts were awarded to private merchants for very long and exclusive terms. Today, many of those contracts are expiring. In addition, the National Park Service can supply you with visitors statistics. To find out more, contact this agency. See Appendix A for more details.

Chapter Wrap-Up

As you can see from this chapter, a whole world of retail location possibilities awaits you. You can use this diversity of location options to your benefit. For instance, if you want to open a restaurant, but don't consider yourself to be a city person or don't do well where large crowds congregate, like a supermall, you might plan your retail business around a location in a small town or in a captive-shopper location, like a national park. In short, you can pick and choose which location best suits both you and your business.

To sum up what you have learned about nonmetropolitan site options, consider the following helpful tips.

- A small town may offer you a customer base with a higher visit frequency rate; remember the monotony factor — people crave new and exciting things.
- Millions of Americans travel the Interstate each day; travelers needs must be filled.
- A real need for many retail items exists in nontraditional retailing areas, such as military bases, resorts, or office buildings.

Whichever location you choose, make sure you carefully follow the guidelines as presented in the first six chapters of this book. If you already have a store and are considering opening a second store, you will find the next chapter especially interesting.

Notes

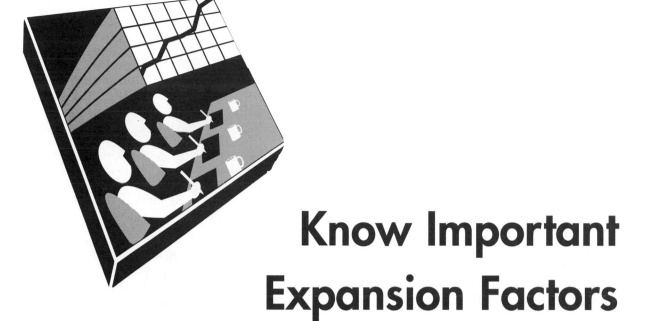

Chapter 9

Know Important Expansion Factors

An entrepreneur or franchisee who already has one or more successful stores faces some interesting challenges when thinking about expansion by opening a second, third, or fourth location. If you want to expand, you will need to consider a multitude of factors. For instance, you want to determine whether there are cases where a large indirect competitor will impact your new store or whether your new store will impact your competitors.

More important, you need to know whether your new store will steal customers from your old store. Further, you must consider the proper distance between your own stores and timing for the openings of a series of stores, and set a strategy for expansion planning. You must ask yourself if it pays to go deeper into the market.

Assuming your old store can survive lower sales when your new store opens, you must decide whether it is realistic to expect your old store to regain its old sales levels without hurting your new store. This chapter addresses these concerns by discussing:

- The effects of market penetration;
- How to measure and handle impact from a new store;
- Ways to maximize the distance between stores;
- The pros and cons of sizes for the various stores;
- How to strategically time store openings; and
- A method to avoid market saturation.

Once you have considered these important expansion factors, you will be ready to put your multistore development plan into action. To assist you, this chapter also highlights the critical steps you must take to develop your new store(s). To start your expansion plans, though, your first priority is to thoroughly understand the effects of market penetration.

Understand the Effects of Penetration

Penetration is the relationship between an existing store's sales and the sales potential of its RTZ. When you place your new store at a certain distance from your old store, you want to achieve a deeper penetration of your market than before the opening of the new store. Otherwise, you will be simply splitting your market share between your two stores. To understand the concept of penetration, consider the following examples of these two franchisees.

There was a McDonald's store in Minneapolis, Minnesota, that had the highest sales of all the McDonald's stores in the Midwest. Analysts went to find out why. At first, the analysts thought its success was due to its franchisee's outstanding efforts. This franchisee had enlarged the store, made it more attractive, and added parking spaces. However, as the analysts' further research revealed, the real reason for the high volume was its market's low penetration level. The store actually served a city area of 30 square miles and there was no other McDonald's located in the entire area. In theory, four more McDonald's stores should have been located there.

In yet another example, a franchisee in Pittsburgh, Pennsylvania, had 18 stores with high sales. When the franchise analysts examined the market potential of the standard metropolitan area (SMA), they realized that the market there could easily handle at least 40 stores. In other words, the area was underpenetrated. In response, the franchisee began plans for additional stores. Today there are 56 stores in that market.

Statistical reports of fast-food restaurants give the number of people per store in the metropolitan statistical areas (MSAs). The numbers vary spectacularly and wildly — 30,000 per store, 244,000 per store, 77,000 per store, and so on. If the stores that have an average of 30,000 people are profitable, just think how many more stores you could place in an MSA with 244,000 people per store. Of equal importance as penetration, impact is of particular interest to franchisees and entrepreneurs with multiple outlets in the same standard metropolitan area.

Use Impact to Your Benefit

Impact is the negative effect that a new store could have on the sales of an existing store of similar format, located at a certain distance. For instance, if you open a similar store on the same side of the street one mile away, most likely it will substantially impact the sales of your existing store — unless there are exceptional business generators in between. Due to this substantial eating up of profits, you may hear some people use the term cannibalization to signify impact. You may prefer not to use that term because it has a negative meaning. Impact, as you will see, can be a positive thing.

Impact can be direct or inverse. Impact is *direct* when you consider the decrease in sales in the existing store. Impact is *inverse* when you consider the potential sales of the new store being negatively affected by the sales of the existing store. In other words, sales of the new store would be higher if the existing store did not exist. Impact resulting from a tight time-distance interval between an existing store and a new location has been the object of heated debate between franchisees and franchisors for a long time. As the debate goes, franchisors like to see more stores in a market to achieve a deeper penetration — or greater market share. Franchisees are afraid that more stores will cut into their sales — particularly in mixed markets, where franchisors and franchisees can open more stores. Check with the secretary of state's office to find out what regulations apply or are proposed for your type of business.

Some franchisors, like McDonald's, give the franchisee an address only, not a clearly defined territory. Hence, the planning of a new store becomes the mutual interest of the franchisor and the franchisee. In other words, both parties need to plan to achieve maximum penetration and minimize the impact on each other's stores. To understand how impact can be a positive thing, take a proactive approach.

Plan for Impact

A market should be planned so that all its retail trading zones (RTZs) overlap each other by a certain percentage. This means that the market should be planned with impact in mind. All stores should be impacted slightly; otherwise, there is no guarantee that all customers will be properly served. In fact, if you leave wide gaps in between, this will cause natural breeding nests for the competition, as shown in Figure 9.1. You must realize that impact will occur. Either you will impact yourself or the competition will. So plan for and manage impact. Now you understand why impact can be positive — it is the price you pay to buy further penetration. The key to managing impact, then, is to have a plan.

The development of McDonald's restaurants in Los Angeles — a market of more than twelve million people — was started with a plan. The plan was to form a constellation of stores within an entire SMA by locating stores approximately two to two and one-half miles away from each other. The plan was made using maps, charts, forms, data, and sales projections. Initially, the plan was based on an instinctive belief that the closer the stores are to people, the more likely

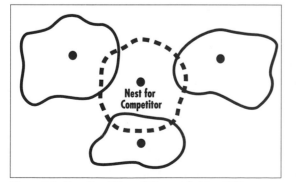

Figure 9.1 Negative Effect of Nonoverlapping RTZs

the stores will get their business. This plan — based on experience and gut feeling — has been followed ever since. The result is that all McDonald's restaurants in Los Angeles have enjoyed high average sales. Many stores were impacted, but the store network is now a most powerful marketing force. The stores are very convenient to people and people know where the stores are. You see, once the market penetration increased — through the opening of more stores — the sales of the stores increased despite the initial impact. After the fallout of impact, more people will come to your place more often, and they will spend more money for more reasons.

Recover from Impact

Recovery from impact is the upward trend of sales in one or more stores after they have been impacted. When existing stores are impacted by new stores, you will pick up new customers in the same market, because there is no better advertising than a beautiful new store in a regional type location. You can measure recovery with the same method by which you measure impact. See the discussion on the Impact Survey later in this chapter.

You will see the sales in most of the stores gradually pick up, reaching a new plateau. Figure 9.2 shows an existing store, represented as X, performing above the market average, represented as an asterisk, before the opening of a new store nearby. The sales of the existing store are immediately impacted by the new store but gradually improve and regain a level above the market average. However, some stores may not respond. In this case, you need to make a full business and marketing evaluation to ascertain the causes. When recovery takes too long or doesn't seem to be happening, it may indicate that some major mistakes were made in location, facilities, and operations.

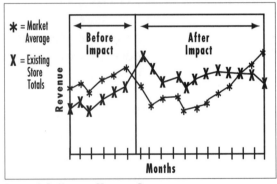

Figure 9.2 How to Measure Recovery

Determine Distance and Size of New Store

If you are planning to open another store, you will need to concern yourself with the distance between your new store and your old store. When deciding the distance between stores, some people use a cookie cutter approach and end up opening a store every two or three miles. These individuals use this approach to reach maximum market penetration because the number of customer visits is the highest in the core and secondary areas of an RTZ. In fact, many business owners have decided to place their stores close enough that the areas they serve become core and secondary areas in the RTZs. And, when you have stores very close to each other, the outer area — or tertiary area — of the RTZ will actually become a secondary area. The secondary area of an RTZ has a higher percentage of customers per grid than the tertiary area. This translates to a definite amount of stores of a certain size and kind within a short distance from one another.

Take caution, however. This approach to a market does not work. It may seem to make sense, but the dynamics of a market will defeat this artificial formula. Remember, an RTZ is the result of human, behavioral, and environmental entities. Because these entities are unpredictable and ever-changing, you cannot deal with them with a rigid approach. If you try to condition the behavior of your customer, don't guarantee it to last. Your best bet is to use the RTZ Survey located at the end of Chapter 4 to give you the information and clues you need to understand the RTZ of the location you intend to choose.

In addition to distance, you will need to decide on the physical size of your new store versus your old store. Keep in mind, even if the old and new stores are of the same type and size, their RTZs are always different in size, shape, kind, and density. Consequently, you cannot keep the physical size of your stores always the same. Some locations have a larger potential; thus, plan for a facility adequate enough to offer more of your goods or services. Although the RTZs will differ in size and shape, you can benefit from the positive overlap of zones.

Rely on a Positive Overlap of RTZs

The limits of an RTZ are dictated by the percentage of business contributed by *grids* — or outlying areas. The grids should be one-eighth of a square mile, and in a CBD, the grids are indicated by its blocks. Some stores of the same type and size have RTZs that may overlap each other partly and, at times, entirely. The overlapping results in a sharing of the market that temporarily diminishes sales. In fact, the shallower the penetration, the greater the impact on the sales of an existing store, even though the new store is located reasonably apart. The penetration is shallow when only a few people spend a little bit of money in getting a certain product or service. Figure 9.3 shows overlapping RTZs. The overlaps themselves represent the impacts.

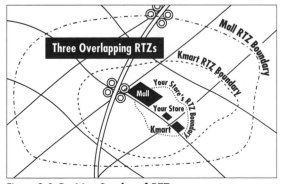

Figure 9.3 Positive Impact on Overlapping RTZs

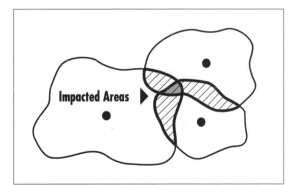

Figure 9.4 Positive Overlap of RTZs

Retailers of a different type and size also have their own RTZ. For instance, look at the Kmart with an RTZ of more than 100,000 people as illustrated in Figure 9.4. If you occupy an in-line store in a community shopping center with this Kmart, you will be surrounded by Kmart's RTZ. You are within the RTZ of Kmart. You have your own customers, plus the customers that Kmart brings from its own, wider RTZ, which will overlap your store in a positive way because it will add more potential customers to your store. Further, if there is a mall three blocks away, its vast RTZ of perhaps 300,000 people will surround both your RTZ and Kmart's RTZ — which creates an even stronger compounded pulling power.

Remember, overlapping RTZs of similar retailers tend to subtract business from each other; but if the retailers are of a different type, the overlapping RTZs strengthen the business of each retailer. To better understand the negative effects of overlapping RTZs, look at Figure 9.5. In this illustration, the stores are represented by the dots, and the darker lines show the stores' RTZs. Notice the overlap of RTZs. Two of the stores almost have the same RTZ. Only one store has its own RTZ to itself. As you can see, if you open stores too close together, they will impact each other considerably. No matter how you look at it, a thorough understanding of your RTZ is necessary to manage impact.

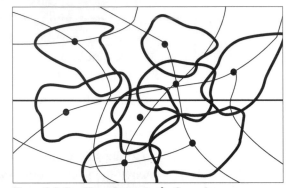

Figure 9.5 Too Many Stores in the Same Area

To rely and plan for a positive overlap of RTZs, consider your original market analysis, as discussed in Chapter 1. This will help you go back to the basics: identify the planned stores' RTZs and their boundaries following the slogan "you walk it, you drive it, you fly it." Outline on a map two RTZ boundaries; for instance, start with the nine-minute drive polygon and the natural and human-made barriers. Compare the results with the RTZ analyses that you already have of existing stores. Then, follow the concept of comparing analogue stores as detailed in Chapter 5 to project potential sales and to rank the RTZs. Another important expansion factor concerns the proper timing of additional store openings.

Develop a Strategy for Timing Openings

When you plan the timing of your new store, you can use a strategic method that will also help you develop your new store's market. This strategic method involves three key phases. First, start from the entire standard metropolitan area and narrow down your analysis to sections of the town, nodes, and nodules of activities that fit your type of industry. Also, study the road system to see how the radial, regional, and quadrant roads connect each part of the town. Second, select the best nodes and nodules, checking it against your demographic and psychographic data. Third, prioritize the major areas you are interested in. Keep in mind, in the initial development stage of a market, you need to plan your locations as far as possible from each other.

Remember, the initial sales impact on each store may be strong. At first, the plan calls for stores far away from each other. Progressively, new stores should be added in between. To better understand this concept, look at it this way. To penetrate a market properly, you must achieve:

• The lowest possible ratio of people per store; and
• The highest possible profitability in each store.

Proper market penetration involves fighting the competition by offering your products or services to the best segments of the market. Consider this lesson that Burger King learned in the mid-1960s. During its beginnings in the 1950s, Burger King allowed McDonald's to select its sites. McDonald's officials repeatedly reported that when a new McDonald's was opened, a new Burger King was about to open a block away. Nearly a decade later, Burger King planners understood that being too close to McDonald's, their stores were too vulnerable. Consequently, they changed their strategy and decided to create their own RTZs by placing their stores in between the McDonald's stores.

You need to plan the number of stores to be opened within a specific time. Do this to achieve a critical mass that will generate top-of-mind awareness and create a marketing punch. Achieving a critical mass means:

- A fair amount of people know what business you are operating and where your stores are located.
- The stores' sales are showing growth.
- The stores are now profitable.

Finally, it means that you are somebody in the market and even more people are noticing you. So, if you plan to open four stores, open them as far apart as possible in distance, but as close timewise as reasonable. Also, you need to plan the timing of openings and their relation in place and distance. You don't want to plan five stores in the southeast of the city and no stores at all on the north side even though the demographics are comparable. To achieve proper penetration, the stores should be distributed harmoniously through the market from the very beginning. Huge markets like New York should be segmented into parts; each part should be treated as a separate SMA. If you open several stores too soon, the market will not be able to absorb the business. It takes time for people to become aware of your place, to find it, and to enjoy your products or services. People are slow to accept a new marketing message. Thus, the rate of development must match the rate of market acceptance of your business. You can help your customers become aware of the new store(s) by preadvertising and premarketing. To save money, you may want to implement your own marketing plan. Obtain a resource book on marketing to help you get started. One excellent guide is *Power Marketing for Small Business* by Jody Hornor. To learn more about this best-selling book, contact:

The Oasis Press
(800) 228-2275 or *www.oasispress.com*

If you let much time go by between your last store opening and a new one, the impetus will disappear. People will forget you and it will take more effort to renew the excitement of your new development(s). Consequently, if you enter a new SMA, don't open a store here and there, one now and one later, or whenever it is convenient for you. If your market analysis tells you there is a potential for five stores, then plan for the maximum penetration — that is, don't open the stores too fast or too slow, and start from the nodes that are most likely to produce the best sales and the best profits. Remember, you need to become the best in town, to get the most dollars from the most people. Everyone must know your business. As a result, you cannot develop a market partially or halfway. Your competitor will quickly realize the opportunity. The five stores now, if properly planned, will have their RTZs touching each other or overlapping each other partially. However, with time, the RTZs of your existing stores will shrink. More areas will open up in between, creating new hubs of opportunity. Be the first to fill in the unserved areas with new stores. But, be cautious and don't jump into these areas. If you are too eager to cover the whole SMA with stores as soon as possible, you are condemned to failure. Never forget that the quality of the location is not only the truth, but the whole truth. A hurried penetration development always causes a deterioration in site selection.

Consider the Time-Convenience Line

The *time-convenience line* is the line of equal convenience in terms of time (isochrones) between an existing site and a proposed site. This line indicates at what geographical point a new site is more convenient to people currently visiting an existing store. The time-convenience line makes it possible for you to measure future impact.

To discover the time-convenience line, follow a drive-and-map procedure. Start by plotting your proposed store and your existing store on a street map. Then, determine four or five potential driving routes between the two sites. Start from the most direct route and add two or three additional routes on either side. Drive each route in each direction and, using a stopwatch, mark the midpoint on the map. Connect the midpoints extending the line to the map boundaries. You now have the time-convenience line. For an illustration of the drive-and-map procedure, refer to Figure 9.6. If the customers are on the side of the line closer to the existing store, it will be less convenient for them to patronize the proposed store. If they are on the side of the line closer to the proposed store, it will be less convenient for them to patronize the existing store. Your understanding of the concept of time-convenience is necessary to complete your own Impact Survey, discussed in the next section.

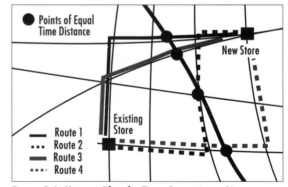

Figure 9.6 How to Plot the Time-Convenience Line

Do an Impact Survey

The Impact Survey focuses on an existing location and a new location to help you discover:

- Which location a customer is likely to patronize; and
- What the financial consequences (impacts) are to each location.

A blank Impact Survey is located at the end of this chapter for your use.

You will need to predetermine the percentage of customers to interview, just like in the RTZ Survey. Although very similar in format, the Impact Survey is not the same as the RTZ Survey. The two types of surveys have different functions and cannot be used interchangeably.

The Impact Survey contains factual questions. Because this survey is based on facts, it is important not to solicit answers that give opinions, desires, or hypothetical judgments. For instance, avoid a question like, "If a store was located in a certain part of town, would you patronize it?" The answer to this question would be unreliable. The questions and answers must relate to actual events. Also, the survey must indicate the frequency of visits. The theory is that heavy users of a store will not be easily swayed to change their habits. Heavy users, as described in Chapter 1, are usually very loyal.

In addition, you must identify the points of departure as either usual or occasional. For example, if a person comes to your store from an accountant's office, it is more than likely a rare occasion. But if another customer comes from home, it is considered usual. The two visits, therefore, have different relevance. There are many more visits that originate from a customer's home than from an accountant's office.

The factual study also involves a map with clearly legible street names. It shows the time-convenience line you discovered during your drive-and-map procedure. The time-convenience line, pre-drawn on the map, will show whether the customer will have to cross it to come to the new facility or not. Each trip pattern will be recorded by the interviewer. The interviewer will mark the points of departure and points of arrival of each customer on both sides of the time-convenience line.

To illustrate this procedure, look at the examples shown in Figure 9.7. Notice the white stars show the points of departure and the black stars indicate the points of arrival. If a customer is and will remain on the side of the time-convenience line where the proposed store will be located, the interviewer will assign the customer's visit to the proposed store. If a customer instead is and will remain on the side of the time-convenience line where the existing store is located, the interviewer will assign the customer's visit to the old store.

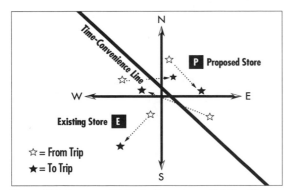

Figure 9.7 Customer Visits to New versus Existing Store

Another factor you must consider involves a customer that has to cross the time-convenience line to go to the new store. In this case, the interviewer must consider the type of product offered. If the customer returns from work to his or her home near the proposed store, he or she might stop at the new convenience store to pick up bread and milk. The store will be given credit for one visit. But if the store is going to be a camera shop, most likely the customer will not stop there at the end of his or her workday. The store will not get credit for a visit. Your interviewers need to know your business well and must predict shopping changes based on the assumption that people will not willingly cross the time-convenience line if there is an alternative.

The results of the Impact Survey will give you an idea of the number of people that will cease to patronize your existing store and will visit the new store for the sake of time-convenience. Knowing the average expenditure per visitor, you will be able to compute the sales losses starting from the opening day of the new store. But counting the customers is not good enough; you must give them a proper weighting. To do this, add two questions to your Impact Survey:

- How often do you visit the store per month?
- What is your average expenditure?

You need to know the percentage of your business generated by heavy and light users. Some customers spend more in a year than others because they visit the store more often. These heavy users may contribute 40 to 50 percent of your sales. Consequently the impact will be higher because the light users are impacted. The heavy users are less likely to be impacted. They are not going to change their habits easily. The first-time customers are also important. They may represent 10 to 20 percent of the business because they don't have any frequency loyalty to your store. Finally, if the new store is functional and attractive and the existing store looks old and tired, there will be more impact.

Measuring impact is very important, because the results will provide you a reference point for future decisions regarding operations, marketing, and market expansion potential. Impact tracking is done by indexing comparable growth of the store to its market and comparing the present revenue levels. Operate your new store for at least six months before starting to measure any actual impact on your nearest store. Remember, the Impact Survey is based on the factors of time and convenience. As a result, the survey works better for commodity products and services. For specialty products and services, people may underplay the importance of time and convenience.

Calculate Impact by Computing Sales

To calculate the impact on an existing store, you need to make comparisons by selecting a number of analogue stores in the SMA and figuring out their sales. Then, determine the sales performance of the new store versus the sales of the selected analogues.

To grasp the idea more firmly, consider this scenario. Suppose you are in the retail hardware business. You opened your first store ten years ago and now have three stores. Soon you will open your fourth store — in an excellent location, but slightly too close to one of your existing stores. You made that decision due to new subdivisions in that part of town and in consideration of zoning plans by the city planning department. You know that your new store will impact your nearest store and want to know how much impact to expect.

To calculate the future impact, you compare the nearest store's revenue with your other stores' (analogues') revenues in the same market. You make the calculations before and after the opening date of the new store. Figure 9.8 illustrates this hypothetical situation in which you prepare to judge the amount of impact your new store will have on your existing store. Compute the sales at your existing store for the full year before the opening of your new store. You will already have the sales data; now adjust your figures for factors like road construction, changes in ingress-egress and changes in traffic, competition, remodelings, special market promotions, and advertising campaigns. For example, suppose your store has a full year's revenue of $750,000. Now that you know your figure, calculate the average hardware store sales in the area. Some people prefer to select as a control — to be used as a comparison — only the stores most similar to the new store. Say you come up with a market average of $600,000. Thus, your existing store's performance is 125 percent of the average store in the hardware market.

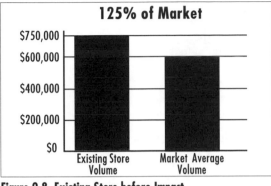

Figure 9.8 Existing Store before Impact

Your impact calculations are shown in Figure 9.9. You wait until the new store has been in operation six months, and then you tabulate the six-month sales of your existing store. You find that your existing store has six-month sales of $348,000, which projects to an annual revenue of $696,000. You compare this to the six-month market average of $300,000, which projects to an annual revenue of $600,000. Your existing store's share of the market is now 116 percent of the average store. You arrive at this figure by subtracting the new percentage from the old percentage — 125 percent minus 116 percent equals 9 percent. Thus, the impact rate is 9 percent. Now you know what effect your new hardware store has had on your existing store. From your analysis you also find out that while the sales of your competitors have been flat, the market itself has grown, and you have absorbed all of the growth.

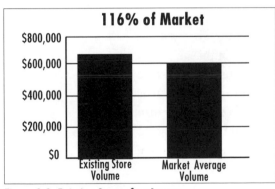

Figure 9.9 Existing Store after Impact

Base Your Analysis on Census Tracts

You can also base your impact analysis on census tracts. Basing your analysis on census tracts is a simple method that measures full or partial census tracts that fall within your store's time-convenience line. When you plan a new store, identify full or partial census tracts that form its estimated RTZ. If the store is already in operation, you know its RTZ via your completion of the RTZ Survey from Chapter 4.

First, draw the time-convenience line (isochrone) between the two locations — the new and existing locations. Then, identify the census tracts that fall within the influence of the new store. Remember, your RTZ Survey will give you the percentage of business that comes from these census tracts. Next, subtract that percentage from the sales of the old store. This method will give you an opinion of impact. It will not be mathematically precise, but you will be able to make a judgment about impact. Then you can determine whether it is acceptable or unacceptable.

Decide How Much Impact You Can Take

When the penetration in an SMA is shallow, the Impact Survey will show bigger impact. Your job is to determine how much impact is acceptable. To know the amount of impact your existing business can handle requires that you analyze each case separately. For example, an impact of five to ten percent may be perfectly acceptable from the point of view of general marketing because you can still completely cover the market without leaving any area unserved. However, the specific store being impacted may not be able to suffer a ten nor a five percent sales loss. If its profitability is already shaky, it would not be wise to push that store to the level of insolvency. Other variables to consider when determining how much impact your store can take include:

- Age of the store;
- Whether its existing sales are low;
- How attractive it is; and
- How adequate the facility is to properly handle the business.

The age of the store is important in the interpretation of the Impact Survey results. If you have created goodwill over the years, your existing store will be less likely to be substantially impacted. You can continue to count on the heavy users to patronize your store steadily. Also, consider whether your existing store has low sales. If the sales are low, look at the store penetration in its RTZ. It is possible that the location, facilities, and operations are not good enough to turn the sales around. However, if the demographics of the RTZ are excellent and there is a high population density, then you can handle the impact if you take other steps. You can:

- Enhance the image of the facility.
- Improve its operational management.
- Increase accessibility.
- Boost marketing and advertising.

Without fail, nicer stores produce more impact. Kentucky Fried Chicken's (KFC) experience within the last two decades illustrates this clearly. KFC had many stores that needed remodeling. They were old and their functionality was poor. However, KFC planners were faced with a dilemma. If they were to open new stores in better locations with better looking facilities, the old stores would be impacted severely. As they quickly learned, customers will drive three to five miles farther just to go to their preferred store — usually the newer and more attractive store — and literally pass in front of the old and tired store. As a result, KFC sometimes closed two stores to open a new, improved one.

Finally, watch the distance factor. You must determine whether customers will spend the same amount annually at the new store as they did at the old store. Are they visiting the old store because they still find it more convenient? When you consider impact, remember, the frequency of visits drops following a decay curve that is specific to your industry. Keep in mind, there is one drawback to the Impact Survey. Because the interviews take place in an existing store, the survey ignores the nonusers. Thus, it doesn't shed light on why these potential customers don't visit the existing store.

In addition to planning for and managing impact and penetration, you need to understand the concept of saturation.

Avoid Saturation by Strategic Evolution

In retail, often people talk about saturation. *Saturation* relates to a market that has no more room for new stores of the same type because they would not produce adequate profits and would excessively impact existing stores. A market can become oversaturated. Avoiding saturation will depend upon you — meaning, you can minimize saturation by strategically evolving your business by continuing to offer your customers more and different reasons to come to your stores and spend more money.

Strategic evolution involves changes made deliberately to match the evolving market demand. The changes or improvements in your business can be in many areas, including:

- Better operations
- Improved amenities
- New products
- Better business positioning
- Improved marketing

Look at ways to improve your products or services. You might make an improvement by adding more and better service employees, improved computer systems, or a drive-thru service, such as in a bank, photo shop, dry cleaner, or liquor store. Also, look for ways to make your production more efficient overall. In addition, you can remodel or rebuild and add better lighting, more attractive facilities, more parking, and a better layout. Further, you can enhance the atmosphere on the inside of your store by improving the landscaping, keeping the premises spotless, and adding interesting architectural touches. You can:

- Increase your store's appeal with new and different products, additions, or substitutions.
- Beat the competition with unique products and services and a special pricing policy.

- Increase your customer awareness with better marketing, advertising, and promotional campaigns.
- Detect new trends in your industry, evaluate them, and be quick to introduce them in your store.
- Be original, creative, daring, and innovative.

Take this attitude: the high sales of a store are never the highest they can be. They must improve the following year and the year after. Consequently, they are moving targets. The best stores become the object of imitation and emulation by other stores, like in the franchise system. They become the analogues to follow. You must visualize the sales of one or more stores increasing forever, given the proper strategic evolution.

Consider the Effects on Your Stores' RTZs

With the addition of new stores in an SMA, the size and the shape of your stores' RTZs change. Their sizes shrink and their shapes assume new boundaries due to:

- Internal competition or impact from same chain stores;
- Outside competition; and
- New static (residences) and dynamic (traffic) elements in the area.

When your RTZs' sizes shrink and your stores' sales volumes increase, you will experience a higher number of customer visits, especially within the core and secondary areas of the RTZs. The frequency of visits from the tertiary areas (off-map) is much less. For instance, if you have three stores in the same part of town, the tertiary areas of their RTZs become the nest for an additional store, as illustrated in Figure 9.10. Any plans for strategic evolution should take into consideration how many stores to place within the available RTZs in a standard metropolitan area.

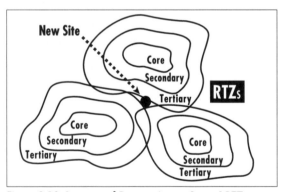

Figure 9.10 Impact and Penetration on Stores' RTZs

An understanding of the concept of strategic evolution will lead you to believe that theoretically there is no end to the number of stores in a market; new unserved areas will be created in the tertiary trade areas of each RTZ. In fact, you can count on a principle that states: the higher the penetration of each store, the smaller the size of its RTZ. The penetration is the result of age, but especially of goodwill created by a business that offers excellent products, services, and value. When considering the right number of stores in a market, take into account these facts.

- Very few retail industries have a penetration of more than 25 percent in any market.
- It is very likely that your industry has a penetration of only 3, 5, or 10 percent.

This means that you have a market potential (people waiting for you) of 97, 95, or 90 percent. Consequently, you may firmly believe that the sales potential is always much higher than normally thought to be.

The single most important factor to help you decide whether you can open another store is what your return on investment (ROI) will be. So if you reach a point at which the economics of the new store do not produce the required ROI, then it is useless to continue to build new stores.

When looking at the ROI for a new location, make strategic business evolution, solid operations, excellent marketing, and financial savvy your top priorities. If one of these is missing, your store development will come to a halt. If all four factors are up to speed and the ROI is right, your store development plan deserves a green light.

Follow a Five-Step Multistore Development Process

Now that you know the critical expansion factors, you are ready to learn the ins and outs of the multistore development process used by companies with multiple corporate and franchise stores. Even if you don't intend on becoming part of one of these larger chains, the planning process tips will help you plan your store's further expansion.

The multistore development process, also referred to as the long-term development planning process in this text, is a five-step process.

- Step 1 encourages the use of a joint effort planning process and shows the benefits of this type of collaboration.
- Step 2 shows the critical need for all members of the planning team to follow an executive decision tree for proper decision making.
- Step 3 lists the important strategy issues to cover as part of a company-wide strategic plan.
- Step 4 gives helpful hints on how to create a development budget plan so all members know their financial boundaries and goals.
- Step 5 gets into the nitty-gritty on the meat of multistore development — that is, the long-range development plan.

Take a close look at each step and you will see what you need to do to begin your business' future expansion.

Step 1 – Use a Joint Effort Planning Process

If you plan to take part in the franchise system, you must be willing to take part in a group planning process. In fact, the long-term development planning process in a company with multiple corporate and franchise stores is the basis for market selection, site selection, the budgeting plan, and the company's strategic plan. Included in the process are not only the projected new stores but also stores that you must relocate, rebuild on the same site with more land and major structural changes, remodel, and redecorate. Thus, be prepared to share the task of site selection with a group of people.

Typically, the real estate representatives in the corporate real estate department are responsible for site selection. Thus, the real estate representatives must have a thorough knowledge of the company's functions — especially of operations. A representative who is only knowledgeable in real estate is dangerous.

At times, operations or marketing people may take over this function. Some companies even have attorneys in charge of retail store development. However, if the function is delegated to separate people, unilateral decisions may be made with little thought given to other overall functions of the company, like finance or construction. In other words, people will consider their own goals and priorities and may not consider the needs of other areas.

- A financial person might select a site that is less expensive.
- A legal person might select one for which he or she can negotiate better legal terms with the landlord.
- A marketing person might select a very good location, but well beyond the scope of the profit and loss capability of the retail business.
- An operations person might give more importance to more immediate factors that will benefit operations with less concern about the future.

Given the complexities of the decision process and the millions of dollars of capital at stake, establish a planning process in which all the aspects of site selection are brought forth, discussed, evaluated, and agreed and disagreed upon, in a free and open exchange of ideas. The planning exercise sends a message to the entire company that its future hinges on the successful opening of new stores. It is a way of leveraging the extensive know-how of the corporate people and the franchisees — free entrepreneurs managing their own dollars.

Step 2 – Follow an Executive Decision Tree

In no way should a corporate committee — made up of people who do not intimately know the areas of the selected locations — make decisions based on completed forms and a few pictures. Instead all parties should follow a clearly laid out executive decision tree. Site approval is a process involving the *line* — a term used to describe those people functioning in an executive capacity — and the *staff* — formed by people who function in an auxiliary, support capacity. The former is often located in various markets away from the company's headquarters.

The executive responsibility for the final approval of a site and the execution of the contracts normally falls on the line and the real estate development department. The line executive — who may be president, division vice-president, or regional vice-president — has the task of operating the future store profitably. That official will be responsible for assisting the franchisees involved in the planning process.

Step 3 – Develop a Company-Wide Strategic Plan

A strategic plan will take into account the macrotrends of the industry, behavior of the consumer, and competitive forces in respect to the products or services you offer. The timeframe for this strategic plan is three, five, or perhaps ten years. The strategic plan should be fully comprehensive and include:

- The design and engineering of the store package — land, building, equipment, signage, and inventory — so that it will be suitable for delivering goods or services efficiently and profitably;
- The development of proper formats that fit real estate retailing needs; some companies have two or three sizes of buildings, some have storefront packages, others have in-line store packages, and still others have a mix of them;
- The setting of the store *hurdle rate* — the return on assets required by the company — so franchisees can also use it as a guide;
- The selection of both big and small markets, in which management intends to develop a brand, like the Gap, Mail Boxes Etc., and Kinkos;
- The establishment of a marketing goal, such as "to open a retail store for every 100,000 people with certain demographic and lifestyle characteristics";
- Further development of existing markets with new stores, relocations, rebuilds, and remodels;
- Decisions concerning which markets are to be corporate, or franchised, or a little of both types; and
- Plans to secure the capital necessary to implement the strategic plan.

Step 4 – Create a Development Budget Plan

The development budget plan is the budget for the first year of the long-range development plan. While the long-range development plan data is purposely vague, the data for the development budget plan must be as objective and reliable as possible. The plan should cover the upcoming twelve months of business. You must carefully weigh all degrees of uncertainty and include some contingencies — events that will more than likely happen. Top management and middle management will sign off on that plan and, if the company is public, the stockholders will expect implementation of the plan.

Because it is the foundation of the development of a retail company, the development budget plan must be refined to the dollar.

- Volume projections must be correct.
- Opening dates must be correct.
- Costs must be correct.
- Number of projected locations must be correct.

Of course, the financial department must be prepared with the correct financing. This is why the financial executive must be a part of the planning process. The franchisees must open their planned stores on time. The operations department must run corporate stores properly with well-trained people. It is like a battle plan to be followed and implemented through the year — day by day, week by week, month by month.

The development budget plan must be managed by the real estate department with extreme care. Such management starts with facilitating communication between corporate headquarters and field operations, which include regional vice-presidents and district sales managers. A weekly conference call between these critical team players is necessary for the smooth flow of directions, followup, counsel, facilitation, and understanding. In other words, corporate should be able to get current information from the field, including production and sales reporting, and a continuous monitoring of the progress made against the original budget plan. Keep in mind, these weekly conference calls must be held in a businesslike manner. It is essential that the regional or division vice-president attend. A weekly development status report will be generated and sent to all team players as a result of the conference calls.

Step 5 – Start a Long-Range Development Plan

The long-range development plan spans five years of projected store development. It includes:

- The development budget plan for the first year;
- Rough-draft plans at various stages of completion for the second and third year that show, as accurately as possible, the projected dates of the contract signings, groundbreakings, and store openings; and
- Summary projections for the fourth and fifth year.

The long-range development plan is general, not too detailed, and concerns itself with areas of interest more than with specific blocks and corners.

Plan each market for each store by using the Long-Range Store Development Plan Worksheet located at the end of this chapter. For instance, in Des Moines, Iowa, a long-range development plan for a home video rental store might call for one store in the northwest part of town to be opened next year; another one in the southeast part to be opened the following year; and finally two more stores in the central business district during the third year. The identified areas are viable retail trading zones — meaning they have all the necessary demographics and psychographics and are currently unserved.

The long-range development plan should cover:

- The type of areas chosen to be developed, like the central business district, suburban areas, shopping centers, small towns, malls, and strip centers;
- Future company and franchise stores; free standing, in-line, and storefront stores; and various format sizes;
- Projected real estate costs;
- Projected construction costs;

- Estimated month in which the property acquisition contracts will be signed by both parties — the seller-lessor and retailer;
- Estimated month of construction groundbreaking;
- Estimated month of store opening; and
- The projected sales volumes.

The development projections for the fourth and fifth year should be kept even more general and vaguely identified because no one can see clearly that far in advance. But they should be recorded as potential opportunities for the retailing of the company's goods and services. It is important to identify the areas as feasible or not feasible, with an index of probability. For example, if the zoning is currently single-residential, then there is zero probability of changing the zoning to commercial.

To clarify the importance of the long-range development planning process, you must spell out its purpose. Parts of that purpose will appear to be obvious, but a misunderstanding of any part of that process could remove some of its value. The purpose, then, of the planning process as well as the long-range development plan itself is to:

- Use in-house knowledge and experience, including marketing, operations, real estate, construction, franchising, and others.
- Inform and educate the members of management and member franchisees about markets, locations, market share, legalities, capital requirements, zoning and environmental requirements, competitive operations, marketing activities and strategies, operations opportunities, and supply problems. All team members will contribute to the plan and will coordinate their respective departments' activities. In short, they will do "their thing."
- Use the information to set up the implementation schedule during the successive periods of the year.
- Encourage every department to organize itself and procure whatever is necessary to implement the plan.

For example, the finance department needs to seek the required capital. The single store franchisee must plan the critical path leading to the opening of his or her store. For more information on a franchisee's critical path, refer to Chapter 10. A multiple store franchisee needs to procure financing and other resources. The corporate human resources department needs to start planning for the personnel needed to run the new stores.

If the fiscal year starts January 1, the schedule of the process should include all steps in proper order.

June through July. During this period, you must survey potential markets and areas of interest and prepare market studies. You will need demographic and lifestyle statistics; trends in open stores' sales and these stores' profitability; market share data; analysis of competition; general marketing data; real estate and construction information; and environmental information, such as zoning and impact studies. Also, you must prepare aerial pictures and maps.

Top management should set aside a full day for the long-range planning session, and the date should be set well ahead of time so that all parties are able to attend, including the franchisees. The meeting should take place in a large conference room with boards on which to display maps, charts, drawings, statistics, and pictures. At best, all attendees will have a clear view of all exhibits. To be comprehensive, the displays will reveal all pertinent information in easy-to-understand form, including:

- Maps of all areas with development potential marked by colored dots that show existing corporate and franchise stores, competitor stores, and legends that indicate yearly sales of each of the company's stores and estimated sales of each competitor store;
- Aerial photos of areas marked for development;
- An outline of basic information about prospective sites, including projected RTZ limits, demographics, psychographics, and time-distance points;
- A chart of market penetration trends;
- Other available marketing information;
- Graphs of traffic counts;
- Zoning information;
- Preliminary site plans;
- Charts that reflect survey results; and
- Maps with colored dots indicating years of openings for all projected locations.

The purpose of the planning session is to collect whatever information the attendees can contribute to the process of site selection. Consequently, the attendees must be the people in the region or division who know the most about the markets and are most capable of intelligently analyzing each site of interest. Thus, the attendees should include the regional and division vice-presidents, district managers, real estate manager, real estate representatives, construction manager, marketing manager, franchisees involved in their markets, and anyone else who lives there and knows the areas intimately. The marketing manager plays a big role in the presentation and should start the session by first covering each area of dominant influence (ADI) markets, pointing out weaknesses and strengths, illustrating the status of the competition, and pointing out marketing factors that may help or hinder the development activity. Then, the real estate manager and real estate representatives of the various markets will present their plans, going into details, area by area. The presentations must include relocations, rebuilds, and remodels, which are closely connected with the future stores.

August. Then, the floor is opened for discussion and questions and answers. At the end of the analysis, the group will draw a conclusion about each selected area of interest, and all areas are rated according to desirability and feasibility.

September. The results of the regional meetings, which have been properly recorded on the Long-Range Store Development Plan Worksheet, are reviewed by the corporate line and staff management. Comments and changes will be communicated to the field.

October through November. The regions and divisions now concentrate on the first year of the long-range development plan and prepare the development budget plan for that year. This plan will start the following January. Therefore, this plan's details must be as correct as possible. The figures must be realistic and obtainable. This plan shows the:

- Number of contract signings;
- Number of openings;
- Number of months in operation;
- Sales estimates;
- Number of groundbreakings;
- Costs; and
- Return on assets (ROA), or the hurdle rate required by the company.

This budget plan has to be in sync with the budget prepared by the finance department. The implementation of the development budget plan begins each January.

Experience shows that these planning sessions are essential for a truly viable store development plan. This kind of development plan, started by McDonald's in 1976, found its roots during a time when there were great dreams of placing McDonald's stores in every area where the stores could run at a profit. The dreams came true, but they came with a synchronized effort and a clear purpose in the minds of all.

This kind of planning process also works for Kentucky Fried Chicken and at Blockbuster Video and has helped both companies achieve great results in their growth rate and quality of development. The process works and will work for you, as well.

The long-range multistore development process is an activity that should be regularly scheduled and repeated every year — reflecting the development already achieved and the knowledge of new areas of opportunity. Each year, the same people should attend the long-range planning meeting. The new people who have more recently joined the region or division should also attend. The combination of old views and new views will greatly assist the overall planning process. In addition, the future opportunities — covering a three- to five-year period — will be reviewed. As a result, new opportunities will be added and old ones removed. The list is changed, perfected, modified, and made realistic and believable. The process will improve as you review, review, review.

As you review your plan, you will achieve the best development professionally possible. The plan will be revalidated each year. After three or four revalidations, the consensus about proposed locations will strengthen or weaken. The locations that stand the test of the critique will have a high degree of potential success.

Chapter Wrap-Up

This chapter has shown you the various expansion factors that can either make or break your plans for future additional stores. To recap, make sure you fully understand the effects of penetration and impact — know how to properly penetrate a market and how to plan for and recover from impact. Remember, you must strategically evolve to avoid oversaturating a market. And, by completing an Impact Survey, like the one on the following pages, you can learn how to master impact.

In addition, you must consider other key factors like distance and size of your new store(s) and how to properly time the openings of new stores. Then, whether you are interested in joining the franchise system or simply opening another store, your knowledge of the five-step multistore development process will give you a head start on planning the expansion of your retail business. When you use these key steps and incorporate your knowledge of expansion, you will be ready to make any future expansion a win-win situation.

Impact Survey Instructions

The sample questionnaire that follows is for a typical Impact Survey. The questions should be directed to the interviewee. The statements in brackets and the physical observations should be done by the interviewer.

If your interviews are for a restaurant that serves inside, provides carryout, and operates a drive-thru, complete three separate surveys — one for inside customers, a second for carryout customers, and a third for drive-thu customers. In each case, the interviews must be done where the customers are, such as the dining area, the carryout counter, and the drive-thru window. Make sure your interviewers specify where in the store the interview took place.

You may wish to design a somewhat different questionnaire. If you do so, be sure to avoid questions that ask for opinions or predictions, neither of which are reliable. Also, be sure to include the points of departure (coming from) and points of arrival (going to) questions.

Impact Survey

[Show interviewee the map and point to store's location.]

Where were you before coming to the store? [Mark the nearest intersection on the map.]

☐ Home   ☐ Church   ☐ Professional appointment

☐ Work   ☐ Recreational activity   ☐ School

☐ Shopping   ☐ Entertainment   ☐ Passing through

☐ Hotel   ☐ Social

☐ Other [specify]: _____

Which road did you take to come here? _____

Where will you be going after you leave this store? [Mark the nearest intersection on the map.]

☐ Home   ☐ Church   ☐ Professional appointment

☐ Work   ☐ Recreational activity   ☐ School

☐ Shopping   ☐ Entertainment   ☐ Passing through

☐ Hotel   ☐ Social

☐ Other [specify]: _____

Please indicate on the map where you live. [Mark the nearest intersection.]

Please indicate on the map where you work. [Mark the nearest intersection.]

How much did you spend today? _____

How many people in your party today? _____

How long did it take you to get here? [Calculate it in minutes.]

By car: _____   On foot: _____   By bus: _____   Other [specify]: _____: _____

Is this your first visit here? If not, how often do you come?

☐ Yes   ☐ No   _____ per week

                  _____ per month

                  _____ per year

Physical Observations [Do not ask interviewee.]

Date: _____   Day of the week: _____   Time of day: _____

Location of interview: _____

☐ Male   ☐ Latin-Hispanic   ☐ African-American   ☐ Native-American
☐ Female   ☐ Asian   ☐ White   ☐ Other [specify]: _____

Long-Range Store Development Plan Worksheet Instructions

Use this strategic planning worksheet to develop multiple stores over a five-year period. Even if you don't intend to become part of a multistore development process, you can still benefit from the detailed planning steps outlined in this worksheet. To help you better understand the long-range planning process, the worksheet is divided into five phases:

- The balance of 1997 (which includes October, November, December)
- All of 1998 (January through December)
- Part of 1999
- Part of 2000
- All projected future openings

To use this form, use the helpful legend in the upper left and bottom left corners of the worksheet. Your main concern is to keep track of three critical planning steps:

- The signing of the purchase or lease contract, indicated by an "S";
- The date construction begins, indicated by a "C"; and
- The projected month of a store's opening, indicated by an "O".

Take a look at the following detailed instructions before you try to use the worksheet. You are given a sample worksheet that has been completed to give you an idea of what the finished product should look like. Then, you are given a blank form for your use. Since this blank form is condensed for the purpose of this book, feel free to enlarge it on your photocopier.

1. In the first column, you will need to identify the store location by its address. For instance, the first entry's address is at the corner of First and Main.

2. In the second column, you will need to identify what type of market it is. Use one of the market acronyms to indicate whether it is a downtown location (DWT), suburban location (Sub), a shopping center location (Sh.C), or a mall (M).

3. In the third column, list what type of deal it will be. For instance, list whether it will be a purchase (P), a lease (L), corporate (Co.), or part of a franchise (F).

4. In the fourth column, indicate the store format — free standing (FS), storefront (SF), or an in-line location (I-L).

5. In the fifth column, you need to project the sales volume — in the millions — for each location.

6. In columns six, seven, and eight, list the projected costs — in the thousands — for the land, site, and construction for each location.

7. Columns 9 through 13 show the actual five-year planning periods. In these columns, you will need to indicate the three planning steps for each location — the signing, construction, and opening. For the years 1999 and 2000, the projections are limited to openings only. It is not possible to project in detail this far in advance. Keep in mind, these preliminary projections will be repeatedly revised and revalidated each year.

8. In column 14, rate the site's quality in terms of sales levels. See the legend at the bottom left corner of the worksheet for ratings.

9. In column 15, you rate the site's feasibility. For instance, a rating of one means that the site has few problems, whereas a rating of four means that, although the site is an excellent location, it is not properly zoned.

Long-Range Store Development Plan Worksheet – Sample

Location Legends

Markets
- DWT = Downtown
- Sub = Suburban
- Sh.C. = Shopping center
- M = Mall

Types
- P = Purchase
- L = Lease
- Co. = Corporate
- F = Franchise

Formats
- FS = Free standing
- SF = Storefront
- I-L = In-line

Planning Legends

Planning Steps
- S = Signed
- C = Construction
- 0 = Open

Desirability Legends

Site Quality
- A = Excellent sales
- B = Average sales
- C = Poor sales

Feasibility
- 1 = Very feasible, little work
- 2 = Feasible, some work
- 3 = Somewhat feasible, substantial work
- 4 = Feasible, but a lot of work

Five-Year Plan

Date: 9/17/96   ADI: Denver, Colorado

Location	Market	Type	Format	Volume Estimate	Land Cost	Site Cost	Constr. Cost	Oct '97	Nov '97	Dec '97	Jan '98	Feb '98	Mar '98	Apr '98	May '98	Jun '98	Jul '98	Aug '98	Sep '98	Oct '98	Nov '98	Dec '98	1999	2000	Future	Site Quality	Feasibility
First & Main	DWT	Co., L	SF	2M		100k	700k	S				C				0										A	1
M & Front	Sub	Co., F, P	M	2M	600k	200k	600k		C					0												A	1
B & Second	Sub	F, P	I-L	3M	700k	250k	700k			0																B	1
New	Sub	F, P	FS									S				C					0					A	1
New	Sub	F, L	FS															S				C		0		A	1
New	Sub	F, L	FS																		S		C	0		A	2
New	Sub	F, L	I-L																				C	C		A	3
New	Sub	P	I-L																	1	1				0	A	4
New	Sub	P	I-L																			2			0	B	1
New	Sub	tbd	I-L											1					1		1	2		2	2	B	1

Totals:	Oct '97	Nov '97	Dec '97	Jan '98	Feb '98	Mar '98	Apr '98	May '98	Jun '98	Jul '98	Aug '98	Sep '98	Oct '98	Nov '98	Dec '98	1999	2000	Future
Signings	1	1		1	1						1				2	2		
Construction starts		1	1	1			1		1					1	1	1	2	
Openings			1				1		1					1		1	2	2
Months in operation			1				1		1					2			2	2

Summary of Activity in this SMA

	1997	1998	1999	2000	Future
Units Existing	6	9	10	12	14
Units Added	1	3	1	2	2
Less Stores Closed	0	0	0	0	0

Chapter 10

Start Your Selection Process

Now that you are aware of the many facets of retail site selection — analysis, research, evaluation, time, and money — you are ready to embark on your search for the right location for your business. The preceding nine chapters have given you the know-how to accomplish the great task ahead of you. Don't be overwhelmed by the many avenues you must take to select a top-notch site. From a thorough market analysis to understanding a city; from researching a specific site to identifying your retail trading zone (RTZ); from knowing how to forecast your future sales to looking for essential location factors; from choosing between an urban location or a rural location or becoming part of a larger corporation with multistores or becoming a franchisee — you are well-equipped for the battle ahead.

Whether you are a first-time retail operator or an established retail business owner of one or more stores, this final chapter will discuss how to:

- Use a tried and proven twelve-step location finding process.
- Envision your future store as the best of all other direct competitor and analogue stores.
- Avoid the temptation of a secondary location.
- Make sure your location is right for your type of business.
- Narrow your search from the top three location choices to the best choice for your situation.
- Make sure your facility is big enough for your type of business.

- Follow a critical site selection path that includes vital real estate, construction, and legal issues.
- Do a post-opening analysis of your store(s).

To supplement this text, you can use two helpful worksheets, including the Real Estate and Construction Checklist and the Post-Opening Analysis Worksheet. To start your site selection process, strictly follow a tried and proven location finding process.

Follow a Twelve-Step Location Finding Process

The process of finding the best location for your business is long and involved — or short and disastrous. To help you avoid the short and disastrous route, you can follow a twelve-step process. The steps to find the best location for your business include:

- Complete a total market analysis.
- Identify and rank major activity nodes — a sure sign of people movement that indicates points of departure and points of arrival.
- Analyze the demographics and psychographics of the area.
- Analyze your competitors.
- Identify traffic generators.
- Analyze traffic.
- Identify natural and human-made barriers.
- Chart equidistant time points (isochrones).
- Analyze the retail trading zone.
- Select the area.
- Select the site.
- Estimate your store's future sales.

The key to the twelve-step location finding process is to do-it-yourself. Resist the temptation to delegate these vital tasks. Allocate time for your research and evaluation. Without your involvement in the entire process, you cannot acquire the understanding you need to make critical site selection decisions.

Although some of the information is available from public records and some from firms that specialize in data gathering and interpretation, a significant amount of information is available only through your own efforts. Even with the best of advice and data gathered from the most reliable sources, your decision to accept or reject a location depends heavily on your first-hand knowledge and diligence in checking out all relevant factors. Remember, one of the best ways to acquire first-hand information is to walk it, to drive it, to fly it. To ensure that you don't miss any relevant factors and that you are well-equipped for each of the twelve steps, you will need to gather some essential pieces of information, including:

- A city map that shows:
  - The estimated limits of your RTZ as determined by the physical or human-made barriers;
  - The limits of the area as determined by the isochrones set, for example, at three, five, and ten minutes, or by the isochrones peculiar to your business;
  - The limits of the RTZ discovered by comparing your area with similar stores' RTZs;
  - The estimated RTZ's core, secondary, and tertiary areas;
  - Circles with one-, two-, three-, four-, and five-mile radiuses to indicate geographical distances; and
  - Relevant traffic generators within one, two, three, five, or more miles;
- Demographic and psychographic data that you obtained from your market analysis as outlined in Chapter 1;
- Notes on relevant competitors;
- Aerial photos taken from the north, east, south, and west, and one from directly overhead that show clear details;
- A proposed facility layout using an existing survey or plot map;
- A listing of both positive and negative physical characteristics of the site;
- A breakdown and evaluation of the off-map traffic;
- Market share data of your business and of the relevant competition; and
- A comparison of your location with the analogue locations — either another store location in the same chain you are linking into, a competitor's location, or a location of a similar but not directly competitive store.

Use a dictaphone when you survey an area. List and evaluate all that you notice. When finished, listen to the tape carefully, examine the map, and follow the route you took. Keep in mind, when you prepare a city map for at least three isochrones of your location's RTZ, the distances are different from one type of business to another. For instance, within one business' RTZ the isochrones will be three, five, and seven miles; for another it might be three, six, and nine miles. Select the version that makes sense for your business.

Some items on the list will not be mathematically precise, like the estimated limits of the RTZ, but it will force you to look at the area with a keen sense of observation. In addition, the aerial photos, especially the shot from directly overhead, should be taken from an altitude low enough to show cars, traffic signals, accesses, pedestrians, and other features. When you have gathered this essential information, analyze your prospective location during the morning, noon, afternoon, evening, and night — to get a clear picture of it at each hour of the day.

A site takes on a completely different meaning after a diligent research of its physical and marketing qualities. You will better understand the visible and invisible factors that will affect the sales greatly. These twelve steps are nothing but a checklist for you — so you will not forget anything. Remember, it only takes one factor to totally change the sales potential of a site or make it unfeasible for your business. For instance, you may have a large frontage, but with no right to open a driveway. You may find it easy to skip a step or two, simply because of self-confidence. This preliminary work is essential: either it will confirm your positive decision or it will help you walk away from a location.

Compare, Compare, Compare

The secret to site selection is to compare, compare, compare. Envision your future store as the best of all other direct competitor and analogue stores. To make proper comparisons, go to the locations of your direct competitors and to the stores of the best nondirect competitors. Go inside each store and look at them with a very critical eye. Be discerning about everything. If you are in the restaurant business, taste the product and try the service. If you do not evaluate the product or service, you cannot properly judge your competitor's RTZ and location. Believing that you have a better product than your competitors is fine, but you will discover that the knockout difference will be your choice of a better location than any of the sites of your competitors.

The process of selecting your retail location is a marketing activity. Think of the ways you will market the location and your business in the future. Don't expect to stand behind the counter and wait for the newspaper ads and TV commercials to kick the customers into your store. You need to market your location just as vigorously as you market your business. Don't select a location that will be difficult to market.

Keep in mind a fundamental factor: Locations are never good or bad because of a variety of small reasons. What makes a location terrible or extraordinary is normally caused by one, two, or a few big, blatant conditions. It is a terrible location because you cannot get to it easily and safely; or you cannot see it very far down the road; maybe it is in the wrong block, or it is in a very small residential RTZ; or there is a lack of traffic generators. It is an extraordinary location because it is on the far corner of a busy road that intersects with a good secondary road, or it has a large population in an expanded RTZ, or it is surrounded by traffic generators. Don't let small factors blind your vision and your professional approach to site selection. Make sure your approach involves a look down the road, too.

Events can transform a poor location into a good one and vice versa. This can happen when:

- A seedy part of town becomes trendy. In that process, some poor locations turn into good ones.
- A freeway is constructed, and what was once a main thoroughfare becomes a service road. Traffic is drastically reduced, and a pretty good location becomes pretty bad.

- The major road in front of your store is converted into a one-way road, is equipped with median strips, or is posted for "no left turns." Sales volumes fall off. A good location becomes not so good.

- The secondary road going past your far corner location becomes a dead end, which results in access cut off from a significant part of your original RTZ. A pretty good location becomes pretty bad.

- The major road in front of your store is widened and becomes an even greater thoroughfare. After the roadwork is completed, your sales volumes go up. A good location becomes excellent.

- Traffic generators are developed nearby. Your RTZ expands. An excellent location becomes stupendous.

- A new signage ordinance restricts size, color, and style of signs. Now you are suddenly hard to find. You no longer stand out. A good location becomes bad.

To successfully look down the road for future positive or negative effects of city development, stay alert to population trends and development plans in the public and private sectors.

Avoid a Secondary Location

Some people advocate the principle that secondary locations, in certain cases, are just fine. In fact, you might find the price of the real estate for a primary location is too high. Instead, you find a secondary location will cost less and therefore you can operate your retail business at a profit even though the sales will be lower. A secondary location can produce profits. The risk of paying high rents and taxes can be reduced. However, consider the ultimate balance between investment and return.

Learn from the example of the franchisee who opted for a secondary location as illustrated in Figure 10.1. This franchisee insisted on acquiring a location one block behind the main intersection in the area. The real estate price of the corner lot, which was the best location choice, was $500,000. The secondary location was only $200,000. The franchisee's rationale was that everybody in the market would know where his business was located. It seemed to be a brilliant strategy — to serve the same RTZ at less than half the price. Although the business was profitable at the beginning, it did not end up that way. A popular restaurant opened on the major corner, and a five-story building was constructed on the corner lot beside the franchisee's location, which totally cancelled the store's visibility from the side street. As a crowning blow, a two-story parking garage was built next to the popular restaurant, and the view of the franchisee's

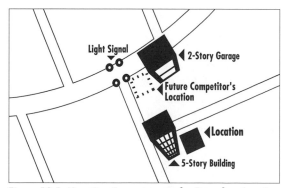

Figure 10.1 Negative Consequences of a Secondary Location

store was obliterated from the major road as well. At that point the business stopped being profitable, not because of high rent, but because of low sales.

At times a secondary location can be profitable, but the long-range risks are great. A business in a secondary location becomes very vulnerable to other market forces, especially to strong competition. A secondary location sends a message to its customers that it is a secondary business. Customers have a keen sense of what is important; they gravitate toward it. They feel more important themselves when they patronize a business at an important location.

Narrow Your Search

Your search for the right location has led you to focus on your top three choices. You are ready to narrow your search from the top three sites to the very best location for your business. To do this, look at the pros and cons for each site and then test and decide.

To illustrate this process, put yourself in this scenario. Suppose you intend to open your free standing retail store in the southeast part of town on a road that runs east–west. You have completed your market research, including the analysis of the demographics and the projection of your RTZ. You have driven the area using the time-distance approach — the three, five, and nine minutes, for instance — and you have walked, driven, and flown the area and the site. You came to the conclusion that the node of activity on the east–west highway is the healthiest and most active in the area. There are three sites with the best appearance. They all look good even though one has an old building on it that will need to be razed. All three sites have the essential location factors — accessibility, visibility, high density, growth, regional exposure, and safety/security — as discussed in Chapter 6. Now is the time to leave no stone unturned. Find out things like:

- Which site has the widest frontage?
- Which site has the largest square footage?
- Which site has a break in the median strip, turn preparation lanes, and a stoplight signal with turn arrows?

Make cardboard templates of the building and parking layout. Design your building and your parking the way you want it. As you do this, be aware of the required landscape area, setbacks, and the rights-of-way. You may find that the first location has an old structure on it, but would offer the best frontage and the best layout. But, can you add $25,000 demolition costs and still be sure that you will have an acceptable bottom-line profit? The other location is almost as good as the first one, with excellent visibility. However, it is irregular. You will have to change the building plans. There is only room for 19 parking spaces. Besides, it requires an expensive retaining wall in the back. The third location is about 200 feet from the corner. How can you get a right-of-way in the back to allow for easy traffic circulation? There are other questions you must ask, such as:

- If your business has a drive-thru, can you superimpose the drive-thru lane over the normal parking layout?
- Where will you put your free standing sign?
- If a sign is not allowed by zoning, how else can you identify your building?
- Should the sign be placed lower than the allowed height to improve visibility, or should you apply for a variance to increase the allowed height? Perhaps you want the sign to be visible from the nearby freeway.

Keep in mind, a sign has the power to transform an average location into a good one. Often, because of expediency, the importance of a sign is not understood. In a real estate deal, the contract or lease comes first and the sign becomes an afterthought. Yet a sign creates a strong awareness in the customer at the crucial point of decision making. It can produce additional sales of 10 to 30 percent. Some smart retailers will not take a site without fully satisfactory signage. However, do not take a secondary site just because you can get a big sign. You need to consider a multitude of factors and compare the positives and negatives of each of the top three choices.

For each of the three sites, drive the road and figure out the greatest distance at which your business will be recognized or identified from both directions, the traffic intervals in minutes or seconds that allow for entrance-exit, and the degree of safety exiting left or right. Also, judge the final look of your facility. Imagine it there — new, beautiful, imposing, and clearly noticeable. Make sure it won't be hidden by other buildings, vegetation, berms, highway embankments, or something else. Is the site a clear compromise or is it a clear winner? Find out whether:

- The traffic is light or heavy enough to allow for impulse shopping during the peak hourly sales of your business.
- There is any possibility of opening your lot to traffic to and from nearby large retailers, such as Home Depot, Wal-Mart, or a grocery store.
- The location is on the better side of the street for your type of business. For example, if you are a home video rental retailer, you want to locate on the going-home side. People don't pick up videos on their way to work.

Further, evaluate the prominence of these locations in relation to your competitors' locations and come up with a list of pluses and minuses. If the pluses of your location outweigh the minuses, you may conclude that your location is better than your competitors' locations.

By this time, you are at a point where you can make an evaluation. The second-best location was eliminated as soon as you rated it second-best. The best location must now pass a six-part test.

Your best location must:

- Have all three basic site requirements — accessibility, visibility, and regional exposure;
- Serve an area characterized by both high density and growth;

- Have more pluses than minuses, and none of the minuses can disrupt the convenience of your customers;
- Have been totally analyzed and scrutinized and have no potential surprises;
- Be financially feasible; and
- Be positioned correctly with respect to your other locations, if you have any.

If your proposed location flunks any part of that test, walk away from it and continue your search. If the location passes every part of that test, you might as well conclude that you were correct in your choice. Now the decision to buy it or rent it is very easy to make.

For an insider's look at buying or selling a business, you may wish to obtain copies of Lloyd Manning's *Business Brokerage: An Opportunity for Real Estate Professionals* and *What's It Worth: A Guide to Valuing a Small Business*. Both provide valuable information and recommendations presented in clear, concise terms. To learn more about these insightful guides, contact:

The Oasis Press
(800) 228-2275 or *www.oasispress.com*

Understand the Critical Path

Once you have decided on the parcel you want, you will be involved in a long list of activities involving real estate, construction, operations, and legal issues. The certain steps you will have to follow for real estate issues are:

- Negotiate your lease or purchase.
- Deposit earnest money.
- Prepare zoning variances, use permits, or public hearings.
- Attend zoning hearings.
- Review progress.
- Deposit balance of funds.
- Secure landlord reimbursements, if any.

When it comes to construction, you will:
- Survey the site.
- Complete soil boring.
- Order a structural analysis of the building.
- Contract a zoning impact analysis.
- Design site plans.
- Order percolation tests.
- Design landscaping plans.
- Outline irrigation plans.
- Comply with environmental requirements.
- Apply for building permits.

- Get approval of survey.
- Obtain approval of soil test.
- Obtain right-of-way permits.
- Get sign permits.
- Attend zoning hearings.
- Apply for other permits, such as curb cuts.
- Select contractors.
- Accept bids.
- Award contract.
- Hold a preconstruction meeting.
- Negotiate with contractor and get a contractor's sworn statement.
- Set a plan for all necessary work.
- Set a system for changes to the original architectural plans.
- Coordinate delivery installation dates with vendors.
- Use a punch list to verify that construction is completed according to plan.
- Apply for licenses.
- Obtain certificate of occupancy.
- Release final retainage of construction money.
- Complete construction.

In terms of operations, you should:

- Plan your preopening.
- Hire and train employees.
- Order beginning inventory.
- Have a dry-run opening or rehearsal.

With regards to the legal matters, you must:

- Get a certified survey, tax bill, evidence of right-to-convey, and preliminary title report.
- Finalize the conditional contract.
- Get approval of the zoning survey.
- Obtain approval of the title report.
- Attend zoning hearings.
- Clear title.
- Verify covenants, conditions, and restrictions (CCRs).
- Verify contract with construction and legal contingencies.
- Get the title policy.
- Close the deal.
- Review the construction contract.
- Sign the contracts.

As you can see, following the critical path involves paying close attention to every real estate, construction, and legal issue. To help you further, make sure you keep track of each phase of the site selection process and use appropriate checklists and worksheets to catch every detail.

Know Every Real Estate and Construction Detail

As part of the site selection process, you will deal with property owners, developers, and real estate people of all kinds. When you work with these people, keep in mind that they look upon their properties as they would look upon their own children — each developer thinks his or her property is the best and most attractive and has no faults or shortcomings. Carefully distinguish between a real asset and a sales talk. When dealing with real estate people, be calm, cool, and analytical. The analysis of the parts will reveal the merits of the whole if there are any to be found.

To analyze the various parts, make sure you look carefully at every real estate and construction factor. To give you an idea of the many things you must consider, use the Real Estate and Construction Checklist located at the end of this chapter. This ten-part checklist includes questions related to:

- Zoning and site development
- Parking
- Signage
- Engineering
- Curb cut and road information
- Building codes
- Fire safety information
- Health safety information
- Unions
- Utilities

You will find the checklist is detail-oriented. Notice the importance of having specific names, measures, quantities, and costs to help you keep track of every facet and document progress. You may need to hire a construction engineer, or architectural professional to find out some of the site specifics that may not appear to a layperson's eye.

Remember, the key to site selection is to overlook nothing — if you overlook something it might end up costing you dearly. For instance, in San Francisco, California, if you don't bother to check a building thoroughly, you may end up spending hundreds of thousands of dollars to bring the whole structure up to the present earthquake requirements. Don't start your site selection process until this checklist, or a similar one, is properly completed by the respective, competent people.

Make Sure the Location Fits

Some people believe blindly in the miracles of a good location. In fact, some new retail chains, in their dreams and enthusiasm, have been selecting outstanding locations and paying a very high price for land, buildings, and equipment. Some have added a heavy pre-investment marketing expense. What is likely to happen to these stores? Even though the sales are excellent, their overall costs are too high.

Think of your retail store as a machine. All its parts must fit; they must work in sync; they must produce a certain amount, at a certain speed; and there must be a profit at the bottom line. If you place your business in a location where the speed of production should be double what the machine can do, you will not be successful. On the other hand, your business may not be as popular as you think. Your machine may not be well designed for those markets: it needs reengineering. If you drive a compact car, don't expect from it the performance of a racing car just because you are driving the Autobahn in Germany. Consequently, you must know the weaknesses and strengths of your retail business and of the right machine you use to exercise it. Obviously, you can force your machine, but make sure all the parts stay together, and you reach your point of destination safely and profitably.

Make Sure Your Location Is Proportional

When you have chosen the product you want to deliver, selected the RTZ you want to serve, found the best location for your facility, and projected the sales and growth you consider realistic, you are ready to turn your full attention to the facility you intend to build or remodel on that site. You may be tempted to skimp on your plans for your store facility, but don't entertain the idea that the smaller your store the higher your sales per square foot. Remember, you are going to be in business for a long time; resist the temptation to downscale to the point where you will lose your customers and the whole market.

There must be a proportion — a balance between location, facilities, and operations. If the location is excellent, the facility must be excellent and your business' operations must be excellent. A poor operation will certainly smother your business. Figure 10.2 shows that if you will serve a big RTZ in size and density, then you will need to have a proportional size facility in which to welcome your customers. On the other hand, if the RTZ is smaller, you will be fine with a smaller facility. Don't forget to allow for possible future expansion.

Consider the example of the franchise operator who had a store operated by five people. The location improved greatly because of new residential and

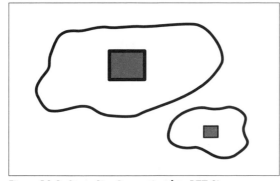

Figure 10.2 Store Size Proportional to RTZ Size

commercial activities. So, the operator demolished the old store and built a much bigger and nicer one — but kept operating it with the same five employees. The business' profits did not increase although the losses did. Ray Kroc, the founder of McDonald's, had his own beliefs: "Size begets volume" and "Do it first, do it now, do it best, and it will pay for itself." Kroc was a visionary.

If you believe as Kroc does, go ahead and do what you believe in. However, you will be best served if you prudently seek proportion between your location, facility, and operations.

Do a Post-Opening Analysis

When a retail store opens, sales volumes generally follow two patterns: 1) sales start at an excellent level and then keep rising steadily, or 2) sales start fairly high, but after a few weeks sales diminish and eventually hit a low level. Through good quality, service, and value the sales gradually start climbing. The market absorbs the new offerings without excitement. People dribble in to see, check, and make a judgment. Sales remain at a low level. When sales start low and stay low, there is a tendency to question the quality of the location and the strength of the RTZ. The problem might be elsewhere.

When sales start high and keep going higher, congratulate yourself or investigate the causes of your success and look for ways to maximize a potential you may have overlooked. In either case, it is time for a post-opening analysis.

The purposes of a post-opening analysis are to:

- Understand your business better.
- Identify your business' problems or elements of potential success.
- Understand your business' positioning with respect to static and dynamic generators.
- Compare your projected RTZ with your actual RTZ after your store's opening.
- Study the parts of the RTZ to identify areas that should be the target of local marketing and promotion.
- Study the internal layout of your store's appearance, accessibility, and visibility for areas of improvement.

A post-opening analysis is best done by the people involved in the day-to-day business operations, including the owner, manager, crew members, and persons involved in marketing, real estate, and construction.

To prepare for a post-opening analysis, you will need:

- Sales information of the store per hour, per day, per week;
- The original RTZ Survey;
- The sales per person in the RTZ;
- The percentage of the RTZ dollar captured by your store compared to your competitors;

- An analysis of similar or competitive stores in your RTZ and a ranking of competitors;
- The average population per store and market share percentage in the total market;
- Quality of service, cleanliness, and value scores of the store relative to comparable stores; and
- An analysis of interior and exterior layouts of similar or competitive stores.

To properly complete a post-opening analysis for your store, use the Post-Opening Analysis Worksheet located at the end of this chapter.

Chapter Wrap-Up

You will want to take into account a range of demands when designing your facility. You can follow seven principles that will form a blueprint for your successful location.

- The best location requires the best facility.
- The retail trading zone potential demands a facility large enough to serve it plus proportional equipment, inventory, staffing, and operation.
- The nature of your business suggests the appropriate design and layout for your facility.
- The demographics and lifestyle of your target customers call for the appropriate ambience, convenience, and quality of service in your facility.
- The visibility of your location needs to be amplified by your signage and by the high-recognition exterior of your facility.
- The easy accessibility of your location must be carried out with the ease of parking and ease of access to your facility.
- Your growth expectations require a facility flexible enough to allow increases in trade volume for five or six years.

When it all comes together — you find you are offering the best values in a product or service that has a heavy demand, customers come in droves to your beautiful store, and your sales volumes far outstrip your costs and quickly return your investment — you will know that you have the best location possible. All the study, legwork, interviews, research, and evaluations you have done has led up to finding the right location. And you will agree it was hard work — just as you were warned — but that it was worth it. Because when it comes to success in retailing, the best location is where you deserve to be.

Real Estate and Construction Checklist Instructions

Once you have chosen a property, you will need to know whether you can use it for your retail business' purpose. The Real Estate and Construction Checklist will help you find this out. This checklist can be used for new and existing improvements.

You will need to hire an architect to work with you and for you — to deal with the various departments of your local city hall, such as the planning department, engineering department, highway department, and fire department. Your architect will also work with a civil and mechanical engineer.

Set a budget for yourself to allow you to fully complete this type of checklist. If the property is not suitable, walk out at the beginning. If you discover problems later, it will be very expensive. This checklist will help you avoid the expense of future problems.

Real Estate and Construction Checklist

Location: _____

Zoning and Site Development

What is the present zoning of the property and adjacent properties? _____

_____

How has this property been used in the past? _____

List any past applications for variances on this site. _____

_____

Who has jurisdiction over property?   ☐ City   ☐ County   ☐ Other [specify]: _____

List any moratoriums or other problems related to utilities. _____

_____

Will tenant share interest in developing off-site utilities?   ☐ Yes   ☐ No   If yes, explain in detail and include source of information. _____

_____

Is the site on a shopping center pad?   ☐ Yes   ☐ No

The shopping center is at what stage?   ☐ Existing   ☐ Proposed   ☐ In development

Are utilities to shopping center parcel in place?   ☐ Yes   ☐ No   If not, who will develop utilities? _____

_____

What is the status of the project with respect to municipal approvals? _____

_____

What contacts have you made with building, zoning, or other agencies? _____

_____

_____

Should tenant remain anonymous during the evaluation to avoid any negative ramifications, like price increases?   ☐ Yes   ☐ No   If yes, explain. _____

Will building appearance have to be approved by agency or private concern?   ☐ Yes   ☐ No
If yes, explain. _____

Individuals to contact (such as, broker, owner, attorney) for further details.

Name: _____   Position: _____

Address: _____   City, State, Zip: _____

Phone: _____   Fax: _____   E-mail: _____

Individuals to contact (such as, broker, owner, attorney) for further details. (continued)

Name: _____ Position: _____

Address: _____ City, State, Zip: _____

Phone: _____ Fax: _____ E-mail: _____

Name: _____ Position: _____

Address: _____ City, State, Zip: _____

Phone: _____ Fax: _____ E-mail: _____

Name: _____ Position: _____

Address: _____ City, State, Zip: _____

Phone: _____ Fax: _____ E-mail: _____

Name: _____ Position: _____

Address: _____ City, State, Zip: _____

Phone: _____ Fax: _____ E-mail: _____

Should the topographical survey be ordered now?   ☐ Yes   ☐ No

Should soil borings report be ordered now?   ☐ Yes   ☐ No

Should title binder be ordered now?   ☐ Yes   ☐ No

Unusual physical site problems: _____

Other pertinent data or comments: _____

Required information and documentation to be attached. [Check off when completed.]

☐ Survey or plot plan of property, from a surveyor and the local city hall, that shows property lines and dimensions, common parking areas, assessments, and other pertinent data. Comments: _____

_____

☐ If parcel is on a shopping center pad, provide a site plan of whole shopping center with subject property outlined, common parking areas, and conflicting easements, if applicable. Comments: _____

_____

☐ Copy of deed with an accurate property description — also referred to as meets and bounds — reviewed by tenant's attorney for accuracy and known restrictions. Comments: _____

_____

☐ Identify any additional zoning information required. _____

_____

☐ Special building department requirements: _____

_____

Date: _____

Source: _____

Phone: _____   Fax: _____

Parking

Note landscape buffer and parking setbacks. (This information is available from the city planning department.)

Front: _____   Property side: _____

Back: _____   Street side: _____

Note landscape buffer and parking setback requirements, if applicable.

Length: _____   Width: _____   Total square footage: _____

Are there minimum 90-degree parking spaces?   ☐ Yes   ☐ No

Should curbs or wheelstops be used in parking spaces?   ☐ Yes   ☐ No

Is two-foot vehicle overhang allowed with minimum parking space?   ☐ Yes   ☐ No

Parking space requirements   Number needed   Size

                for customers: _____   _____

                for employees: _____   _____

                for disabled individuals: _____   _____

What are the minimum drive-aisle widths?   Two-way: _____   One-way: _____

The number of spaces required for the proposed building is based upon this formula. _____

_____

Minimum percentage of on-site parking spaces: _____

Contact the city planning department to find out whether there is a requirement for a screening hedge or wall. If there is, give details. _____

_____

Are there any trees on the property protected by local ordinances?   ☐ Yes   ☐ No   If yes, describe and locate on sketch. _____

Local method of irrigating landscaped areas: _____

Date: _____

Source: _____

Phone: _____   Fax: _____

Signage

Pylon sign   Amount allowed: _____   Maximum area of each face: _____

                                    Maximum height: _____   Minimum setback: _____

Monument sign   Amount allowed: _____   Maximum dimensions: _____

High-rise sign (if needed)   Recommended height: _____ Recommended size: _____

                                    Allowable height: _____   Allowable size: _____

Shopping center sign (if needed)   Recommended height: _____ Recommended size: _____

                                    Allowable height: _____   Allowable size: _____

Is the sign criteria controlled by the developer?   ☐ Yes   ☐ No   Or lessor?   ☐ Yes   ☐ No

Will you have to share sign square footage with other tenants?   ☐ Yes   ☐ No

Are auxiliary signs, like smaller entrance-exit signs, permitted?   ☐ Yes   ☐ No

Describe any unusual sign restrictions. _____

_____

_____

List any variances required for any sign listed above. _____

_____

What size and height will be requested? _____

What sign supplier is recommended? _____

Does tenant apply for sign permits?   ☐ Yes   ☐ No

Date: _____

Source: _____

Phone: _____   Fax: _____

Engineering

How is storm runoff handled? [check one]:

☐ Sheet drain to right of way   ☐ Tie into storm drain

☐ On-site retention   ☐ Other [specify]: _____

Contact the engineering department of the local city hall to find out the storm drainage design criteria.

Year installed: _____   Duration: _____   Intensity: _____

Minimum flood plane criteria elevation: _____

Is a hydrologic study required for storm drainage system design?   ☐ Yes   ☐ No   If yes, attach sample study.

What are the off-site requirements for construction of public improvements that may affect your location?

Sidewalks: _____

Curbs and gutters: _____

Drainage: _____

Paving: _____

Other off-site construction requirements: _____

_____

_____

Estimate of engineering costs. [Provide plans of existing improvements, if available.] $_____

Date: _____

Source: _____

Phone: _____   Fax: _____

Curb Cut and Road Information

Street jurisdiction(s):

☐ City   ☐ County   ☐ State   ☐ Federal

☐ Other: _____

Are there any future changes planned, such as a road widening?   ☐ Yes   ☐ No   If yes, submit plans and comments. _____

_____

Describe any proposed or pending plans that could result in a partial or total condemnation of this site. _____

_____

_____

Curb limitations [Attach standard curb cut and driveway details.]

Frontage	Maximum Number	Two-Way Width Max/Min	One-Way Width Max/Min
_____	_____	_____/_____	_____/_____
_____	_____	_____/_____	_____/_____
_____	_____	_____/_____	_____/_____

Minimum distance in feet between driveways: _____

Minimum distance in feet between driveway and side property line: _____

Minimum distance in feet between driveway and street intersection: _____

Is a deceleration lane required to provide a safe left turn?   ☐ Yes   ☐ No   If yes, what is the possibility of obtaining a median cut? _____

Date: _____

Source: _____

Phone: _____   Fax: _____

Building Codes

Applicable building code: _____   Year: _____

Applicable plumbing code: _____   Year: _____

Applicable mechanical code: _____   Year: _____

List any unusual structural requirements.

    ☐ Snow loads: _____   ☐ Seismic zone: _____

    ☐ Wind loads: _____   ☐ Other [specify]: _____

Does the building have to conform to any aesthetic requirements?   ☐ Yes   ☐ No   If yes, explain. ___
_____

What is the minimum finish floor elevation, such as feet above grade or crown? _____

Date: _____

Source: _____

Phone: _____   Fax: _____

Fire Safety

Fire zone: _____   Comment on zone restrictions: _____

Is there a fire flow ordinance?   ☐ Yes   ☐ No   If yes, give details. _____
_____

Are you required to install a fire hydrant or firewall?   ☐ Yes   ☐ No   If yes, include cost in construction cost estimate. _____

Is panic hardware required on exterior doors?   ☐ Yes   ☐ No

Is a fire sprinkler system required?   ☐ Yes   ☐ No   If so, what is the approximate cost? $_____

Is a separate water service line required for a fire sprinkler system?   ☐ Yes   ☐ No   If yes, give details.
_____

Other fire code requirements: _____
_____

Is a special fire department connection required?   ☐ Yes   ☐ No

Date: _____

Source: _____

Phone: _____   Fax: _____

Health and Safety

Outline any hose bib requirements in the dumpster enclosure. _____

Is a sanitary drain required in the dumpster enclosure?   ☐ Yes   ☐ No

Is a roof required for the dumpster enclosure?   ☐ Yes   ☐ No

Minimum size in gallons of grease interceptor: _____

How many fixtures are required in restrooms?   In men's restroom: _____   In women's restroom: _____

Are separate employee restrooms required?   ☐ Yes   ☐ No   If so, give details. _____

_____

Describe any special requirements for dressing rooms. _____

_____

Describe any other pertinent requirements. _____

_____

Date: _____

Source: _____

Phone: _____   Fax: _____

Unions

Is the site located in an area where there are unions?   ☐ Yes   ☐ No

How should you bid the project?   ☐ Union   ☐ Nonunion

Utilities

[Include all fees, deposits, and charges in construction cost estimate.]

Water:

    Location of main: _____

    Size: _____   Approximate connection fee and deposit: $_____

Date: _____

Source: _____

Phone: _____   Fax: _____

Sewer system:

    Location of line: _____

    Size and type: _____ Approximate connection fee and deposit: $_____

Date: _____

Source: _____

Phone: _____ Fax: _____

Electricity:

    Location of main breakers (also referred to as primaries): _____

    Available power characteristics, such as voltage: _____

    Connection charge, if any, for pad-mounted transformer: $_____

    Minimum distance between transformer pad and building: _____

Date: _____

Source: _____

Phone: _____ Fax: _____

Natural gas:

    Location of main: _____

    Size: _____ Approximate connection fee and meter deposit: $_____

Date: _____

Source: _____

Phone: _____ Fax: _____

Liquid petroleum gas:

    Name of local supplier: _____

    Minimum distance between tank and building: _____

    Does the tank have to be installed underground?   ☐ Yes   ☐ No

    Approximate service charge, if any: $_____

Other alternatives if services are not available or there are moratoriums on the use of some utilities: _____

_____

_____

Date: _____

Source: _____

Phone: _____ Fax: _____

Site Final Assessment

List any citizens, homeowners, or political groups in the community that might oppose your application on this site.

_____
_____
_____
_____
_____
_____

Assess the degree of difficulty to obtain all necessary approvals. _____

_____
_____
_____

How many months will it take to obtain all approvals and permits? _____

Describe below any and all zoning changes, variances, or special approvals that will be needed in connection with this project. _____

_____
_____
_____
_____
_____

List below, in time sequence, any and all city, county, or state government bodies that must approve the project.

_____
_____
_____
_____
_____
_____

Describe any other related issues. _____

_____
_____
_____
_____

Post-Opening Analysis Worksheet Instructions

Completing a post-opening analysis of your store is a vital part of the overall site selection process. A post-opening analysis confirms your location decision and helps you identify your store's areas of improvement. In short, by doing this type of analysis you will know your store's weaknesses and its strengths so you can work on making your store a step above and beyond your very best competitor.

This simple, easy-to-use worksheet is divided into several sections. To begin, you will need to drive the area to identify and evaluate the major traffic generators in all three major divisions of your store's RTZ. Make sure your test runs are during the most relevant business hours.

Next, you will need to compare the results of your original location analyses — original RTZ Survey, original Competitor's Location Analysis, and original Competitor's Strategy Analysis — with the actual results of operating your store for one year. From these worksheets you can compile the demographic information that led to the logic you used to choose your store's location. Determine whether your projections were accurate and, if not, find out how you can enhance your store's image and marketability in your RTZ.

Then, you will need to see how your store fares against three of your direct and indirect competitors. You can evaluate these competitors by simply counting the number of cars on each lot during peak hours and customers in each store for each competitor and your store. Rank each location's total number of cars and customers compared to your location.

In addition, you will find areas on the post-opening analysis where you can grade (poor, average, or great) your operation, customers, and physical premises. Finally, you will need to ask yourself some important yes/no questions regarding operation, service, facility, and marketing. This will help you formulate a list of areas you can improve during your next year's operation.

If you do a post-opening analysis each year, you will continue to refine your store's products, operation, interior and exterior appearance, and sales and marketing approach.

Post-Opening Analysis Worksheet

Traffic Generation Analysis

Major traffic generators in the first radius: _____

_____

_____

Major traffic generators in the second radius: _____

_____

_____

Major traffic generators in the third radius: _____

_____

_____

Original Logic Evaluation

_____

_____

_____

_____

_____

_____

_____

_____

_____

_____

_____

Traffic Comparison Analysis

Subject Stores	Number of Cars	Number of Customers	Rank (1–10)
Direct competitor 1	_____	_____	_____
Direct competitor 2	_____	_____	_____
Direct competitor 3	_____	_____	_____
Indirect competitor 1	_____	_____	_____
Indirect competitor 2	_____	_____	_____
Indirect competitor 3	_____	_____	_____

Operational Quality Analysis

	Great	Average	Poor
Quality of product offered	☐	☐	☐
Efficiency of service	☐	☐	☐
Merchandising	☐	☐	☐
Value offered	☐	☐	☐
Pricing strategy	☐	☐	☐

Customer Analysis

_____
_____
_____
_____
_____
_____
_____

Physical Premises Analysis

	Great	Average	Poor
Daytime signage	☐	☐	☐
Nighttime signage	☐	☐	☐
Exterior illumination	☐	☐	☐
Interior illumination	☐	☐	☐
Accessibility	☐	☐	☐
Driveways and curbs	☐	☐	☐
Visibility	☐	☐	☐
Buildings	☐	☐	☐
Height of signs	☐	☐	☐
Attractiveness	☐	☐	☐
Ease of parking	☐	☐	☐
Conditions of parking lot	☐	☐	☐
Drive-thru layout	☐	☐	☐
Landscaping	☐	☐	☐

Operation   Yes   No

	Yes	No
Is the operation up to standard?	☐	☐
Is the product excellent?	☐	☐
Is the product consistent?	☐	☐
Is the store clean, neat, and manicured?	☐	☐
Is the inventory adequate?	☐	☐
Is the packaging adequate?	☐	☐

Service

	Yes	No
Is service prompt and efficient?	☐	☐
Is service friendly, and offered with a smile?	☐	☐
Are product suggestions offered to customers?	☐	☐
Does management do its job well?	☐	☐
Is store staffed properly?	☐	☐
Are service representatives well trained?	☐	☐
Is service system adequate?	☐	☐

Facility

	Yes	No
Is signage highly visible and attractive?	☐	☐
Is access easy and safe?	☐	☐
Is the parking layout functional?	☐	☐
Is facility equipped well enough?	☐	☐

Marketing

	Yes	No
Have you conducted attitude surveys of customers or focus groups?	☐	☐
Are you spending a reasonable amount for advertising?	☐	☐
Do you have a public relations campaign?	☐	☐
Are you targeting any special customer groups?	☐	☐
Do you conduct any local store marketing?	☐	☐

Construction

What needs to be replaced or improved?

☐ Driveway   ☐ Heating

☐ Lighting   ☐ Air conditioning

☐ Signs   ☐ Other [specify]: _____

☐ Landscaping   _____

Notes

Site Selection Resources

Listed here are some major contacts for finding the right location for your business. There are numerous publications on nationwide retail trends that can help you keep up-to-date on store design and layout, shopping centers and individual retail outlets, and merchandising and pricing. Helpful franchising publications and contacts are included for those interested in becoming part of a franchise. Also, there are key contact organizations listed for retailers interested in opening a store in a captive-shopper location.

Retail Trends

Chain Store Age Magazine
Lebhar-Friedman
425 Park Avenue
New York, NY 10022-3556
(800) 216-7117

Dollars and Cents of Shopping Centers
Urban Land Institute
1025 Thomas Jefferson Street, NW, Suite 500 West
Washington, DC 20007-5201
(202) 624-7000
(800) 321-5011

Journal of Retailing
Babson College
Babson Park, MA 02457-0310
www.babson.edu/jr
(781) 235-1200

Retail Observer
1442 Sierra Creek Way
San Jose, CA 95132
www.retailobserver.com
(408) 272-8974
(800) 393-0509

Retail Trends (continued)

Shopping Center World
Intertec Publishing
6151 Powers Ferry Road, NW
Atlanta, GA 30339
www.interlec.com
www.scwonline.com
(770) 955-2500
FAX (770) 618-0349

Shopping Centers Today
Value Retail News
**International Council of Shopping Center
    Developers**
1221 Avenue of the Americas
New York, NY 10020-1099
www.ICSC.org
(646) 728-3800
FAX (212) 589-5555

Store Equipment and Design
Macfadden Communications Group LLC
233 Park Avenue South
New York, NY 10012
www.storequip.com
(212) 979-4800

Visual Merchandising and Design Publications
ST Media Group
407 Gilbert Avenue
Cincinnati, OH 45202-2285
www.stpubs.com
(513) 421-2050
FAX (513) 421-5144

Notes

_____
_____
_____
_____
_____
_____
_____
_____
_____
_____
_____

Franchising

Franchise Annual Directory
Info Press, Inc.
P.O. Box 826
Lewiston, NY 14092
www.infonews.com/franchise
e-mail: infopres@infonews.com
(716) 754-4669
FAX (905) 688-7728 (Canadian office)

Franchise Bible
The Oasis Press
P.O. Box 3727
Central Point, OR 97502
www.oasispress.com
(541) 245-6502

The Franchise Handbook
1020 North Broadway, Suite 111
Milwaukee, WI 53202
www.franchisehandbook.com
(414) 272-9977

The Franchise Redbook
The Oasis Press
P.O. Box 3727
Central Point, OR 97502
www.oasispress.com
(541) 245-6502

Franchising World
International Franchise Association
1350 New York Avenue, Suite 900
Washington, DC 20005
www.franchise.org
(202) 628-8000
FAX (202) 628-0812

Notes

Captive Shopper Location Contacts

American Association of Airport Executives
601 Madison Street
Alexandria, VA 22314
www.airportnet.org
(703) 824-0500

American Logistics Association
1133 15th Street, NW, Suite 640
Washington, DC 20005
www.ala-national.org
(202) 466-2520

Army & Air Force Exchange Service (AAFES)
3911 South Walton Walker Boulevard
Dallas, TX 75236-1598
www.aafes.com
(214) 312-1101 (switchboard)
(800) 527-2345 (catalogue)

Marine Corps Exchange
3044 Catlin Avenue
Quantico, VA 22134-5103
(703) 784-3826
FAX (703) 784-3826

National Park Service
1849 C Street NW
Washington, DC 20240
www.nps.com
(202) 208-6843

Navy Exchange Service Command (NEXCOM)
3280 Virginia Beach Boulevard
Virginia Beach, VA 23452-5724
www.navy-nex.com
(800) 628-3924

Notes

Demographic Resources

Because demographic data is crucial to selecting the right site for your business, you must be prepared to readily obtain and identify the demographic makeup of the customers that exist in your store's RTZ. With this in mind, the market research companies and magazines listed here will give you the jump-start you need to understand the multifaceted world of gathering demographics. Both mailing addresses and web-site addresses are listed for most of the following invaluable resources.

Market Research Companies

Anysite Technologies, LLC
1201 Dove Street, Suite 200
Newport Beach, CA 92660
www.anysite.com
(800) 489-8829
(949) 885-4900   FAX (949) 885-4901

The Internet's easiest-to-use site for advanced demographic reports and presentation quality maps. Designed specifically for professionals in retail, restaurant, real estate, and financial service industries.

Caliper Corporation
1172 Beacon Street
Newton, MA 02461-9926
www.caliper.com/mtudinfo.htm
e-mail: sales@caliper.com
(617) 527-4700   FAX (617) 527-5113

Producer of Maptitude, a system for developing maps, pin maps, dot-density maps, color-coded maps, scaled symbol maps, maps with integrated pie and bar charts, and other graphic devices.

213

Market Research Companies (continued)

Claritas, Inc.
1525 Wilson Boulevard, Suite 1200
Arlington, VA 22209
e-mail: jlevy@claritas.com
(703) 812-3628   FAX (703) 812-2701

This resource produces the Conquest market system family, which contains census-based data, business line data, retail data, and health care data. The psychographic module is Clusterplus. It also produces Atlas GIS — a system that allows you to map and analyze statistical data geographically. For example, trading areas for a chain of retail outlets can be determined based on sales volumes, the addresses of customers, demographics, and any other data available. Data, software, and services of the company are seamlessly interconnected.

Claritas Express
53 Brown Road
Ithaca, NY 14850
(800) 234-5973 (Sales)
(800) 780-4237 (Technical support)

Instant access to demographic reports and maps. Business retail potential, daytime employment, shopping centers, and segmentation data is also available for fast access to the information you need.

Compusearch Micromarketing Data and Systems
330 Front Street West, Suite 1100
Toronto, Ontario M5V 3B7
www.mapinfo.com
(416) 348-9180

This company provides demographic, geographic, and marketing data, including census data, estimates and projections of households and income, consumer potential, and location data for stores.

Demographic Information Sources
CACI Marketing Systems
1100 North Glebe Road
Arlington, VA 22201
(800) 292-CACI (2224)
(800) 394-3690 (West Coast offices)

This resource develops demographic estimates and forecasts. Scan/US is the company's geomarket analysis tool. It provides a map-based view of demographic data from the U.S. census and other sources.

Demographic Surveys Division
U.S. Census Bureau
4700 Silver Hill Road
Suitland, MD 20233
www.census.gov/
(301) 457-4608

This resource contains information about population, housing, economy, and geography. It provides data access tools, information about the Bureau of the Census, and guidance in information gathering.

Earth Resources Observation Systems (EROS)
U.S. Geological Survey, EROS Data Center
47914 252nd Street
Sioux Falls, SD 57198-0001
http://edcwww.cr.usgs.gov/
(800) 252-4547
(605) 594-6151   FAX (605) 594-6589

The EROS Data Center is the world's most extensive civilian repository of remotely sensed data (via satellites) on the Earth's land surface. The center also operates an archive of more than eight million photographs taken from aircraft.

Market Research Companies (continued)

Environmental Systems Research Institute, Inc. (ESRI)

380 New York Street
Redlands, CA 92373-8100
www.esri.com
(800) 447-9778 or (909) 793-2853

This resource provides use of ArcView, a system for accessing, displaying, querying, analyzing, and publishing organizational data. It links traditional data analysis tools, such as spreadsheet and business graphics with maps, tables, and charting capabilities for an integrated analysis system. ArcView can be used as a standalone system or extended into an entire department, division, or organization.

Genomics, Inc.

geovue
200 Lincoln Street, 5th Floor
Boston, MA 02111
www.geonomicsinc.com
(617) 451-2520   FAX (617) 482-3066

This is a GIS company providing iSITE, a powerful, easy to use mapping and demographic software product, used for site analysis by real estate developers and retailers.

Geographic Data Technology (GDT)

11 Lafayette Street
Lebanon, NH 03766
www.geographic.com
(800) 331-7881

GDT develops and sells geographic digital street network and boundary databases, geocoding software, and custom geographic services. It is a leading supplier of geographic data to all major GIS and desktop mapping vendors. It also provides vehicle registration and lifestyle information.

MapInfo

One Global View
Troy, NY 12180
e-mail: custserv@mapinfo.com
www.mapinfo.com
(518) 285-6000
(800) FASTMAP   FAX (518) 285-6070

This resource provides demographic data products, including Claritas, a desktop mapping system combining data and geographic positioning.

Mapsmart

12758 Treeridge Terrace, Suite 200
Poway, CA 92064
www.mapsmart.com/
(858) 513-0903

Mapsmart produces radii and drive-time reports and maps, and include a executive summary and site location map.

Paul Kagan Associates

126 Clock Tower Place
Carmel, CA 93923
www.Kagan.com
(831) 624-1536

Media analysts who provide valuation and strategic consulting services as well as market share data for media and communications properties, Kagan offers seminars, newsletters, and a vast array of research reports.

Sites USA, Inc.

1553 West Todd Drive, Suite 204
Tempe, AZ 85283
www.sitesusa.com
e-mail: info@sitesusa.com
(480) 491-1112   FAX (480) 491-6633

Market Research Companies　(continued)

This firm provides complete, cutting-edge desktop mapping solutions, demographics for site analysis, custom store modeling, and special software for the commercial and retail real estate industry.

The NPD Group, Crest Division

900 West Shore Road
Port Washington, NY 11050
www.npd.com
e-mail: info@npd.com
(516) 625-0700　　　　　FAX (516) 625-2347

With nine offices across the United States and Canada, this firm identifies, describes, and communicates the dynamic factors that drive sales in the restaurant business. Focusing on consumer restaurant behavior, this company can help identify a restaurant's market share position to ensure its marketing efforts are properly measured.

Market Research Publication

Statistical Abstract USA

U.S. Census Bureau
P.O. Box 277943
Atlanta, GA 30384-7943
www.census.gov/stat_abstract/
e-mail: compendia@census.gov
(301) 457-4100　　　　　FAX (888) 249-7275

This resource is a collection of statistics, tables, and graphs on social, economic, and international subjects. It is also a guide to census data sources.

Market Research Magazines

American Demographics; Demographics USA; Forecast; and *Marketing Tools*

www.demographics.com
(800) 420-4223

Consumer Research

250 S. Wacker Drive, Suite 1150
Chicago, IL 60606
(312) 980-3776　　　　　FAX (312) 980-3135

Analogue Data Development

The study of existing stores that are similar to your store's overall operation is an integral part of proper site selection. By using the concept of analogue — or stores that are analogous to yours — you can accurately forecast your store's future sales. As detailed in Chapter 5, you have five sales forecasting methods based on the analogue concept from which to choose. Ideally, you will want to use all five methods for the most accurate sales projections. To assist you with these methods, this appendix contains four worksheets, including the:

- Analogue Study Worksheet
- Analogue Rating Score Sheet
- Hourly Sales Analysis
- Success Model Worksheet

Just like all other worksheets in this book, these worksheets are preceded by helpful instruction pages that give details on how to properly complete each. To get the most out of these worksheets, make sure you have read Chapter 5.

Analogue Study Worksheet Instructions

If you are a new retailer — this will be your first store — you must take the time to fully consider four kinds of analogue data. To begin, you can complete this four-part worksheet on at least three analogue stores versus your potential store. Make enough photocopies of all four parts of the Analogue Study Worksheet so you can properly analyze the analogue stores.

Part 1: Demographic and Lifestyle Data
You can obtain this information from:

- Real estate brokers;
- Real estate developers;
- On-line information;
- A demographic service company;
- The planning division of your local city hall;
- The local utilities companies;
- Your local public library;
- Your local college library; and
- Your local chamber of commerce.

Part 2: Site Data
You will identify various site characteristics via a thorough personal survey of each site. To do this you must walk, drive, and fly the locations.

Part 3: Facility Data
A personal survey will generate this information. When you examine the analogues, you will want to determine things about the store, such as:

- Sizes and types;
- Outside architecture;
- Inside layout and decor, including shelving and sales area; and
- Outside features, including parking, landscaping, and signage.

Part 4: Sales Data
To obtain sales dollars and trends that will impact your store, you must analyze your best competitor in the area where you want to locate your store. Use the Competitor's Location Analysis from Chapter 1 to help you locate your best competitor. Remember, competitors can be direct or indirect. For example, if you sell men's clothing, you can also study a women's clothing store.

Analogue Study Worksheet Instructions (continued)

No competitor will give sales information to strangers. So, you have to be tactful and diplomatic. You could:

- Introduce yourself to the store manager and offer to take him or her to lunch.
- Talk to some employees of the competitor.
- Check various sales at the cash register.
- Talk to some customers.
- Talk to some suppliers.

If you are part of a multistore corporate or franchise entity, the company might be able to give you the four types of information. Several multistore companies collect data and computerize it by using a special software that answers questions like:

- Which corner location has the highest sales?
- What are the site demographics?
- Which is the best end cap location?
- What is the average sales of the in-line stores?
- Which are the stores with the biggest facilities?
- What is the sales trend of a store front location, on Tuesday, in the month of March?

With this computerized information, you can use it to project sales of new locations. The concept is to compare analogue locations — existing and new ones — to learn the traffic generator that you can add and subtract to help you know your potential sales. For example, a retail location near a Wal-Mart may do better than another location without any major traffic generators.

The type of information to gather and computerize depends upon your industry. The four types of data included in this worksheet will help most types of retail businesses. However, you can customize the data to fit your business' needs. For example, you can include special traffic generators that are peculiar to your business like:

- A drugstore near a major hospital;
- A sporting goods store in a recreational area; or
- A beach attire store in a lakefront region.

Analogue Study Worksheet – Part 1: Demographic and Lifestyle Data

	In RTZ	Within 1/2 mile	Within 1 mile	Within 2 miles
Population Growth				
Current estimated total population	_____	_____	_____	_____
Current estimated daytime population	_____	_____	_____	_____
Current estimated total households	_____	_____	_____	_____
Previous five years' population growth rate percentage	_____	_____	_____	_____
Previous five years' total household growth rate percentage	_____	_____	_____	_____
Percentage of customers in each age group:				
under 18	_____	_____	_____	_____
18–34	_____	_____	_____	_____
35–44	_____	_____	_____	_____
45–54	_____	_____	_____	_____
over 54	_____	_____	_____	_____
Income				
Median household income	_____	_____	_____	_____
Average household income	_____	_____	_____	_____
Percentage of customers' household incomes:				
less than $15,000	_____	_____	_____	_____
$15,000–24,999	_____	_____	_____	_____
$24,000–34,999	_____	_____	_____	_____
$35,000–49,999	_____	_____	_____	_____
$50,000–74,999	_____	_____	_____	_____
more than $75,000	_____	_____	_____	_____
Gender				
Percentage of male population	_____	_____	_____	_____
Percentage of female population	_____	_____	_____	_____
Ethnic Background				
White	_____	_____	_____	_____
African-American	_____	_____	_____	_____
Latin-Hispanic	_____	_____	_____	_____
Asian	_____	_____	_____	_____
Native-American	_____	_____	_____	_____
Other [specify]: _____	_____	_____	_____	_____

Analogue Study Worksheet – Part 1 (continued)

Socioeconomic Status	In RTZ	Within 1/2 mile	Within 1 mile	Within 2 miles
Percentage of population in average units (apartments and houses)	_____	_____	_____	_____
Percentage of population in rental units	_____	_____	_____	_____
Percentage of households with children	_____	_____	_____	_____
Percentage of population with high school diploma	_____	_____	_____	_____
Percentage of population with college degree	_____	_____	_____	_____
Percentage of white-collar employees	_____	_____	_____	_____
Percentage of blue-collar employees	_____	_____	_____	_____

Lifestyle

Choose the right lifestyle profile for your industry and fill in the blanks. For example, the first line might read "Percentage of households with well-educated, affluent suburban professionals," and the second line might read "Percentage of households with urban, mobile professionals, and few children."

Lifestyle Profile	In RTZ	Within 1/2 mile	Within 1 mile	Within 2 miles
_____	_____	_____	_____	_____
_____	_____	_____	_____	_____
_____	_____	_____	_____	_____
_____	_____	_____	_____	_____
_____	_____	_____	_____	_____
_____	_____	_____	_____	_____
_____	_____	_____	_____	_____
_____	_____	_____	_____	_____
_____	_____	_____	_____	_____
_____	_____	_____	_____	_____
_____	_____	_____	_____	_____
_____	_____	_____	_____	_____
_____	_____	_____	_____	_____

Analogue Study Worksheet – Part 2: Site Data

Site address: _____

Area of dominant influence: _____

Standard metropolitan area: _____

Closest major intersection: _____   Dimensions of property: _____

Location Type

[check one]

☐ Urban   ☐ Rural

☐ Suburban   ☐ Other [specify]: _____

Lot Type

[check one]

☐ End cap   ☐ In-line

☐ Free standing   ☐ Other [specify]: _____

☐ Shopping center pad

Visibility

[check one]

☐ Regional

☐ Neighborhood

Road Classification

[check one]

☐ Radial   ☐ Collector

☐ Quadrant arterial   ☐ Neighborhood road

☐ Minor arterial   ☐ Other [specify]: _____

Type of Road

[check one]

☐ Frontage road   ☐ Left

☐ Side road   ☐ Right

Store Position

[check one]

☐ Midblock   ☐ Near corner

☐ Corner   ☐ Adjacent to corner

☐ Far corner   ☐ Access to side street

Traffic Conditions

[check any that apply]

☐ Going-home side   ☐ Left-turn possible

☐ Going-to-work side   ☐ Right-turn possible

☐ Stoplight   ☐ Median on primary

☐ Stop sign   ☐ Median on secondary

Analogue Study Worksheet – Part 2 (continued)

Traffic Conditions (continued)

Average daily traffic (cars that pass by during each 24-hour period): _____

Peak A.M. traffic hours: _____

Peak P.M. traffic hours: _____

Lanes of traffic: _____

Speed limit: _____

Percentage of living traffic: _____%

Percentage of work traffic: _____%

Percentage of long-distance traffic: _____%

Visibility distance on same side: _____

Visibility distance on opposite side: _____

Accessibility

[check one] ☐ Excellent   ☐ Good   ☐ Poor

Number of Parking Spaces

Front: _____   Side: _____   Back: _____

Number of Nearby Public Transportation Modes

[check one] ☐ Bus stops: _____

☐ Subway entrances: _____

☐ Train stations: _____

☐ Other [specify]: _____

Exterior Signage

[check any that apply] ☐ Pylon sign (on a pole)

☐ Monument sign (attached to building or close to ground)

☐ Visible sign on building

Number of Curbs

Front: _____   Side: _____   Back: _____

Shopping Center Type

[check one] ☐ Strip   ☐ Neighborhood   ☐ Mall   ☐ Outlet

Setback

Front: _____   Side: _____   Back: _____

Shopping Center Size

[check one] ☐ Less than 100,000 square feet   ☐ More than 300,000 square feet

☐ 100,000–300,000 square feet

Analogue Study Worksheet – Part 2 (continued)

Traffic Generators	Distance from Your Store	Name	Contribution to Sales
Major generator adjacent to site	_____	_____	$_____ / _____%
General merchandise stores	_____	_____	$_____ / _____%
Minor grocery stores	_____	_____	$_____ / _____%
Major grocery stores	_____	_____	$_____ / _____%
Drugstores	_____	_____	$_____ / _____%
Others (like Wal-Mart)			
_____	_____	_____	$_____ / _____%
_____	_____	_____	$_____ / _____%
_____	_____	_____	$_____ / _____%
_____	_____	_____	$_____ / _____%

Three Complementary Businesses within Two Blocks (not necessarily major traffic generators)

Name	Type
_____	_____
_____	_____
_____	_____

Modes of Transportation People Use (percentage)

Car: _____%

Walk: _____%

Public transportation: _____%

Other [specify]: _____ : _____%

Analogue Study Worksheet – Part 3: Facility Data

Building Type

[check one]
- ☐ Free standing
- ☐ End cap
- ☐ In-line
- ☐ Storefront
- ☐ Other [specify]: _____

Building Construction

[check one]
- ☐ New
- ☐ Remodeled
- ☐ Rebuilt
- ☐ Relocated

Square footage of building: _____

Width of frontage: _____

Square footage devoted to sales: _____

Square footage devoted to service: _____

Square footage devoted to storage: _____

Number of seats (if it is a restaurant): _____

Number of sales stations: _____

Building Features

[check any that apply]	Yes	No	[check any that apply]	Yes	No
Distinctive frontage	☐	☐	Efficient merchandising layout	☐	☐
Wide windows	☐	☐	Excellent exterior lighting	☐	☐
Attractive decor	☐	☐	Spotless premises – exterior	☐	☐
Excellent interior lighting	☐	☐	Rear area lighting	☐	☐
Spotless premises – interior	☐	☐	Manicured landscaping	☐	☐
Parking area lighting	☐	☐			
Feeling of safety	☐	☐	A drive-thru service	☐	☐
Easily recognized	☐	☐	If so, number of cars in both lanes: _____		
Distinctive architecture	☐	☐	If so, number of drive-thru windows: _____		

Analogue Study Worksheet – Part 4: Sales Data

Competitor Identification

	Site Rating (1–10)	**Estimated Yearly Sales**
Names of Major Competitors (within one mile)		
_____	_____	$_____
_____	_____	$_____
_____	_____	$_____
_____	_____	$_____
_____	_____	$_____
_____	_____	$_____

	Site Rating (1–10)	**Estimated Yearly Sales**
Names of Minor Competitors (within one-half mile)		
_____	_____	$_____
_____	_____	$_____
_____	_____	$_____
_____	_____	$_____
_____	_____	$_____
_____	_____	$_____

Previous Twelve-Month Revenues (by day for the last twelve months)

Sunday: $_____   Tuesday: $_____   Thursday: $_____

Monday: $_____   Wednesday: $_____   Friday: $_____   Saturday: $_____

Daily Percentage (%) of Revenues (previous twelve months)

7:00–8:00 A.M. _____%	3:00–4:00 P.M. _____%	11:00–12:00 P.M. _____%
8:00–9:00 A.M. _____%	4:00–5:00 P.M. _____%	12:00–1:00 A.M. _____%
9:00–10:00 A.M. _____%	5:00–6:00 P.M. _____%	1:00–2:00 P.M. _____%
10:00–11:00 A.M. _____%	6:00–7:00 P.M. _____%	2:00–3:00 A.M. _____%
11:00–12:00 A.M. _____%	7:00–8:00 P.M. _____%	3:00–4:00 A.M. _____%
12:00–1:00 P.M. _____%	8:00–9:00 P.M. _____%	4:00–5:00 A.M. _____%
1:00–2:00 P.M. _____%	9:00–10:00 P.M. _____%	5:00–6:00 A.M. _____%
2:00–3:00 P.M. _____%	10:00–11:00 P.M. _____%	6:00–7:00 A.M. _____%

Visits per week: _____   Visits per month: _____   First-time visitors: _____

Analogue Study Worksheet – Part 4 (continued)

Number of Current Transactions

7:00–8:00 A.M. _____	3:00–4:00 P.M. _____	11:00–12:00 P.M. _____
8:00–9:00 A.M. _____	4:00–5:00 P.M. _____	12:00–1:00 A.M. _____
9:00–10:00 A.M. _____	5:00–6:00 P.M. _____	1:00–2:00 P.M. _____
10:00–11:00 A.M. _____	6:00–7:00 P.M. _____	2:00–3:00 A.M. _____
11:00–12:00 A.M. _____	7:00–8:00 P.M. _____	3:00–4:00 A.M. _____
12:00–1:00 P.M. _____	8:00–9:00 P.M. _____	4:00–5:00 A.M. _____
1:00–2:00 P.M. _____	9:00–10:00 P.M. _____	5:00–6:00 A.M. _____
2:00–3:00 P.M. _____	10:00–11:00 P.M. _____	6:00–7:00 A.M. _____

Average dollar amount per check: $_____

Highest Sales Hours in a Week

Day	Hour		Day	Hour	
Sunday	_____	A.M./P.M.	Thursday	_____	A.M./P.M.
Monday	_____	A.M./P.M.	Friday	_____	A.M./P.M.
Tuesday	_____	A.M./P.M.	Saturday	_____	A.M./P.M.
Wednesday	_____	A.M./P.M.			

Number of hours open: Weekdays: _____   Saturdays: _____   Sundays: _____

Restaurants

Percentage of sales in dining room: _____%

Percentage of sales for carryout: _____%

Percentage of sales at drive-thru: _____%

Distance

Percentage of customers that come from: 0–1/2 mile: _____%

1/2–1 mile: _____%

1–11/2 miles: _____%

11/2–2 miles: _____%

2–3 miles: _____%

3–4 miles: _____%

Average Yearly Sales $_____

Analogue Rating Score Sheet Instructions

The purpose of the Analogue Rating Score Sheet is to assign a rating based upon the relevant factors that will generate sales in your new store. This score sheet will allow you also to rate the factors that actually generate the sales in three existing analogue stores.

To evaluate each factor, remember the slogan: you walk it, you drive it, you fly it. Then, you can begin to formulate your opinion of the relevance of the factors that contribute to sales. For instance, when looking at the residential factor, ask yourself: How important is it for generating sales? Very important? Not so important? You will rate each factor (1–10). If residential is very important, give it a rating of 8 or 9 or 10. If it is not, give it a rating of 2 or 3. Remember that you are rating these factors so you can tally the scores for all three analogues and your prospective store.

You will rate each factor on the score sheet in this manner, with a slight deviation for the competition factor. For example, if the competition factor is great, it will obviously weigh against the sales potential for any given store in the areas in which you look. Thus, if the competition is high, instead of assigning a rating like 8 or 9, you will assign a reverse rating like 2 or 3. Remember, you are rating these factors so you can tally a score for all three analogues and your prospective site.

Analogue Rating Score Sheet

Date: _____   Rated by: _____

Relevant Factors	Analogue Store 1	Analogue Store 2	Analogue Store 3	Prospective Location
Residential	_____	_____	_____	_____
Employment	_____	_____	_____	_____
Shopping	_____	_____	_____	_____
RTZ size	_____	_____	_____	_____
Population	_____	_____	_____	_____
Visibility	_____	_____	_____	_____
Accessibility	_____	_____	_____	_____
Facility attractiveness	_____	_____	_____	_____
Income	_____	_____	_____	_____
Total traffic	_____	_____	_____	_____
Local traffic	_____	_____	_____	_____
Competition	_____	_____	_____	_____
Tourism	_____	_____	_____	_____
Other: _____	_____	_____	_____	_____
Other: _____	_____	_____	_____	_____
Other: _____	_____	_____	_____	_____
Other: _____	_____	_____	_____	_____
Total score	_____	_____	_____	_____
Twelve-month sales	$_____	$_____	$_____	$_____

Hourly Sales Analysis Worksheet Instructions

You will also need to project the yearly sales revenue for the three analogue stores and your new store. If you are part of a franchise system, you can obtain this information from your franchisor. If your business is a startup, then you will need to use the Hourly Sales Analysis Worksheet. The Hourly Sales Analysis Worksheet will help you track the total sales of a given store — hour by hour, week by week.

You can learn the sales totals by doing some creative investigation. For instance, in the fast-food business, operators used to look at the total number of hamburger bun deliveries to give them an idea of total sales. Also, you can talk to the analogue stores' managers, employees, former employees, customers, suppliers, and neighbors. These individuals can provide a wealth of knowledge that will give you a good idea of existing sales.

Although it may seem time consuming and inaccurate, you will be surprised at the accuracy and relevance of this method. Finally, it is necessary that the same person rate the factors of all three stores and the prospective store. The same person will use the same judgment and the scores will be more consistent with each other.

To use this worksheet, you must do an hour-by-hour analysis for your existing analogue store versus your future store. Thus, for each hour ask yourself:

- Will my new store produce more sales or fewer sales than my existing store?
- What traffic generators contribute to the sales?
- Are there any significant missing traffic generators?

Based on the answers to these questions, you can estimate the dollar amounts of sales for both stores. For instance, suppose you analyze the traffic flow between 12:00 P.M. and 1:00 P.M. At the existing store you observe a large office complex with numerous employees who patronize your restaurant during their lunch hour. So, in the space above the slanted line, you put down $200 in sales. Then, you evaluate your projected store by observing the flow of traffic. It may not have the substantial traffic generator that your existing store does. As a result, you will estimate $50 in sales between 12:00 P.M. and 1:00 P.M. and note this in the space below the slanted line. Do this for each hour to give you a clear comparison of hourly sales for both stores.

Hourly Sales Analysis Worksheet

Date: _____   Rated by: _____

	Monday	Tuesday	Wednesday	Thursday	Friday	Saturday	Sunday
11:00 A.M.							
12:00 P.M.							
1:00 P.M.							
2:00 P.M.							
3:00 P.M.							
4:00 P.M.							
5:00 P.M.							
6:00 P.M.							
7:00 P.M.							
8:00 P.M.							
9:00 P.M.							
10:00 P.M.							
11:00 P.M.							

Success Model Worksheet Instructions

This simple worksheet will give you another projection of your store's future sales. To complete the worksheet, answer yes or no to the list of characteristics on the worksheet. Add up the yes and no columns. If you sense there are too many no answers, reconsider whether you have picked the right location serving the right RTZ. While checking off the yes and no boxes, score those same characteristics, using a rating system of 1–10. Add up these numbers also.

If your worksheet has 36 questions, then a perfect score, which is highly unlikely, would be 360. How high a score your location should have is strictly the result of your judgment, but do not entertain the idea that a score of 180 means that your sales will be half of what a perfect location would generate. Keep in mind, the number of questions vary in type and in number.

Success Model Worksheet

Characteristics	Score (1–10)	Yes	No
Big, attractive, and well-illuminated exterior signs	_____	☐	☐
Signs visible from four blocks away	_____	☐	☐
Building visible from at least two blocks	_____	☐	☐
Easy and safe entrance-exits	_____	☐	☐
Parking layout easy for safe movement	_____	☐	☐
At least 40 customer parking spaces, plus parking for the employees	_____	☐	☐
Regional exposure	_____	☐	☐
Major traffic generators in the area	_____	☐	☐
Nearby recreational generators (theaters, sports areas, bowling alleys, recreational parks, or parks)	_____	☐	☐
At least three major grocery stores with fully stocked shelves	_____	☐	☐
Very important main road crossing the city	_____	☐	☐
Main road carries heavy work traffic both ways	_____	☐	☐
Main road carries heavy living traffic	_____	☐	☐
Main road carries long-distance traffic	_____	☐	☐
Traffic continues late into the night	_____	☐	☐
Traffic on weekends and holidays	_____	☐	☐
Part of a community shopping center	_____	☐	☐
Major blue-collar employers within one-quarter to one mile	_____	☐	☐
Major white-collar employers in the area	_____	☐	☐
Location within the core or secondary parts of the RTZ	_____	☐	☐
Stable area (not in transition)	_____	☐	☐
Up to 30 percent of your business from one-quarter mile	_____	☐	☐
About 50 percent of your business from one-half mile	_____	☐	☐
Subtotal	_____	_____	_____

Success Model Worksheet (continued)

Characteristics	Score (1–10)	Yes	No
Heavy residential within one mile	_____	☐	☐
Dense, multiple, and multistory residences	_____	☐	☐
Neat, clean, and attractive residences	_____	☐	☐
High percentage of two income families	_____	☐	☐
Affluent households	_____	☐	☐
Large number of families with children	_____	☐	☐
Apparent growth (new homes, offices, and factories)	_____	☐	☐
Significant construction in progress	_____	☐	☐
Bus or train stations relevant to the store	_____	☐	☐
Weak direct and indirect competition in the area	_____	☐	☐
Impact on other stores likely	_____	☐	☐
Big successful competitors	_____	☐	☐
Competitor will take less than ten percent of your business	_____	☐	☐
_____	_____	☐	☐
_____	_____	☐	☐
_____	_____	☐	☐
_____	_____	☐	☐

Subtotal   _____   _____ _____

Subtotals from previous page   _____   _____ _____

Totals   _____   _____ _____

Glossary

Acceleration lane. A short expansion of a road that allows a vehicle to enter the traffic flow after building up speed. Compare: deceleration lane.

Activity generator. An establishment that draws people to a site, such as a recreation area, school, office, or shopping center.

Analogue store. A competitive store that is similar in important characteristics to a prospective store. The performance record — sales, customers, market, and facility — of an analogue store is used to forecast the sales of a prospective store.

Anchors. The most important retailers in a shopping center that are joined by several smaller retailers.

Area of dominant influence (ADI). An area dictated by the radius of the television signal that identifies each market. This is usually monitored by Nielsen Media Research.

Arterial roads. Important roads without which a city or sections of a city could not exist or function.

Average daily traffic (ADT). This 24-hour traffic count can generally be obtained from city traffic engineers, the department of transportation, county planning commissions, and police departments.

Barrier. A natural or human-made obstacle that hinders traffic movement.

Block. The smallest type of census geographic area, which averages 100 people and is usually bound by four streets or some other physical feature.

Block group (BG). A group of city blocks with an average population of 1,000. Block groups are used in place of enumeration districts in areas where block statistics are tabulated.

Captive-shopper location. A confined area with retail potential, such as an airport, where customers are typically located because of nonretail activities.

Cash flow. The current cash return on a cash investment (exclusive of the mortgage) made in a property.

Census tract. A permanently established geographic area as defined by the U.S. Bureau of Census. It contains an average population of 4,000 persons.

Central business district (CBD). The center or core of a city; also known as the downtown of a city.

Common areas. The areas in a building or shopping center that tenants share, such as corridors, elevators, sidewalks, parking, and rights-of-way.

Community shopping center. A center that provides convenience goods and shopping goods. There are generally between 25 and 45 stores with three larger tenants as the principal stores, including a supermarket, drugstore, and a variety store, home improvement store, or department store. The site is usually ten to thirty acres with 60,000 to 300,000 square feet with a median gross lease area of 150,000 square feet.

Consumer price index (CPI). A measure of the prices over time of basic consumer goods and services.

Cross easement parking. The right by result of an attained easement to use someone else's property for a purpose.

Customer profile. The demographic and psychographic description of a customer.

Deceleration lane. An expansion of a road that allows a vehicle to reduce speed in preparation for a right or left turn.

Demographics. A study of the characteristics of the population of an area regarding its size, growth, and vital statistics.

Designated marketing area (DMA). An area dictated by the radius of the radio signals. This is usually monitored by the Arbitron Company, which services and updates radio listening habits.

Destination point. An assembly of important traffic generators with strong interest gravitation. See also: interest gravitation.

End cap. A term used to describe both ends of a strip center, whether the center is linear, L-shaped, or U-shaped.

Equity. The value of a property minus the amount owed on it.

Far corner site. A corner site located on the right side of a road just across an intersecting road.

Four-way intersection. An intersection of two main roads, two secondary roads, or a main and a secondary road on which more than 70 percent of the traffic goes straight through the intersection rather than turning. Both roads have two-way traffic.

Free standing. A building that is separate from others. Compare: in-line store.

Freeway. An interstate or intrastate highway with certain distinguishable free-way facilities and features, such as service islands, lighting, signage, offramps, controlled access, no stop signs or traffic lights, and a high maximum speed limit.

Frontage. The width of the front of a parcel that is located on a major highway and is occupied by a retailer.

Frontage road. A road that runs parallel to or adjacent to a highway; also called a service road.

Gross square footage. The total floor area designated for tenant occupancy, including basements, mezzanines, and upper floors, if any. All of an area on which tenants pay rent.

Hub. The point at which all radial roads in a particular area merge.

Impact. The effect of a new store opening on an existing one in terms of declining sales volume.

Impulse shopper. A person who suddenly becomes consciously aware of an unfulfilled need or whim.

Income, family. The amount of monies brought in annually by all members more than 14-years-old of a family unit.

In-line store. A retail outlet designed to meet certain criteria with adjacent surroundings, such as a mall.

Interest gravitation. Also called the wind, interest gravitation is a force or attraction that orients and moves people toward one or more directions where there are places, objects, and activities of great interest.

Interstate system. A system of federal highways, officially established in 1956, that crisscrosses and serves the entire United States.

Isochrone. An imaginary line that connects points that are time-equidistant from a point of departure or a point of arrival.

Land use control. Rules and regulations concerning the use of land that are enacted and governed by political jurisdictions in each city.

Lifestyle. A mode of behavior that is based on personal philosophies with special needs and purchasing patterns, regardless of traditional demographic characteristics.

Living traffic. Traffic that is comprised of people who need to travel to acquire basic necessities for their own everyday needs.

Macroarea. The larger, total standard metropolitan area. Compare: microarea.

Main road. The most important road in a particular node or nodule.

Major recreation area. An area that attracts people from areas beyond two miles several times a year for recreation, such as a beach, park, or lake.

Market share. The ratio of the dollars spent in your industry within an SMA versus your total business sales.

Microarea. A small geographic area within the parameters of a larger macroarea.

Near corner site. A corner site located on the right side of a road before an intersecting road.

Neighborhood shopping center. A center that offers daily living goods and services for sale, such as food, drugs, and toiletries. A supermarket and a drugstore are generally the principal tenants. The site is usually four to ten acres with a gross square footage of up to 100,000 square feet or an average gross lease area of 50,000 square feet and usually 10 to 15 stores.

Net lease. A long-term lease, usually 20 to 25 years, in which a tenant agrees to pay a fixed minimum rent and all operating expenses, including his or her share of real estate taxes, insurance, utilities, and repair and maintenance costs.

Node. A major collector of traffic generators that support a central business district or are independent and self-sustaining.

Nodule. A minor collector of traffic generators supporting one or more nodes.

Outlet mall. Also known as an off-price center, an outlet mall, or factory outlet, contains specialty stores that offer merchandise substantially below regular retail prices.

Outlot. A parcel of land or building located on the perimeter road of a mall or on the connector roads immediately leading to a mall.

Penetration. The relationship between an existing store's sales and the sales potential of its RTZ.

Percentage rent. Rent that is contingent upon — and based upon — a percentage of a commercial tenant's gross dollar volume of business and is paid in addition to the minimum rent agreed to in a lease; also called overage rent.

Planned unit development (PUD). Property platted and zoned for specific uses.

Plat. A parcel of land surveyed and divided into lots.

Plat plan. A drawing of the legal boundaries of a property and the location of buildings within these boundaries.

Power centers. A huge retail complex featuring discount centers, superstores, food stores, and other mass merchandisers.

Primary trading area (PTA). Residents and other business-generated activity that accounts for a minimum of two-thirds of a store's sales.

Psychographics. Data that describes the personality, lifestyle, and spending habits of an individual.

Quadrant road. These straight roads generally run parallel or perpendicular, or both, to one another.

Radial road. A main road, like the spoke of a wheel, that leads directly to and from a central business district.

Radio metro market. The area of a metropolitan statistical area covered by a radio signal.

Recovery. The time it takes for the sales of an impacted store to gain or surpass previous sales levels.

Regional exposure. A location on a wide road with multiple lanes that carry living, work, and long-distance traffic and serve a big section of a city.

Regional shopping center. A center or mall that offers a variety of shopping goods comparable to a central business district. There are usually two or three department stores as principal tenants and 50 to 75 stores. These sites are 30 to 60 acres or more with 500,000 to 750,000 square feet of total leasable area.

Regression model. A statistical tool used to fit a set of historical data to a theoretical line or curve to minimize the difference between the projected line and the historical data.

Relocation. The closing of an existing store and moving that facility to a more desirable location.

Retail trading zone (RTZ). The area around a store from which it gets approximately 75 percent of its business. An RTZ has different shapes, sizes, and depths, and is bound by natural and human-made boundaries, such as mountains, highways, and bridges.

Return on assets (ROA). Income divided by equity plus debt.

Return on investment (ROI). Income divided by the investment.

Saturation. Saturation relates to a market that has no more room for a new store of the same type because it would not produce adequate profits and it would impact existing stores excessively Compare: impact.

Setback. The distance of the building from the middle of the front road.

Spokes. Radial roads that expand in various directions from their hubs or points of confluence.

Standard Metropolitan Area (SMA). A geographical area consisting of a large population nucleus with adjacent communities that have a high degree of economic and social integration.

Storefront. An in-line store located on a ground floor of a building that is at least two stories high and normally located in a downtown area (CBD).

Strip center. A series of small, one-story high stores that are adjacent to each other.

Supermall. A super regional shopping center that provides a larger variety of shopping goods and services than a regional shopping center. There are usually four or more department stores as major tenants, each generally not less than 100,000 square feet in size, and between 75 and 150 additional tenants. The sites are generally 50 acres or larger with one million square feet or more gross leasable area.

Swing corner. The corner around which the majority of cars turn left or right at an intersection.

Target market. The segment of a population base that is considered to produce the highest sales for a given retail chain, such as persons earning $30,000–$35,000, 30- to 45-years-old, owning two automobiles, and with three persons per household living in a single unit.

Time-convenience line. An imaginary line between two or more locations that a customer finds inconvenient to cross because of time or convenience.

Top-of-mind awareness. An awareness in the minds of your customers that means when asked about your product, your customers think of your business first.

Traffic aggregate. The combination of three types of traffic — living traffic, work traffic, and long-distance traffic.

Traffic inhibitors. Characteristics or conditions that affect the accessibility of a site. Common traffic inhibitors include medians in front of a site, one-way streets, traffic congestion, lane change problems, high speed, or any other relevant condition.

Visibility time. Number of seconds from when a site is recognizable to the time it takes a customer to reach a site while driving at a normal traffic speed.

Work traffic. Traffic that is generated by people traveling to and from work. Compare: living traffic.

Zoning. Government regulations that control the development of land for the common health, safety, and welfare.

Bibliography

Alexander, Ian C. *The City Center Patterns and Problems*. Perth, Australia: University of Western Australia Press, 1974.

Applebaum, William. "How to Measure the Value of a Trading Area." *Chain Store Age*. Nov. 1940: 111–114.

Applebaum, William, et al. *Guide to Store Location Research With Emphasis on Super Markets*. Reading, MA: Addison-Wesley, 1968.

Applebaum, William, and Richard F. Spears. "How to Measure a Trading Area." *Chain Store Age*. Jan. 1951: 149–154.

Berry, Brian J. L. *Geography of Market Centers and Retail Distribution*. Englewood Cliffs, NJ: Prentice-Hall, 1967.

Castle, Gilbert H., III, ed. *Profiting from a Geographic Information System*. Ft. Collins, CO: GIS World Inc., 1993.

Claus, R. James, and Walter G. Hardwick. *The Mobile Consumer: Automobile-Oriented Retailing and Site Selection*. Canada: Collin-MacMillan, 1972.

Davies, R. L., and D. S. Rogers, eds. *Store Location and Store Assessment Research*. New York: Wiley, 1984.

Ghosh, Avijit, and Sara L. McLafferty. *Location Strategies for Retail and Service Firms*. Lexington, MA: Lexington Books, 1987.

Haber, Ralph Norman, and Maurice Hershenson. *The Psychology of Visual Perception*. New York: Holt, Rinehart and Winston, 1973.

Laulajainen, Risto. *Spatial Strategies in Retailing*. Dordrecht, Holland: D. Reidel Publishing, 1987.

Llewellyn, Thomas E. "Movement of the Eye." *Scientific American.* August 1968: 88–99.

Lynch, Kevin. *The Image of the City.* Cambridge, MA: Technology Press, 1960.

————. *Site Planning.* 2nd ed. Cambridge, MA: MIT Press, 1971.

Melaniphy, John C. *Restaurant and Fast Food Site Selection.* New York: Wiley, 1992.

Morris, Robert. *Annual Statement Studies 1994.* Philadelphia: American Institute of CPAs.

Murphy, Raymond E. *The Central Business District.* London: Longman, 1972.

Porterfield, Gerald A., and Kenneth B. Hall, Jr. *A Concise Guide to Community Planning.* New York: McGraw-Hill, 1995.

Reilly, W. J. *The Law of Retail Gravitation.* New York: Knickerbocker Press, 1931.

Richard, Nelson L. *The Selection of Retail Locations.* New York: F. W. Dodge, 1958.

Roca, Ruben A., ed. *Market Research for Shopping Centers.* New York: International Council of Shopping Centers, 1980.

Thompson, John S. *Site Selection.* New York: Lebhar-Friedman Books, 1982.

Watter, Paul A. *The Structure of Retail Trade by Size of Store.* New York: Arno Press, 1979.

Whitehouse, Kay. *Site Selection: Finding and Developing Your Best Location.* Blue Ridge Summit, PA: Liberty House, 1990.

Index

THE OASIS PRESS

A Complete Franchise Solution.
From The Oasis Press®

Understand the nuances of running a franchise or turning your existing business into a successful franchise model. Each of these books offer unparalleled expertise in helping you make the most of operating a franchise in today's marketplace...

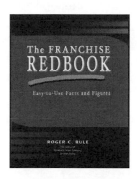

The Franchise Redbook
Roger C. Rule

An accurate and user-friendly reference that will help determine your best franchise opportunity. The Franchise Redbook is up-to-date, comprehensive, and by far the easiest to use for determining your franchise options. Ideal for selecting a franchise, doing market and comparative analysis, preparing a marketing or business plan, preparing contact lists, or doing any other research on franchises.

Paperback $34.95   750 Pages   ISBN 1-55571-484-6

No Money Down Financing for Franchising
Roger C. Rule

An essential resource for securing finances and building the foundation to a winning franchise. Broken down into three logical progressions, this book explores every resource available for franchise financing, including many methods that require no money down and explains the vital points that will prepare you in obtaining these goals.

Paperback $19.95   240 Pages   ISBN 1-55571-462-5

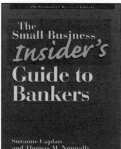

Franchise Bible (4th ed.)
Erwin J. Keup

Equally useful for the prospective franchisee or franchisor. This complete and practical guide, including sample documents and checklists, explains in detail what the franchise system entails and the precise benefits it offers. The book will familiarize you with the terms and conditions of a franchise agreement while providing you with the latest federal regulations.

Paperback: $18.95   163 Pages   ISBN: 1-55571-400-5

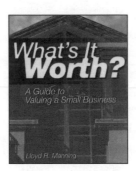

The Oasis Press®
Successful Business Library
Tools to help you save time and money.

businessplan.com *(2nd ed.)*

Now you can ready your business for the age of digital commerce. *businessplan.com* is a step-by-step guide for creating your Web-woven plan. It gives you the tools to integrate your real and virtual offices for increased profits and efficiency. Updated and revised, this second edition is a leading-edge, innovative business tool that will help you get your start in the world of eCommerce. Reach beyond old-school planning models and take advantage of the unprecendented opportunities.

L. Manning Ross   Paperback: $19.95   ISBN: 1-55571-531-1

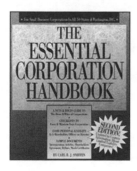

Improving Staff Productivity

In today's business climate, it is increasingly important to maintain a competitive edge. By following the easy-to-implement techniques, you can expect to potentially generate significant time and money savings and improve your overall operations and custom service by learning to monitor your own company's progress to eliminate inefficiencies that could be dragging your comapnay's profits down.

Ben Harrison Carter   Paperback: $16.95   ISBN: 1-55571-456-0

The Essential Corporation Handbook   *(3rd ed.)*

The Essential Corporation Handbook takes the mysteries out of corporate formalities, and shows owners what they must do and what they may do with their corporations. By knowing the rules to follow, you can avoid time-consuming, expensive mistakes, and you can keep your energy focused where you want it – on running your business.

Carl R.J. Sniffen   Paperback: $21.95   ISBN: 1-55571-560-5

Your one-stop resource to starting a business

**COMPREHENSIVE,
STATE-SPECIFIC
GUIDE TO
STARTING OR
EXPANDING YOUR
BUSINESS**

**SAMPLE FORMS,
BUSINESS PLAN
AND THE LATEST
CONTACT INFOR-
MATION FOR STATE
AGENCIES**

**NOW AVAILABLE
FOR 46 STATES &
THE DISTRICT OF
COLUMBIA**

SmartStart
Your (State) Business

Clear. Complete. Concise.

SmartStart Your (State) Business was designed to eliminate financial and bureaucratic confusion by providing you with the most
current contact information for federal, state, and local agencies. Its
appendices contain brief descriptions of each regulatory agency
and include addresses, phone numbers, and links to World Wide
Web information. Detailed, accurate, and jargon-free, SmartStart is
an invaluable reference for any business.

Just look at what SmartStart Your (State) Business includes:
- Sample forms
- Sample business plan
- Detailed economic and demographic information
- Comprehensive guide to money resources

SmartStart Your (State) Business is designed to help you:
- Determine if you should operate as a sole proprietorship,
  partnership, or incorporation
- Register trademarks and apply for local permits
- Protect yourself and your business through proper tax
  planning
- Anticipate the basic issues of expansion, relocation, and
  interstate commerce

"... good 'how-to' books (that) provide lots of practical information."
- Inc. Magazine

"... clarifies the most perplexing issues facing the entrepreneur."
- BusinessLife Magazine